Andrew M. Fairbairn

Studies in the Philosophy of Religion and the History

Andrew M. Fairbairn

Studies in the Philosophy of Religion and the History

ISBN/EAN: 9783337241988

Printed in Europe, USA, Canada, Australia, Japan

Cover: Foto ©Lupo / pixelio.de

More available books at **www.hansebooks.com**

STUDIES IN THE

PHILOSOPHY OF RELIGION AND HISTORY

By A. M. FAIRBAIRN

" Τὸ γνωστὸν τοῦ Θεοῦ φανερόν ἐστιν ἐν αὐτοῖς
ὁ Θεὸς γὰρ αὐτοῖς ἐφανέρωσεν."
ROM. i. 19.

WILLIAM MULLAN & SON
34 PATERNOSTER ROW, LONDON
4 DONEGAL PLACE, BELFAST
1877

"*And hath made of one blood all nations of men for to dwell on all the face of the earth, and hath determined the times before appointed, and the bounds of their habitation; that they should seek the Lord, if haply they might feel after Him, and find Him, though He be not far from every one of us: for in Him we live, and move, and have our being: as certain also of your own poets have said, 'For we are also His offspring.'"*—
ACTS xvii. 26-28.

PREFACE.

THE resolution to issue in a collected form the following "Studies" was come to after considerable hesitation. They are mostly tentative. They embody, indeed, the results of much thought and not a little inquiry; but they were, and still are, intended to be "Studies" preliminary to what should be at once a Philosophy and a History of Religion. They pretend to be no more; but may, even as such, have some worth for an age which seeks to increase by a Science of Religion the number of the already recognized and cultivated Sciences.

The first and third Essays, and part third of the fourth, originally appeared in the *Contemporary Review*. The other parts of the latter formed the substance of two Lectures delivered in the winter of 1874 to the Philosophical Institution, Edinburgh. The second paper was written in the summer of 1875, but has not before been printed.

ABERDEEN, *June* 1876.

CONTENTS.

I.

THE IDEA OF GOD — ITS GENESIS AND DE-
VELOPMENT, ... 1—57

	PAGE
The question as affected by Modern Science and Philosophy,	3
I. The Genesis,	7
Natural Histories of Religion,	7
Whether Fear created the Idea,	10
Or Revelation,	13
Our Inquiry in the Historical Method,	14
Philosophy not Creative of the Religious Idea,	17
The Indo-European Mythologies; the Older the Simpler,	18
Oldest Name for God,	23
Oldest General Term,	25
How they are Related and what they Signify,	27
Nature-Worship—What does it Mean?	32
Paternal Element in the Indo-European Idea of God,	34
The Primitive Indo-European Idea,	37
Its Factors,	38

	PAGE
11. The Development,	44
Influence of Imagination and Conscience,	45
The Theogonic Process,	47
Anthropomorphism and Apotheosis,	51
The Struggle after Unity,	54
Conclusion,	55

II

THEISM AND SCIENTIFIC SPECULATION, 59—105

The Religious and Scientific Conceptions of the World,	61
The New Search after a Cause,	63
Scientific Speculation,	65
Theism and Science,	66
"Theology is Anthropology,"	71
Relation of God to the World variously conceived,	73
Whether Teleology be necessary to Theism,	75
How the Hebrew conceived the Relation of God to the World,	77
Whether the Greeks conceived their Gods as Creators,	78
The Technic Theory of Creation Scientific, not Religious,	82
Effect of the Scepticism of Hume and Criticism of Kant,	84
How are we to conceive the Relation of God to the World?	88
Theism necessary to the Scientific Interpretation of Universe,	90
Evolution: a Moral or Causal Theory of Creation?	91
The Cause—Mr. Spencer's "Unknowable,"	94
Man the Interpretation of Nature,	100
Mind in Premiss and Conclusion,	103

III.

	PAGE
THE BELIEF IN IMMORTALITY,	107—230
PART I.—INTRODUCTORY,	109—122
I. The Belief and the Philosophies,	109
II. The Origin and Evolution of the Belief,	115
III. Significance of its History for Modern Thought,	120
PART II.—THE BELIEF IN INDIA,	123—167
1. The Hymns of the Rig-Veda,	123
2. The Brahmanas,	135
3. The Upanishads,	142
4. The Laws of Manu,	151
5. The Philosophical Systems,	155
6. Buddhism,	160
7. The Reformed Brahmanism,	164
PART III.—THE BELIEF IN GREECE,	168—230
I. Introductory, Order and Development of Religious Thought in Greece,	168
II. Homer,	175
III. Hesiod,	194
IV. The Mysteries,	196
1. The Eleusinian,	197
2. The Orphici,	203

		PAGE
V. The Pre-Sokratic Philosophy,		. 207
1. The earlier Ionians,		207
2. Pythagoras and the Pythagoreans,		. 208
3. The Eleatics,		. 211
4. Herakleitos,		. 212
5. Empedokles,		. 213
6. Anaxagoras,		. 214
VI. The Lyric and Tragic Poets,		. 217
1. The Lyric Poets,		. 218
2. The Tragic Poets,		. 219
VII. Plato,		. 223

IV.

THE PLACE OF THE INDO-EUROPEAN AND SEMITIC RACES IN HISTORY, 230—402

PART I.—COMPARATIVE PSYCHOLOGY AND THE PHILOSOPHY OF HISTORY, 230—264

1. Comparative Psychology,	. 233
Its Problems,	. 234
Mind and Nature,	. 235
Mind Progressive because Free,	. 238
Motives, while not necessitating, necessary to Choice,	. 240
Origin and Influence of Ideals,	. 242
Dynamic Force of the Great Man,	. 243
Comparative Psychology the Psychology of Peoples,	. 245
Its Subjects and Method,	. 247
Relation to other Comparative Sciences,	. 252
And Philosophy of History,	. 255

CONTENTS.

	PAGE
II. The Races to be studied,	259
Their Limits, Branches, Names,	259
Their distinctive qualities,	261

PART II.—THE RACES IN CIVILIZATION, . 265—301

I. Civilization,	265
Relation of Modern to Ancient,	267
The Individual and Society,	269
II. The Races—Their Pre-Historic State,	272
The Indo-European,	272
The Semitic,	273
III. The Fresh Races and the Old Cultures,	281
The New Civilizations not simply imitations of Old,	283
Their efficient and their suggestive cause,	284
Influence of Geographical position and Ethnic relations,	287
1. On Assyria,	287
2. On Phœnicia,	291
Semitic Character of their Civilizations,	287
Greece,	298
Rome,	299

PART III.—THE RACES IN RELIGION, . 302

I. Religion and Man,	302—351
Cause of its Universality,	303
,, Variety,	304
Differences of Religious Faculty in Peoples,	306
Forms under which the Religious Faculty works,	312
Whether Semites possess a Monotheistic Instinct,	314

CONTENTS.

	PAGE
II. The Religions of the Races—Their Characteristic Principles and Differences, .	316
1. The Semitic Religions, .	316
Their Names for God,	316
Their Theocratic Character,	319
Ethical and Authoritative, .	321
Symbolism, . . .	322
The Semitic Idea of Deity, .	325
The Hebrew Religion,	327
2. The Indo-European Religions, .	332
Their Names for Deity,	333
Their Naturalism, . .	334
The Limitations it imposed on Deity, .	336
Effect on Idea of Man, . .	337
Their Political Character,	339
Hellenism, . .	342
III. Their Respective Contributions to Christianity,	346
Hebraism and Hellenism, . .	346
Their Parts in the *Preparationes Evangelicæ*,	348

PART IV.—THE RACES IN LITERATURE AND PHILO-
SOPHY, .   352—402

I. Literature and Culture,	352
II. Language and Literature, .	356
The Languages of the Two Races, . .	357
Their Literatures, . .	360

CONTENTS.

		PAGE
III. Their Mythologies and Poetries,	.	362
Source of their Differences,	.	363
Indo-European Mythologies,		364
Semitic, ,,	.	366
Indo-European Poetry,	.	367
Semitic ,,	.	369
IV. The Races in Philosophy,	.	371
I. The Ancient Philosophic Peoples,		371
Non-Semitic,	.	371
Chiefly Indo-European, and Why?		373
The Hindu and the Greek,	.	375
II. The Schools of Alexandria,	.	385
Judeo-Greek Philosophy,	.	387
Neo-Platonic,	.	389
Christian Conception of God,	.	391
III. The Arab Philosophy,		394
Character of People,	.	394
Of their Philosophy,	.	397
Influence on Modern,	.	398
Spinoza,	.	399

THE IDEA OF GOD: ITS GENESIS
AND DEVELOPMENT.

A

THE IDEA OF GOD: ITS GENESIS AND DEVELOPMENT.

MODERN Science, on the one hand, and modern Philosophy, on the other, have raised in the most distinct and precise form the question as to the Genesis of the Idea of God. Religion is practically co-extensive with man; its presence, even among savage tribes, is the rule, its absence the exception. Peoples the most distant, and indeed opposite, in genius and culture and geographical position, with languages, institutions, and civilization in every shade and degree of difference, have yet a religion as their common characteristic, have never as peoples outgrown it; and though they may have changed its form, have only done so to find in a reformed religion renewed life. A nation's genius rises as its consciousness of God deepens, and the one is highest when the other is most intense.* The point

---

* M. Renan finds the characteristic which mainly distinguishes the Indo-European and Semitic from the other races of mankind to be their moral and religious superiority (*Histoire des Langues Sémitiques*, pp. 500 ff. (4th ed.).

where the genius and culture of Greece culminated was the very point where it had come to realize most vividly the being and government of God. The two eras in our English history most distinguished for genius and heroism, were also the most distinguished for intensity and sincerity of religious life.

Religion thus seems so necessary to the nature of man, so pervades and determines his individual and social life, that Science, in its inquiries into the origin, constitution, and original condition of man, has come face to face with the questions, How did man become religious? What was the earliest form of his religious faith? How can the practical universality and apparent necessity of his belief in one God, or in many gods, be explained? The answers have, on the whole, been growingly adverse to belief in a primitive Theism. The extreme antiquity of man which Geology is inclined to affirm, the aboriginal barbarism Archæology claims to have proved, the primitive Nature-worship Comparative Mythology is said to reveal, the savage condition which Ethnology exhibits as the point from which civilization starts, and, lastly, Mr. Darwin's attempt to trace the "Descent of Man" from a "hairy" ancestor, seem to demand a natural descent of Theism from Atheism, of our religious ideas from the rude fears and frightful dreams of anthropomorphous animals.

The question has also been raised, quite as sharply

THE IDEA OF GOD.

too, in the proposition which Positivism has enunciated as the law of historical progression. Comte's law of mental evolution is too well known to require statement here. The "theological or fictitious" is the first stage of our knowledge, "the necessary starting-point of the human mind."* Here individual and race must alike begin. In this first stage there are three progressive sub-stages—Fetichism, Polytheism, Monotheism, each transitional, each fictitious. To Positivism the primitive faith of the world is a Fetichism common to infant and savage, dog and monkey,† and the English disciples who on other points differ most from their master are yet at one with him here.‡

Of course, the agreement on this point of Science and Positivism is superficial, and should not be allowed to hide the fundamental difference of their principles and aims. Science does not, but Positivism, as Comte understood it,§ does, pronounce against the truth of theology. Mr. Darwin thinks his speculations in no way hostile to belief in the being of God,|| but M. Comte could not allow the "fictions" of the theological stage any

---

* "Cours de Philosophie Positive," vol. i. p. 3.

† Ib., vol. v. pp. 30 ff.

‡ J. S. Mill, "Auguste Comte and Positivism," p. 12, pp. 18 ff.; "System of Logic," vol. ii. p. 528. G. H. Lewes, "Hist. of Philos.," vol. iv. pp. 248 ff. (ed. 1852). Herbert Spencer, *Fortnightly Review*, vol. vii. (N.S.) pp. 536—550.

§ "Cours de Philos. Posit.," vol. i. pp. 4—10; Mill, "Comte and Positivism," p. 14. || "Descent of Man," vol. i. p. 65.

place among the facts of the positive. The difference between Science and Positivism is thus fundamental. It is the accident of the one to ignore, but the essence of the other to contradict, theological belief. Their accidental agreement on the point in question only helps to sharpen their essential antithesis. Science does not seek by its theories to supersede or abolish religion; but Positivism dogmatically promulgates its fundamental law that it may evolve the Atheism which claims to be the new religion of humanity.

The question to be here discussed is the question which modern Science and Positivism have thus combined to raise—How did the idea of God arise? What was its earliest form? What the law or what the process of its development? The questions are certainly in some respects grave enough, touch not only a point at which Christian thought and scientific inquiry come into the sharpest collision, but also the speculative tendencies most threatening to religious truth. Neither religion in general, nor Christianity in particular, depends on the answer to any question in physical science, and our faith has nothing to fear from the most searching investigations into the origin and primitive condition of man. But the tendency, on the one hand, to erect a law of evolution, enacted and administered without any conscious moral law-giver, into the grand principle of human progress, and the tendency, on the other hand, to resolve religion into the expression of subjective states, the externalization in forms and acts of the religious consciousness, are much more dangerous; because they contain, in so far as the one seeks order and progress in the history of humanity, and the other the explanation of the various ethnical religions in the nature and faculties of man, elements of neglected but most significant truths. Our essay, which is meant to deal, more or less directly, with each of these phases of modern thought, falls into two parts. The first will discuss the genesis of the idea of God, therefore the question raised by Science. The second will discuss the development of the idea, therefore the question raised by every theory of evolution, whether coming from the transcendental or positivist side.

I.

"Natural Histories of Religion" are as old as Scepticism. Doubt has always been forced, all the more because exceptional, to justify itself against belief. Coarse or shallow minds have snatched at the readiest and least creditable explanation. Religion is an invention of priests, or poets, or rulers. This explanation was not unknown to the ancient world, figured largely in the anti-religious French and English literature of last century, and still plays a part in the lower infidel discussions of to-day. But the explanation is so manifestly superficial and unsatisfactory, that it falls to pieces the moment the inquiry becomes earnest and searching. Subtler minds saw that a phenomenon so universal as religion must have its roots in the nature of man, and his relation to the world around him. Hence the Epicurean, who hated a *curiosum et plenum negotii deum*,* held that fear had created the gods. The terrible forms seen in dreams, the system of the heavens, the seasons, tempests, meteors, and lightnings, created the notion of invisible or spiritual beings, of gods, and the terror which they inspired gave birth to religion.† Hume, with a rare subtlety of analysis and felicity of illustration, tried to evolve the idea of gods out of the ignorance and fear that personified the "unknown causes" of the accidents and eccentricities of Nature, the idea of one God or Monotheism out of the gradual concentration of flattery and offerings on one of these personifications.‡ Hence Polytheism was the deification of many unknown causes of natural phenomena; Monotheism, the deification of one unknown cause. Dupuis held that all religions had their origin

---

* Cicero, "De Nat. Deor.," lib. i. 20.

† Sext. Empir. Adv. Math., ix. 25; Lucretius, v. 1161—1240. The notion that fear is the mother of religion runs through the whole poem of Lucretius and crops out everywhere. Yet the fine invocation of *Alma Venus*, with which his poem opens, shows what a fascination the idea of the divine had for him. It was the actual religion he saw around him which he hated, for "Sæpius illa Religio peperit scelerosa atque impia facta" (i. 82).

‡ "Natural History of Religion," sections i—viii.

in a worship of nature pure and simple, and that "les Dieux sont enfans des hommes."* But he did not explain the one thing needing explanation—how and why man had begun to worship at all. Comte supposed the primitive Fetichism to rise from infant or savage, by a tendency which they had in common with dog or monkey, ascribing to natural objects, organic or inorganic, a life analogous to their own.† Sir John Lubbock thinks that the rudest savages, representatives of aboriginal man, are actual Atheists, ‡ and describes the transition to Fetichism § somewhat as Lucretius did,—the explanation of the Roman Epicurean, however, being, on the whole, the more philosophic and elevated. Herbert Spencer considers that the rudimentary form of all religion is the propitiation of dead ancestors, who are supposed to be still existing, and to be capable of working good or ill to their descendants.‖ Mr. Darwin's theory is eclectic, and seems to combine the various elements of an ascription of life to natural objects, dreams, and fears.¶

* "Origine de Cultes," vol. i. p. viii. and pp. 3—42.
† "Cours de Philos. Posit.," vol. v. p. 37.
‡ "Origin of Civilization," p. 119.
§ The main factors in the change are dreams (p. 126), disease (p. 131), divination, and sorcery (p. 141); see also p. 221.
‖ *Fortnightly Review*, vol. vii. (N.S.) p. 536. Mr. Spencer has now more fully developed his views, profusely illustrating them, as his way is, in his "Principles of Sociology," cc. ix. ff. I regret that they cannot be here noticed in detail. Chap. xx., on "Ancestor-Worship in general," specially invites criticism, were it only for the curious misapprehensions it contains.
¶ "Descent of Man," vol. i. pp. 65—68.

An analytic and categorical criticism of these Natural Histories of Religion cannot be attempted here and now. But it may be observed that, amid minor differences, they agree in their three main propositions—(1) that man was originally destitute of religious belief; (2) that delusions due to ignorance, fear, or dreams were the causes of his earliest faith; and (3) that the primitive religion was one of terror, a series of rude attempts to propitiate supposed unfriendly beings. Religion is thus derived from the lower faculties and passions of man, and, as a necessary result, its form is low—lower, one would think, than the aboriginal Atheism. It is, too, in its nature false and delusive, without objective reality, the creation of miserable ignorance and trembling fear, a very torment to the minds that had created it. It is hard to see how a religion so produced, and of such a nature, could be otherwise than injurious to man, its terrors fatal to his incipient moral nature, its delusions bewildering and oppressive to his intellect, its entire influence tending to throw the savage back into the animalism from which he had lately emerged. Such a religion could only increase the difficulties in the way of progress, make civilization less possible. Then, how can the admitted virtues and graces of religion be evolved from this barbarous faith? *Ex nihilo nihil fit.* The highest moral qualities do not spring from the lowest. This "Natural History of

Religion" would require an inverted actual history of religion, the reversal of its historical place in society and the State. It is not without significance that, while M. Comte was introducing his law of evolution to the world, finding the roots of religion in Fetichism and the final and perfect system in a Positivism without God, the two profoundest thinkers then living were formulating very different doctrines—the one the doctrine that a nation and its religion rose together, that, apart from religion, a nation, with its institutions and laws, was impossible;* the other, that "the religion and foundation of a State are one and the same, in and for themselves identical," and that "the people who has a bad conception of God has also a bad State, bad government, and bad laws." †

Before finally dismissing these theories, it may be

---

* Schelling, "Philosophie der Mythologie," i. 63.

† Hegel, "Religions-philosophie," i. p. 241. A sketch of the German philosophies of religion, in so far as they touch the genesis of the idea of God, although a very tempting subject, is not one that can be touched within the limits of a short essay. It would have to start with Lessing, Herder, and Kant, and come down to the younger Fichte, Von Hartmann, and Pfleiderer, and would lead us into the very heart of the questions that have agitated the German philosophic schools for now almost a century. German thought on this matter forms, on the whole, an admirable counteractive to English and French. The elements the one ignores are, as a rule, the elements the other emphasizes, though English empirical and physico-scientific thought is beginning to tell at the close of this century in Germany, very much as English rationalistic thought told at the beginning of last.

well to notice a few of their assumptions. They assume the truth of an empirical philosophy. They resolve religious ideas into impressions of sense. Man's faculty or tendency to believe in invisible beings is unexplained. If infant and dog, savage and monkey, alike think natural objects alive, the man does, the animal does not, formulate his thoughts into a religion. Why? If man can get out of the Fetich stage, he can also get into it. Why? Faith is not the result of sensations. Mind is not passive, but active, in the formation of beliefs. The constitutive element is what mind brings to nature, not what nature brings to mind, otherwise no spiritual and invisible could be conceived. Our theorists assume, too, that the aboriginal state of our cultured peoples was similar to that of the lowest living savages. But surely the difference of their conditions, the one savage, the other civilized, hardly warrants such an assumption—implies rather original differences, physical and mental, fatal to it.* Then they assume a theory of development which has not a single historical instance to verify it. Examples are wanted of peoples who have grown, without foreign influence, from Atheism into Fetichism, and from it through the intermediate stages into Monotheism; and until such examples be given, hypotheses claiming to be "Natural Histories of Religion" must be judged

* Renan's "Histoire des Langues Sémitiques," p. 495.

hypotheses still. "Spontaneous generation" is as little an established fact in mental as in physical science, and its truth need not be assumed until it be proved.

We cannot, therefore, accept any hypothesis which would evolve the idea of God from delusions, or dreams, or fears. Shall we trace it, then, to a supernatural source, to a primitive revelation? But a primitive revelation were a mere assumption, incapable of proof—capable of most positive disproof. Although often advanced in the supposed interests of religion, the principle it assumes is most irreligious. If man is dependent on an outer revelation for his idea of God, then he must have what Schelling happily termed "an original Atheism of consciousness."* Religion cannot, in that case, be rooted in the nature of man—must be implanted from without. The theory that would derive man's religion from a revelation is as bad as the theory that would derive it from distempered dreams. Revelation may satisfy or rectify, but cannot create, a religious capacity or instinct, and we have the highest authority for thinking that man was created "to seek the Lord, if haply he might feel after and find Him"—the finding being by no means dependent on a written or traditional word. If there was a primitive revelation, it must have been—unless the word is used in an unusual and misleading sense—either written or oral. If written, it

* "Philos. der Mythol," i. pp. 141, 142.

could hardly be primitive, for writing is an art, a not very early acquired art, and one which does not allow documents of exceptional value to be easily lost. If it was oral, then either the language for it was created or it was no more primitive than the written. Then an oral revelation becomes a tradition, and a tradition requires either a special caste for its transmission, becomes therefore its property, or must be subjected to multitudinous changes and additions from the popular imagination—becomes, therefore, a wild commingling of broken and bewildering lights. But neither as documentary nor traditional can any traces of a primitive revelation be discovered, and to assume it is only to burden the question with a thesis which renders a critical and philosophic discussion alike impossible.

The natural and supernatural theories, as they may be termed, may here be dismissed. Let us now attempt to approach the question in what may be termed the historical method. This method is, indeed, of limited application. The history of no people reaches back to a very remote antiquity. Then, the religions of the ancient world are, with one exception, polytheistic in their earliest historical form, and their Polytheism so developed as to indicate ages of growth. They seem like an ancient forest in which the underwood has become so dense as to render any attempt to pass through it, or discover the order and time of growth, alike hopeless. But, happily, many labourers, long engaged in clearing the underwood, have met with such success, that diligent search, such as is now possible, among the roots of the old mythologies, may bring us near the discovery of the thing we seek.

In this inquiry we must confine ourselves as much as possible to the limits within which the method is applicable. Adopting, as meanwhile the most convenient, the familiar division of the race into the Indo-European, Semitic, and Turanian families, we shall confine ourselves to the first, leaving aside, though for opposite reasons, the second and the third. This limitation has a double advantage. It connects the discussion with ourselves. The religious ideas whose origin and evolution are to be examined were the ideas of our forefathers. There is no proof that the lake-dwellers of Switzerland, the flint-hatchet makers of Abbeville, or the aborigines of Scotland, were either our ancestors or their kindred; but there is the most positive proof that we are the lineal descendants of the Indo-Europeans who emigrated from North-western Asia. The other advantage is, that the Indo-European family seems to offer decisive disproof of a primitive Theism. If there have been in certain branches of the Semitic family tendencies to Monotheism, the most distinctive branches of the Indo-European have tended towards the most extravagant and multitudinous Polytheisms. No Indo-European people has had a Jahveh like the Hebrews, or an Allah like the Mohammedans;* nor has any one had a prophet, save the partly exceptional Zoroaster, authoritative like Moses, or exclusive like Mohammed.† The Indo-European has been, as a rule, tolerant of the different gods of different nations; the Semite intolerant of all gods except his own. The tolerance, in the one case, has increased the tendency to multiply gods; the intolerance, in the other case, has intensified the passion for unity. But under this difference there lies what at first seems similarity, but becomes on deeper examination a sharp antithesis. Indo-European man has had his passion for unity, but his unity has been abstract, impersonal. Unity of person has been the goal of Semitic thought, but unity of conception the goal of Indo-European.‡ The highest being of the first was personal, masculine, Jahveh, Allah; but the highest being of the second was impersonal, neuter, Brahma,§ τὸ ὄντως ὄν. We must therefore distinguish between the religious and philosophic forms

* Lassen, "Indische Alterthumskunde," vol. i. p. 496 (2nd ed.).

† Renan, "Histoire des Langues Sémitiques," p. 8, compares, not very happily, I think, the Semitic prophet to the Indian *Avatar*. The two are, save in one or two superficial points, essential contrasts. The Indian *Avatar* doctrine rests on the communicableness of the divine nature, but Hebrew prophecy on its incommunicableness.

‡ This is only another side of the contrast Renan points out between the capacity of the Indo-European race to produce original philosophies, and the incapacity of the Semitic to do so ("Histoire des Langues Sémitiques," pp. 9 ff.).

§ Brahmâ (mas.) is the first god in the Hindu Trimurtti, but Brahmâ (neut.) is the universal soul or substance of Hindu philosophy.

of the idea of God. The Indo-European tendency was to religious multiplicities, but to philosophic unities. The unity or monism, which was the product of the speculative reason in the historic period, was by no means a Monotheism; while the multitude of mythological persons which sprang up in the pre-historic period certainly formed a Polytheism.

It is the more necessary to emphasize this distinction as so much has been written about the development of Monotheism among the Greeks. It is not time yet to discuss that part of our question. And here we can only note the contrast between the Deity of a philosophy, and the God of a religion. The one is an object of worship, the other a product of speculation. In the one case, God must be conceived as a person or power standing in a certain relation to the worshipper; in the other, Deity is the first or final proposition forming the base or the summit of a system of reasoned truth. Religion may exist without philosophy, has always existed before it, and may, when it has passed from the instinctive and imaginative stages into the reflective, attempt to represent in system, or justify to thought, its idea of God; but while the two may thus become allies, they can never, save in the mind of some transcendentalist, be identical. Religion has often given the idea of God to philosophy, but philosophy has never given a God to religion. The speculative God of the Brahmans remained an object of speculation.* And not one of the Greek schools gave a God to Greek worship. The development of abstract conceptions—space, time, the infinite, the absolute, the supreme good—is not the development of Monotheism, just as a system of thought is not a religion.

We return to our problem. What was the genesis of the religious idea of God? Our first step must be to determine the primitive form of that idea among the Indo-European peoples. Here we assume (1) the original unity of the Indo-European family of nations; (2) that the rudimentary form of their civilization was in existence prior to their separation;† and (3) that the Indo-European mythologies send their roots into that distant time, are branches whose parent stem is the faith of the still united family. Discussion of mythological theories is here unnecessary. Our own view, and the reasons for it, will appear in the sequel.‡

Let us start, then, from the well-known fact that, while the Indo-European mythologies in their earliest

---

* Nor does the worship of Brahmâ (mas.) seem to have been general (Lassen, "Indis. Alterthumsk., i. p. 776, 1st edition). He was too much a product of the reflective priestly consciousness to be a people's god.

† See pp. 272 ff.

‡ A most exhaustive and philosophic discussion of mythological theories, combined with a triumphant assertion of the origin of mythology in the religious conceptions of a people, will be found in Schelling's "Philos. der Mythol.," vol. i. *Erstes Buch.*

THE IDEA OF GOD.

literary forms reveal developed and multitudinous Polytheisms, their elements become simpler and fewer the farther they are traced back.* The more cultured Greeks believed that the religion of the ancients had been much simpler than that of their own age, and that the mythical elements had been added either for poetical or political purposes.† While each philosophic school had, according to its own fundamental principles, a different—either allegorical, physical, or historical—method of interpreting the national mythology, each agreed with the others in repudiating the literal and popular sense.‡ In the Homeric and Hesiodic poems fragments can be found which seem like the survivors of an earlier faith, and look, even in the old epics, like the curiously carved stones of an ancient Gothic cathedral built into the walls of a modern church, or, to use Welcker's figure, like the fauna and flora of a lost world preserved in the successive strata of the earth's crust.§ The simpler Polytheism standing behind

---

* Welcker, "Griechische Götterlehre," vol. i. p. 129; Blackie, "Homer and the Iliad," vol. i. p. 23.

† Herodotus, lib. ii. 53; Plato, "De Repub.," lib. ii. §§ 18 ff., vol. vi. pp. 380 ff. (Bekker); Aristotle, "Metaphys.," lib. xi. 8; Creuzer, "Symbolik und Mythol. der Alten Völker," i. pp. 3 ff.

‡ Zeller, "Philosophie der Griechen," ii. 305 ff., 554 ff. (ed. 1846), iii. 299 (ed. 1865); Max Müller, "Lectures on the Science of Language," ii. lect. ix.

§ Creuzer, "Symbolik und Mythol.," iii. pp. 64—67; Welcker, "Griechis. Götterlehre," i. pp. 5—8.

the Greek epics can, in great part, be deciphered, and the several streams whose confluence form it traced to their respective Indo-European, Pelasgic, Hellenic, Oriental, and Egyptian fountain-heads. The process is thus one of increasing simplification. Diversity and multiplicity alike tend to disappear as historical analysis dissolves the tribal and temporal accretions, and resolves the faith of the early Greek settlers into its primal elements.

What is true of the Greek branch of the Indo-European mythology is also true of the Indian. The Vedic hymns represent a much earlier phase of mythological development than the Homeric poems.* If we may use Schelling's terms,† changing somewhat their sense, we would say, the Homeric Polytheism is successive, *i.e.*, its gods have each a history and a place in a definite system; but the Vedic Polytheism is simultaneous, *i.e.*, has no developed system‡—now one god, now another, is supreme.§ The simultaneous is much

---

* Muir's "Sanskrit Texts," v. pp. 3, 4; Müller, "Chips from a German Workshop," i. p. 26.

† "Philosophie der Mythologie," i. p. 120.

‡ Lassen, "Indis. Alterthumskunde," i. 908.

§ Müller's "Hist. of Ancient Sans. Lit.," p. 546. Since the above was written I have read the first of a series of papers entitled, "Veden-studiën," in *De Gids* for June 1871, by Mr. P. A. S. van Limburg Brouwer. The writer gives a fresh and interesting, but I think, in some respects, incorrect interpretation of Vedic Polytheism. The several gods are personalized natural phenomena, but God the power in nature which

more primitive than the successive stage. There has been time to create, not to systematize. But behind the Vedas lies a still earlier faith, or rather a series of earlier faiths, which can be determined partly from the hymns themselves, and partly from a comparison of Vedic deities with those of other Indo-European peoples. Indra is the supreme Vedic god,* but his origin cannot be placed earlier than the immigration into India,† where he soon thrust the older and, morally, higher Varuna into the background,‡ as Varuna seems at a still earlier period to have superseded Dyaus. Then, many gods known to the Indian are unknown to the other Indo-Europeans, and can only be regarded as additions to the primitive faith held by the undivided family. But centuries behind the Vedas we find a point where a still earlier phase of Indo-European mythology can be studied—the point where the two branches that had grown longest together parted, to form the Indian and Iranian peoples, and to develop religions almost the exact anti-

---

produces them. There is apparent plurality, but actual unity.—*De Gids*, June, pp. 395 ff.

* Of course only comparatively supreme. See former reference to Müller, and also Lassen, "Indis. Alterthumsk.," i. pp. 893—895; Muir's "Sanskrit Texts," v. sec. v.

† Benfey, "Orient und Occident," i. pp. 48, 49, note 275; Muir's "Sanskrit Texts," v. 118.

‡ Muir's "Sans. Texts," v. p. 116.

thesis of each other.* Here literary documents fail us, but comparative philology sheds a light that can hardly be called dim. By this light we can perceive that there are fewer gods than in the Vedic age, but more than had existed prior to the departure of the European branches.† The elaboration and increased importance of the worship, the appearance of a professional priesthood, the rise of new gods like Soma-Haoma, Mitra-Mithra, and other things indicative of growth in religious doctrines and rites, can be discovered from a comparison of the names and words existing at this period with those common to the Indo-European family as a whole,‡ while the absence of gods afterwards well known, of ceremonies and castes raised at a later period to prime importance, can be ascertained from a comparison of the Iranic-Indian deities, religious terms and rites, with those of the Vedas.§ The process of simplification thus continues; the younger the Polytheism the fewer its gods.

But behind the Homeric poems, and the Vedas,

---

* Lassen, "Indis. Alterthums.," p. 617; Spiegel, "Erânische Alterthumsk.," i. 489.

† Spiegel, "Erânische Alterthumsk.," pp. 432 ff.

‡ Spiegel, *ut supra*. Some excellent materials for such a comparison can be found in Fick's "Vergleich. Wörterb. der Indoger. Sprachen," ii. Wortschatz.

§ Muir's "Sanskrit Texts," i. pp. 289—295, where views of Dr. Martin Haug bearing on this point are stated.

and the separation of the Iranic-Indian branches, lies the period when Celt and Teuton, Anglo-Saxon and Indian, Greek and Roman, Scandinavian and Iranian, lived together, a simple single people. And at this point comparison can be again instituted. The germs of many subsequent developments in arts and institutions can here be discovered; but the one thing sought, meanwhile, is, What can be determined as to the religious faith then held? The points of radical and general agreement are few. Resemblances that may be classed as coincidences evolved in the course of subsequent development, must, of course, be excluded. Under this head many of the points comparative mythology seizes may be comprehended. The same faculties in men of the same race, working under different conditions indeed, but with kindred materials, could hardly fail to produce similar results. The most of those Myths of the Dawn which Max Müller has so ingeniously analyzed and explained;* gods of the stormful sky, like the German Wodin and the Indian Rudra; gods of the sea, like the Indian Varuna in his later phase, and the Greek Poseidon; gods of the sun, like the Indian Savitri and Surya and the Greek Helios— are, whatever their mythical resemblances, developmental coincidences, creations of the Aryan genius, nationalized yet retaining its family features. Excluding, then, the

* "Science of Language," ii. lect. xi.

coincidences natural to related peoples developing the same germs, we find two points of radical and general agreement—the proper name of one God, and the term expressive of the idea of God in general. The name is the Sanscrit *Dyaus*, the Greek *Zeus*, the Latin *Ju* in Jupiter, the Gothic *Tius*, the Anglo-Saxon *Tiw*, the Scandinavian *Tyr*, the old German *Ziu* or *Zio*. On this point scholars are agreed. Sanskritists like Dr. Muir[*] and Professors Müller,[†] Aufrecht,[‡] and Lassen,[§] Greek scholars like Curtius[||] and Welcker,[¶] German like Jacob Grimm,[**] and Celtic like M. Adolphe Pictet,[††] unite in tracing the cognates back to a common root, and, therefore, to a primitive name. A name for God had thus been formed before the dispersion. It remained the name, too, of the Supreme Deity of the Greeks and Romans. A distinguished Sanskritist supposes Dyaus to have been before the rise of Indra the highest God of the Indian, as well as of the other Indo-Europeans,[‡‡] and

---

[*] "Sanskrit Texts," vol. v. p. 33.
[†] "Science of Language," ii. pp. 425 ff.
[‡] Bunsen's "Christianity and Mankind," vol. iii. p. 78.
[§] "Indis. Alterthumsk.," i. 891.
[||] "Grundzüge der Griech. Etymol.," p. 222 (3rd ed.).
[¶] "Griech. Götterlehre," vol. i. pp. 131 f.
[**] "Deut. Mythol.," vol. i. p. 175.
[††] "Les Origines Indo-Européennes," vol. ii. pp. 663 ff.
[‡‡] Benfey, "Orient und Occident," vol. i. pp. 48, 49, note; Muir's "Sanskrit Texts," v. pp. 118, 119, where the greater part of Benfey's note is translated, and the similar views of M. Michel Bréal stated.

THE IDEA OF GOD.

his supremacy may have extended into the period of the Indian and Iranian unity.* The German scholar most distinguished for research in the mythology of his own land, thought he had discovered traces of the original supremacy of Tius or Zio among the Teutonic tribes;† and a brilliant philologist has generalized these facts and opinions, and argued that Jupiter was the supreme Indo-European God.‡

Perhaps it is too much to argue that the general eminence and prevalence of this name proves the supremacy of the God it designated. Two inferences, however, may be meanwhile allowed—(1) that the word in its primitive form was the name of a deity, (2) that the deity it denoted was acknowledged and worshipped by the Indo-European family as a whole. Let us turn, before attempting any more definite deduction, to the term expressing the idea of God in general. This term is in Sanskrit *deva*, in Zend *daeva*, in Greek θεός (?),§ in

---

* Spiegel, "Eränische Alterthumsk.," p. 436.
† Grimm, "Deut. Mythol.," vol. i. pp. 77 ff.
‡ Müller, "Science of Language," ii. lect. x.
§ Skt., *deva*, Zend, *daeva*, Pers., *dew*, Lat., *deus*, Lith., *déva-s*, Old Prus., *deiwa-s*, Old Ir., *dia*, Gen., *déi*, Cym., *dew*, Armor., *doué*, Corn., *deu*, Old Nor., *tiva-r*, are certainly cognates, but there is by no means the same certainty as to θεός. The current of philological opinion, once strongly in favour of identifying its root with that of *deva* and *deus*, seems now to have set as strongly against it. Bopp ("Compar. Gram.," i. pp. 4 and 15), Lassen ("Indis. Alterthumsk.," i. p. 755), Grimm ("Deut. Mythol.," i. p. 176), Welcker ("Griech. Götterl.," i. p. 131), Pictet ("Les Origines Indo-Europ.," ii. p. 653),

Latin *deus*, in Lithuanian *déva-s*, old Prussian *deiwa-s*, old Irish *dia*. The very existence of such a term is remarkable.* It indicates that the united Indo-Europeans had advanced so far in religious thought as both to form and formulate a conception of God. Names may express perceptions of sense or presentations of imagination, but general terms imply more or less practised powers of comparison and judgment, abstraction and generalization. But why had the general term come into use? In the sphere of theological thought, if the theology be an

Max Müller ("Science of Lang.," ii. pp. 405, 454), make *deva*, *deus*, and θεός cognates. But Curtius ("Grundzüge der Griech. Etymol.," pp. 222, 466—473), G. Bühler ("Orient und Occident," i. pp. 508 ff.), Mr. Peile ("Introduct. to Greek Etymol.,"), Fick ("Vergleich. Wörterbuch," pp. 96, 368), hold θεός to have no connection with *deva-deus*. Their objections appear to me to be valid. The Greek θ and the Latin *d* do not correspond. Curtius is uncertain as to the etymology of θεός, but supposes it may be from a root θεσ, whence θεσ-σά-μενοι, which he had connected in his first and second editions with the Latin *festus*, *festum*, *festivus*, but not in his third, doubts having been started by the objections of Corssen and Pott as to the correctness of his earlier view. Fick derives it from a word *dhaya*, from a root *dhî*, to shine, to look, to be devout ("Vergleich. Wörterb.," pp. 368, 102). If the latter etymology be correct, the word coincides in meaning with *deva-deus*. Then there is a significant and appropriate progress in the meaning of the word. The primary sense of this root is to shine (*scheinen*); then to look at, contemplate (*schauen*) what shines; then finally, what results from the contemplation, to be devout (*andächtig sein*). The difference of root thus only leads back to identity of meaning, while it helps to show how the contemplator became the worshipper.

* Max Müller, "Hist. Ancient Sans. Lit.," p. 527. "Words like *deva* for 'God' mark more than a secondary stage in the grammar of the Aryan religion."

absolute Monotheism, denominative and appellative will be identical.* The Hebrews, indeed, had a specific name, Jahveh, and a general term, Elohim. But the first, whatever may be said as to its meaning, was introduced because of the growing latitude in the use of the second. In Christian countries, again, where the very idea of God is exclusive, denominative and appellative tend to coalesce. We no longer distinguish between Jahveh and God; to us they are one and the same.

The formation of a term to express God in general seems possible in one of two ways—either by the gradual extension of a name to various objects of the same nature as the one first designated, or by the creation of a new word to express the new conception. Either explanation implies, so far as concerns our present subject, a growing Polytheism, and various things indicate that gods had begun to multiply before the dispersion.

Perhaps it is perilous to conjecture as to the order Indo-European thought and language here followed. But there are some significant facts. The general term, even without the Greek θεός, has a wider prevalence than the proper name. The Celts must have been the first, or

* The Hebrew prophets knew the power of a single name. Zechariah (xiv. 9) says of the time when the knowledge of the true God shall be universal, "In that day shall there be one Lord, and His Name one," while nothing was more characteristic of Polytheism than gods like Διόνυσος πολυώνυμος, or Ἶσις μυριώνυμος.

among the first, to leave the common home, but the several Celtic dialects, Irish, Cymric, Armorican, Cornish, have the cognates of *deva*, but not of *dyaus*.* It seems an almost allowable inference that the Indo-Europeans had not begun to distinguish between the individual and the general, God and gods, when the earliest departures occurred. Then the Lithuanian has *deva-s*, old Prussian has *deiwa-s*, but neither has preserved the proper name. That *deva* had been undergoing a process of deterioration in very early times is also evident from its complete change of meaning in Zend, where *daeva* is no longer God, but demon. This is all the more significant as the Iranians are representatives of an Indo-European monotheistic tendency, and their repudiation of the deity of the *daevas* may be interpreted as their protest against the growing Polytheism. If, then, these facts may be held to indicate the extension of an individual name so as to embrace a genus, the individual must have formed the starting-point. And if the inter-relations of *dyaus* and *deva* be studied, whatever the order of their application to the Divine Being, this aboriginal individualism becomes apparent. They spring from the same root—are branches of a common stem.† The unity of root indicates unity

---

* Pictet, "Les Origines Indo-Europ.," vol. ii. pp. 653, 663.

† The inter-relations of the words and their relation to the common root, *di*, to shine, may be studied as exhibited in Fick, "Vergleich. Wörterbuch," pp. 93—96, and Max Müller, "Science of Language."

of thought. If *Dyaus* was first, then a *deva* was a being who had the nature of *Dyaus*, *Dyaus* was *deva*, Ζεύς ὁ θεός. The qualities perceived in him were the qualities conceived as constitutive and distinctive of a god. If *deva* was first, then *Dyaus* was the *deva par excellence*, the being to whom the qualities held to be divine belonged. Inquiry as to the order in which the words were applied to God may be useless enough, but their common root seems to indicate that the primitive Indo-European mind had conceived *Dyaus* and *deva* as ultimately identical; just as the Hebrew—though here the verbal does not indicate the mental connection —identified in his ultimate thinking Jahveh and Elohim.*

The radical connection thus existing between the words may be held as an evidence that a radical connection existed in the Indo-European mind between the idea of God and a specific God. However this connection is explained—whether *Dyaus*, or *deva*, or neither, but a thought anterior to both, is made the parent conception —the result is the same, a Theism which we may term individualistic. But now the question rises, What thought lay at the root of both words? The common

---

ii. pp. 449 ff. *Dyaus* seems to have as a word a simpler and more rudimentary structure than *deva*, but simplicity of structure may not always be evidence of priority of use in a given sense.

* Ewald, "Geschichte des Volks Israel," vol. i. p. 138 (2nd ed.).

root, *div*, means, as is well known, to beam, to shine; hence *Dyaus*, resplendent, light-giving Heaven; *Deva*, the bright or shining one. And so the conclusion has often been drawn, the worship of the primitive Indo-Europeans was a Nature-worship,[*] an adoration of the elements, of the phenomena and powers of Nature. Confirmation is found in the Nature-worship so evident in the Vedas, so visible in the background of the Greek mythology. Then, again, Heaven is married to Earth, Dyaus to Prithivi, Zeus to Hera; and this marriage, as a French author has told us, "forms the foundation of a hundred mythologies."[†] But, beginning with the last, we inquire, Is this marriage a primitive belief, or the creation of a developed mythology? Certainly there is no evidence that Earth is as old a goddess as Heaven is a god—very decided evidence to the contrary. Dyaus was known to almost all the Indo-European peoples, but each people, and often the several tribes composing it, had a different name for the Earth-goddess. Prithivi was known to the Indians alone. Zeus, in his several forms, Pelasgian and Hellenic, was one in name and the ultimate elements of his character; but almost every Greek tribe had its own Earth-mother. The place Hera

---

[*] Renan, "Hist. des Langues Sémit.," p. 496; Bunsen, "God in History," vol. i. p. 273.

[†] M. Albert Réville, "Essais de Critique Religieuse," p. 383, quoted in Muir's "Sanskrit Texts," vol. v. p. 24.

occupies in the Olympian system is given by many of the local worships of Greece to different goddesses; and Homer, in elevating the Hellenic Hera to the throne, has to reduce the old Pelasgic Dione to a mere "lay-figure."* The German Zio, too, has no consort, the Hertha of Tacitus being altogether a local goddess.† The separation of the sexes implies an anthropomorphism,‡ rudimentary, perhaps, but real; and the marriage of Heaven and Earth, although "the foundation of a hundred mythologies," is built upon the conception that the life in both is akin to, indeed the parent of, the life in man. Since the idea of difference of sex among the gods must precede the idea of marriage, the latter must be a later mythical product than the former, and, as names like Juno and Dione witness, the bright divinity of Heaven may have been sexualized and married to a goddess of Heaven before the mythical faculty in its career of unconscious creation deified Earth and married it to Heaven.§ Developmental coincidence can explain the uniformity of the association, but no theory which assumes it as the common starting-point of the Indo-

---

* Gladstone, "Juventus Mundi," pp. 198, 238 ff., 261 ff., 264 ff.
† "De Germania," 40 ; Grimm, "Deut. Mythol.," vol. i. 230.
‡ Creuzer, "Symbolik und Mythol.," vol. i. p. 24.
§ Even Demeter may have been originally no earth goddess, but Dyâvâ Mâtar, the Dawn, corresponding to Dyaushpitar, the sky. So M. Müller, "Lectures, Science of Lang.," ii. p. 517. The marriage of Heaven and Earth is too artificial to be a very primitive conception.

European mythologies can explain the general preservation of the name in the one case and the universal loss of it in the other.

But now we come back to the Nature-worship theory, and ask, What does such a worship mean? The Nature is now limited—excludes Earth. The worshippers turned to Heaven. But it does not follow that because they named God Heaven, they thought Heaven God. It is, perhaps, no longer possible to us to personalize Heaven, but it might have been as impossible to the primitive Indo-European to conceive it as impersonal. The belief difficult to the philosophic man is easy to the imaginative child. The most natural thought to a child-like mind is, as every natural historian of religion witnesses, that Nature is animated—acts by virtue of an immanent life. The Indo-European placed the seat of this life in Heaven, worshipped no fetich or idol, but the bright resplendent Dyaus. Heaven was to him living—a being capable of feeling and exercising influence, to whom he prayed and offered sacrifices. That primitive man knew what obedience was, strove to shape his life in such a fashion as Heaven might approve, termed the being he worshipped up there Bhaga, the Distributor or the Adorable.* He had not learned to localize the

---

* The original meaning of Bhaga seems uncertain. Bopp ("Compar. Gram.," p. 1217, note) and Pictet ("Les Origines Indo-Europ.," ii. 654) derive it from a root signifying to worship, to adore, to love; hence

deity upon earth, and hence had no temple—to fear him, and hence had no priest.* The home, or the meadow, or the shadow of a giant oak, like that which stood in old Dodona, or those under whose spreading branches the Germans of Tacitus gathered to worship the invisible Presence,† was the temple, and the patriarch of the family was the priest. That worship may be termed a Nature-worship, because the one word was the name of Heaven and of God, but Nature is here only a synonym for God. The Nature was living, and the life in it was to our primitive man divine. Man had not learned to dualize his own being, nor the great being that stood around and above his own. A stranger to the philosophic thought that divides man into body and spirit, and the universe into nature and God, he realized in consciousness the unity of his own personal being, and imagined a like unity in the light and life-giving *Dyaus*. The glory of the blue and brooding heaven was the glory of the immanent God.

This primitive worship is also sometimes termed a personification of natural forces and objects. It depends very much on what personification means whether the explanation be true or false. Our personification is a

Bhaga, the adorable being. But Fick ("Vergleich. Wörterbuch," p. 133) derives it from a root signifying to distribute. Hence Bhaga, the Distributor ("Zutheiler").

* Pictet, "Les Origines Indo-Europ.," vol. ii. p. 690.

† "De Germania," 9; Welcker, "Griech. Götterlehre," vol. i. p. 202.

conscious act—the investing material things with the character and attributes of living beings. But in no respect whatever was primitive worship personification in this sense. The imagination was not consciously creative. There was no intentional investiture of natural objects with divine powers. That, indeed, would have implied cultured thought and developed belief. Personification involves the idea of person. If man personifies a natural object as a god, he must have the idea of God. A strict Naturalism, without belief in invisible powers, cannot personify—can create a fetich as little as a god. Hence Nature personified can only mean Nature conceived as living, as vital with creative and preservative powers. To worship Nature, or natural elements and objects thus conceived, is to worship neither the Nature of material forces and laws known to science, nor the Nature of imaginary voices and shapes known to poetry, but the Nature known to the primitive man-child as the body and home of the immanent God.

But there is one element of the Indo-European conception of God too characteristic to be overlooked—the element of Paternity. He was conceived as Father—father of man. The Indians called him Dyaushpitar. The Greeks invoked Ζεῦ πάτερ—could so little forget this essential attribute of their family deity that they transferred it to the great Olympian, Father of gods and men. The Romans blended name and character in Jupiter. The

Germans, though they displaced the ancient Zio, did not forget his fatherhood,* and so loved the thought of a father-god † as to make the stormful Wodin *Alvater*. This is, perhaps, the characteristic which most distinguishes the Indo-European from the Semitic conception of God—the parent, too, of all other differences. Neither as Monotheisms, nor as Polytheisms, do the Semitic religions attribute a fatherly, humane character to their gods. Even the Old Testament knows only an abstract ideal fatherhood, which the Hebrews as a nation realize, but the Hebrew as a man almost never does. The Semitic God dwells in inaccessible light—an awful, invisible Presence, before which man must stand uncovered, trembling; but the Indo-European God is pre-eminently accessible, loves familiar intercourse, is bound to man by manifold ties of kinship. The majesty of God in an exalted Monotheism, like the Hebrew, is sometimes so conceived as almost to annihilate the free agency and personal being of man; but the Indo-European, as a rule, so conceives his Deity as to allow his own freedom of action and personal existence full scope. The explanation may, perhaps, be here found of the Hebrew horror at death, almost hopeless "going down to the grave," the often-asserted and often-denied silence of the Old Testament as to the immortality of man. So much is certain, whether the Warburtonian or the more orthodox

---

* Grimm, "Deut. Mythol.," vol. i. 178.   † Ib., pp. 20, 149 f.

theory be held, the doctrine of a future state occupies a less prominent and less essential place in the religion of the Old Testament than in the Indo-European religions in general.* The belief in immortality was before Christ more explicit and more general among the Greeks than among the Jews. The conception of God, in the one case, seems to have almost annihilated the conception of man; but in the other, the two conceptions were mutually complementary,—God incomplete without man, man without God. Then, while the father in the Indo-European religions softens the god, and gives, on the whole, a sunny and cheerful and, sometimes, festive character to the worship, the god in the Semitic annihilates the father, and gives to its worship a gloomy, severe, and cruel character, which does not indeed belong to the revealed religion of the Old Testament, but often belongs to the actual religion of the Jews.† The Indo-European loves the gay religious festival, the Semite the frequent and prolonged fast. The Semitic Polytheisms showed very early their fiercer spirit in the place they gave and the necessity they attached to human sacrifices; but the Indo-European religions, although perhaps, even in the earliest times, not altogether innocent of human sacrifices,‡

---

* Ewald, "Geschichte des Volks Israel," vol. ii. 172 ff.

† Kalisch, "Leviticus," vol. i. pp. 381—416.

‡ Muir's "Sanskrit Texts," i. pp. 355 ff. Weber, "Ueber Menschenopfer bei den Indern der Vedischen Zeit.," Indis. Streifen, pp. 54 ff.

yet entered on their more dreadful phase only after they had fallen under malign influences, home or foreign.* The contrast might be pursued to their respective priesthoods, where, indeed, exceptions would be found, but only defining and confirming the rule. These characteristic and fundamental differences in feeling, thought, and worship can be traced to the primary difference in the conception of God. The one class of religions developed themselves from the idea of Divine Fatherhood, but the other class from the idea of Divine Sovereignty, severely exercised over a guilty race. The subjective Semite found his God in himself, and offered a worship such as would have been acceptable to him had he been Deity. The objective Indo-European found his God without and above him, and rejoiced in a religion as full of light and gladness as the resplendent heaven.

We may now attempt to formulate the primitive Indo-European idea of God. We can at once exclude the fancy that it was a fetich or an idol-god, such as the savages of the South Sea Islands may now worship. The God of our fathers was no ghost of a deceased ancestor seen in feverish dreams. They stood in the primeval home in the highlands of North-western Asia, looked, as

---

* Pfleiderer, "Die Religion," vol. ii. 128, ascribes the myth of Kronos devouring his own children to Oriental, *i.e.*, Semitic influence. Gladstone, "Address on the Place of Ancient Greece in the Providential Order of the World," pp. 35, 36.

Abraham once did, at the resplendent sun flooding the world with life and light, at the deep, broad, blue heaven, a bosom that enfolded earth, bringing the rain that fertilized their fields and fed their rivers, and the heat that ripened their corn, at the glory its sunlight threw upon the waking, its moonlight upon the sleeping, earth, and at the stars that "globed themselves" in the same boundless Heaven, and went and came and shone so sweetly on man and beast, and they called that far yet near, changing but unchangeable, still but ever-moving, bright yet unconsumed and unconsuming Heaven, *deva*— God. To Indo-European man, Heaven and God were one, not a thing but a person, whose *Thou* stood over against his *I*. His life was one, the life above him was one too. Then, that life was generative, productive, the source of every other life, and so to express his full conception, he called the living Heaven, Diespiter, Dyaushpitar—Heaven-Father.

The primitive form of the Indo-European idea of God, so far as it is discoverable, now lies before us. We must now see what light the form can throw upon the genesis of the idea. It certainly shows the theories before examined to be historically untenable. Terror, distempered dreams, fear of the unknown causes of the accidents and destructive phenomena of nature, the desire to propitiate the angry ghosts of ancestors deceased—none of these could have produced the simple, sublime faith of our Indo-European man-child. The religion whose earliest form embodies neither terror nor darkness, but a spirit glad and brilliant like the light of Heaven, cannot have risen out of the ignorance and fears of a soul hardly human. The object selected for worship was the sublimest man could perceive, and even the inquirer most inclined to deny spiritual and theistic elements to the first religion, must concede to its Indo-European form rare elevation of object and sunniness of aspect, and to the men who held it a force of thought and strength of imagination incompatible with what we know to be the mental and moral condition of savages. The idea formulated in Heaven-Father was no product of the reasoning or reflective consciousness, because the conclusions of the one and the creations of the other are abstract, bodiless, not concrete, embodied, living. There were two real or objective, and two ideal or subjective, factors in the genesis of the idea. The two real were the bright, brooding Heaven and its action in relation to Earth. The two ideal were the conscience and the imagination. The real factors stimulated the action of the ideal. The ideal borrowed the form in which to express themselves from the real. Conscience knew of relation, dependent and obligatory, to Some One. Imagination discovered the Some One on whom the individual and the whole alike depended in the Heaven. Neither faculty could be satisfied with the subjective, each was driven by the law of its own constitution to seek an objective reality. Conscience, so far as it revealed obligation, revealed relation to a being higher than self. Imagination, when it turned its eye to Heaven, beheld there the higher Being, the great Soul which directed the varied celestial movements, and created the multitudinous terrestrial lives. Without the conscience, the life the imagination saw would have been simply physical; without the imagination, the relation the conscience revealed would have been purely ideal—the relation of a thinker to his thought, not of one personal being to another. But the being given by the one faculty and the relation given by the other coalesced so as to form that worship of the bright Dyaus, which was our primitive Indo-European religion.

These, then, were the two faculties generative of the idea of God, *i.e.*, from their action and inter-action the primitive religion sprang. Of course, in terming these "the faculties generative of the idea" we do not mean that they acted alone. No faculty can be isolated in action, whatever it may be as an object of thought. We only mean that these, for the time being the governing faculties of the mind, were the two from whose combined instincts and actions the idea of God rose into form. That conscience was a main factor of our Indo-European faith is evident, setting aside psychological considerations, from that faith itself. More moral

THE IDEA OF GOD.

elements can be found, comparatively speaking, in its earlier than in its later forms. The proofs of its Naturalism, as of its Polytheism, are derived from the developed national religions, not from the rudimentary and common faith. But it is certain that some of these grew from a (comparative) Spiritualism into an almost pure Naturalism. It was almost certainly the conflict of the spiritual and sensuous forms that separated the Iranian and Indian branches.* In the Rig Veda the younger and more physical faith is seen superseding the older and more moral.† Varuna has a "moral elevation and sanctity" of character "far surpassing that attributed to any other Vedic deity."‡ Yet he is seen undergoing a twofold process, one of supersession and another of deterioration, until, in the later Vedic hymns, the God, in his older and nobler character, almost entirely disappears. The God that supersedes him is Indra, a splendid physical figure, no doubt, "borne on a shining golden car with a thousand supports," drawn by "tawny steeds" "with flowing golden manes," hurling his thunder-bolts, drinking the soma-juice, slayer of Vritra, but the moral elements in his character are far fewer and inferior

* Professor Roth, "Zeitschrift der Deut. Morgenländ. Gesellschaft," vol. v. pp. 76 ff.
† Ib. Also Muir, "Sanskrit Texts," vol. v. pp. 116—118, where an epitome is given of Roth's views.
‡ Muir, "Sans. Texts," v. p. 66.

to those in Varuna's.* Behind the latter the still more ancient *Dyaus* stands, and his character, though shadowy and fragmentary, reveals moral elements transcending the conception of a mere physical deity. In the religion behind the Vedas and Avesta we see the point where mind becomes conscious of a dualism in its faith, and by exclusion of the moral element, the Naturalism of the first is developed, by exclusion of the physical, the Spiritualism of the second. But behind this point stands the ancient and common Indo-European faith in which the two elements existed together as matter and form, spirit and letter, not in a consciously apprehended dualism, but in a realized unity. In this oldest religion worship,† sacrifice,‡ prayer,§ and such rudimentary ideas as faith, piety,∥ holiness,¶ can be discovered, and their existence implies, as the creative faculty, a moral sense. The acquired conscience of Utilitarianism cannot explain these acts and ideas, because they rise with the Indo-European people, create, are not created by, its religious experience, are deteriorated rather than improved by certain later developments. The oldest is here the highest. The physical eclipses the moral, the moral does not rise by hardly perceptible gradations from the physical.

---

* See the admirable and exhaustive exhibition of Indra in the fifth volume of Dr. Muir's "Sanskrit Texts," sec. v.

† Pictet, "Les Origines Indo-Europ.," vol. ii. 690.

‡ Ib., p. 702. § Ib., p. 699. ∥ Ib., p. 696. ¶ Ib., p. 694.

We require, therefore, a faculty generative of these primary religious acts and ideas, and we have it in conscience. Consciousness and conscience rose together. Mind conscious of self was also mind conscious of obligation. The "I am" and the "I ought" were twins, born at the same moment. But to be conscious of obligation was to be conscious of relation, and so in one and the same act mind was conscious of a self who owed obedience, and a Not-Self to whom the obedience was due.

The idea of God was thus given in the very same act as the idea of self; neither could be said to precede the other. Mind could be mind as little without the consciousness of God as without the consciousness of self. Certain philosophies may have dissolved the first idea as certain others may have dissolved the second, but each idea is alike instinctive, rises by nature, can be suppressed only by art. But we must try now to define the nature of this πρώτη θεοῦ ἔννοια. Our ordinary terms are so associated with modern ideas as to be inapplicable to this aboriginal idea. We cannot call it a Monotheism, for, as Preller rightly remarks, "Monotheism rests essentially on abstraction and negation,"* while here the very idea of other gods has not as yet been formed. Schelling terms the primitive faith *relativer Monothe-*

* Quoted in Welcker, "Griech. Götterlehre," iii. p. xiv.

ismus,* but this phrase is hardly descriptive and definite enough, is also, perhaps, properly denotive of a Monotheism which admits a number of divine beings as intermediate between God and the world, as contrasted with an absolute Monotheism, which draws the line of a sharp and rigid dualism. Max Müller uses the term *Henotheism*.† This is better; but we would prefer, as more intelligible, the terms, individual Theism, or simply Individualism. It is a Theism, as opposed to Naturalism, in so far as it makes Dyaus conscious, creative, moral. It is an individual Theism, as opposed to an abstract and exclusive Monotheism, on the one hand, and a Polytheism, on the other, in so far as it affirms God is, but neither that there are or are not other gods. These, indeed, were questions the primitive mind could neither raise nor answer. Centuries of unconscious creation were needed to raise the one—centuries of conscious reflection to raise the other.

II.

We come now to the development of the idea. It was in its earliest form essentially capable of evolution. A pure Monotheism or an actual Polytheism is, each in its own way, an ultimate form, which may be developed as to its accidents, but not as to

---

* "Philos. der Mythol.," i. 126.

† "Chips from a German Workshop," vol. i. p. 355.

its essence. Revolution must precede further evolution. But the primitive idea was germinal, held in it many evolutional possibilities, was a point from which the human mind could start, but at which it could not permanently stand. Had reason been cultivated, or had an instinct anticipated its action, the evolution might have been to an abstract and exclusive Monotheism; but the primitive Indo-European had neither a cultured reason nor a monotheistic instinct. Of the faculties generative of the idea, conscience was unifying, demanded an individual deity, demanded no more; but the imagination was multiplicative. Then, the very conception of a life immanent in the luminous and impregnating Heaven strengthened the multiplying as opposed to the unifying tendency. The variety and contrasts of Nature helped the imagination to individualize the parts. A different spirit seems to animate the calm, smiling Heaven from what animates a heaven tempestuous and thundering. Night seems distinct from day—the brilliant, beneficent spirit of the one from the revealing yet enfolding, distant yet near, spirit of the other. So the imagination, which had discerned and localized the God conscience demanded, pursued its creative career, not now in obedience to the moral faculty, but only to its own impulses. And so its creations graduated to Naturalism, became more physical, less moral—simple transcripts of the phenomena and aspects of Nature. The Indian Varuna, the Greek Uranos, marks the first step of the evolution to Naturalism. The conceptions so agree as to warrant the inference that the deification had begun before the Greeks left for Europe, but so differ as to imply that the creation was recent, the character of the new deity still fluid, unfixed.* He represented the covering, enfolding Night-Heaven, as opposed to the luminous Dyaus. The two had seemed so different as to suggest distinct individuality; two aspects of the same object were apprehended as two beings. When next comparison can be instituted, a new deity stands beside Varuna—Mitra, the God of Light.† The creation of the one had necessitated the creation of the other; deified Night was incomplete without deified Day. But though the conceptions graduate to Naturalism, they are not yet purely natural—creations, indeed, of the imagination, but of it as still influenced by the moral faculty.

But the conscience also acted indirectly on what we may term, after Schelling, the theogonic process.‡ In prompting to worship, it furnished objects that could be personalized. The earliest worship was, indeed, simple, but its tendency was to multiply acts and

---

* Muir, "Sanskrit Texts," vol. v. p. 76.
† Spiegel, "Erânische Alterthumsk.," p. 434.
‡ "Philos. der Mythol.," vol. i. pp. 193, 204.

ceremonies. The first priests were the fathers of the family; but as life became more toilsome and occupied, the father was fain to delegate his priestly office to another. The sense of faults and sins, too, began to affect the worshipper, to force him to distinguish between secular and sacred, until he came to think that the man acceptable to God must be a man divorced from secular and devoted to sacred things. Hence, a professional priesthood was formed, and, as a matter of course, forms of worship increased. Each reacted on the other. The worship became more elaborate as the priesthood became more professional, and the ritual the priest developed the imagination idealized—the form became to it the matter of religion. What could reveal deity was deified. What made the worshipper accepted, forgiven, was idealized into the accepter, the forgiver. And hence sacerdotal deities were evolved alongside the natural. The same period that witnessed the creation of Varuna-Mitra witnessed also the creation of Soma. The juice of the plant used in sacrifice to God became itself a god, just as to a certain section of Christians the symbol of Christ's sacrifice has become the sacrifice itself.

The theogonic process thus operates at the beginning in two distinct spheres—the natural and the sacerdotal. Its action is influenced in the one by geographical conditions, in the other by social and political. The natural objects deified are borrowed from the Nature presented to the imagination. It was only after the Indians had descended into the hot plains of India, lived under its bright, burning sky, wearied and prayed for softening and cooling rain, that Indra was created. It was up among the mountains of Kashmir, where frequent tempests rage, that the blustering and furious Rudra took his rise.* The Germans, wandering under the cloudy and tempestuous skies of the north, forgot the bright face of Zio, and worshipped the stormful Wodin and the thundering Thor; but the Greeks, under their sunny sky, and in their land of many mountains and rivers and islands, washed by the waves of the sparkling Ægean, remembered Zeus, and called around him innumerable bright deities of mountain and river and sea. Geographical conditions thus very much determined the character and number of the natural deities. A land of severe climate and uniform scenery could not have the wealth of mythical gods and legends natural to a beautiful and varied land like Greece. The Vedic natural deities but embody the splendour of Indian nature; but the rough, yet kindly, German gods reproduce the boisterous, yet warm-hearted, Fatherland.

Political and social conditions in India favoured the growth there of a sacerdotal caste, and that was the

* Weber, quoted in Muir's "Sanskrit Texts," vol. iv. p. 335.

Indo-European land pre-eminent in sacerdotal deities. The struggles, conquests, and changes that issued in the rise of the Brahmans do not concern us meanwhile, but their rise indicates profound religious convictions. It dates from the Iranian and Indian unity, and many things prove that to have been a period of extraordinary spiritual fervour and growth. The inner and moral forces then active the Iranians carried away, but the Indians the outer and formal. The genius of each people took thus a different direction—the one tended to develop the spiritual, the other the external, side of religion. The most extreme sacerdotalism is the least spiritual. It changes the form into the matter of religion—augments and emphasizes it. Hence from the separation, when its moral spirit departed with the Iranians, the sacerdotalism of India increases. The very natural deities have more or less a sacerdotal character. Indra loves the soma-juice, which he "drinks like a thirsty stag," is thereby exhilarated and propitiated.* Agni is the sacrificial fire deified, and so is the mediator between gods and men, "the priest of the gods," "commissioned by gods and men to maintain their mutual communications."† Brahmanaspati is an "impersonation of the power of devotion," "a deity in whom the action of the worshipper upon the gods is

---

* Muir's "Sanskrit Texts," vol. v. pp. 88 ff.
† Ib., pp. 199 ff. ; Lassen, "Indis. Alterthumsk.," vol. i. p. 760.

personified."* He is sometimes the representative of Indra, sometimes of Agni, the idealizing faculty halting uncertain as it were between a new creation or the sublimation of an old.† The imagination which found so much to deify in the sacerdotalism of India, was less successful in the same sphere in other Indo-European countries. Greeks and Germans, Latins and Celts, held the instruments of worship to be sacred but not divine. Oaks and groves were believed to be the haunts of deities, sacrifices were thought to persuade the gods, certain ceremonies and symbols to have peculiar sanctity, but without the necessary social conditions the act of deification was impossible.

The mythical faculty pursued in each sphere a different course—descended in the one, ascended in the other. Thus in the Rig Veda, where Naturalism stands in its purest form, we have as the background and starting-point two conceptions—Heaven as luminous, Dyaus; then as immense, boundless, Aditi.‡ The dissolution of Aditi into the Adityas yields a number of deities, each partly natural, partly spiritual—as the first associated with the greater phenomena of Nature, as the second representatives of functions like government, or

* Professor Roth, quoted in Muir's "Sans. Texts," vol. v. pp. 272 ff.
† Muir, ib., p. 281.
‡ Professor Roth, "Zeitschrift der Morgenländ Gesells.," vol. vi. pp. 68 ff.

virtues like the mercy that forgives. Then single objects are deified, like the sun as Surya or Savitri, or the dawn like Ushas, or the storm as the Maruts. The process goes on descending till rivers like the Sarasvati and Yamuna, and mountains like the Himalaya, are deified. But the theogonic process in the sacerdotal sphere begins with the soma-juice, ascends through Agni and Brahmanaspati, till it culminates in Brahma, the supreme deity. This difference in the order of evolution is instructive. The first shows how an exalted idea has been materialized and depraved, the second how a low idea can be, by abstraction and negation, raised and rarified till it becomes the highest deity of speculation, but not a god to be worshipped. The living god which the process of degradation ruins the process of elevation cannot restore.

But now, while this double theogonic process goes on, exhausting the natural and sacerdotal objects it has to deify, the necessary evolution of the human mind leads to another theogonic process, also double, and starting from two opposite sides. This process, as it affects the gods, is anthropomorphism; as it affects man, apotheosis. The first, by ascribing human forms and relations to the gods, prepares the way for the second, the deification of man. The one springs from the worship, the other from the unconscious poetry, of a people. Every god who is the object of worship is conceived more or less under human forms. The feelings, relations, and acts attributed to him, the influences brought to bear upon him in prayer and sacrifice, are the results or expressions of an anthropomorphic conception. Thus, as worship becomes more elaborate and important, the gods become more manlike. Sacrifices persuade them as gifts persuade men. The soma-juice, or the wine of the libation, exhilarates gods as well as men. They are pleased with those who worship them, displeased with those who do not. So essential is this anthropomorphic conception to worship, that the pure Monotheism of the Hebrews could not, when made the basis of an actual religion, dispense with it. It forms the foundation of every successive Polytheism, changes the character, modifies the history and relations, of every deity, natural or sacerdotal. When the anthropomorphic process is well advanced, apotheosis begins. Gods have been changed into the similitude of men, men can now be changed into the similitude of gods. The tendency to apotheosize was always strong in Indo-European man. Love of the fathers has ever been one of his characteristics. The heroic age lay behind, and the fathers were the heroes. Indian and Teuton, Greek and Latin, alike reverenced their ancestors, and the unconscious poetry of the popular mind transformed the splendid figures of the past into minor deities. The primitive Indo-European faith, which attributed paternity to God, favoured the apotheosis of the fathers. The first men were the sons of Dyaushpitar—partook of his divine nature—were divine. The anthropomorphic process introduced human elements into the idea of God; apotheosis introduced divine elements into the idea of man. Each widened the circle of Polytheism, allowed the imagination to deify men as easily as it had once deified natural and sacerdotal objects. The idea had ceased to be exclusive and become comprehensive. The difficulty was now to determine not what was, but what was not, divine. And at this very point the mythical faculty became exhausted. It was crushed beneath the multitude of its own creations, died because it had driven the idea with which it started into regions where it could no longer live.

But at the point where creation ends combination begins. The gods of different tribes and nations become blended together. Foreign worships are naturalized, and their legends adapted to their new homes. The religion of the Indian aborigines affected, modified, that of the Aryans—certain gods of the soil conquered the conquerors. Simple as was the German mythology, it was an amalgam of elements derived from various sources. And every one knows how many mythologies and worships coalesced in those of Greece and Rome. The age of combination culminates in the epics. They are a conscious effort to weave into historical harmony and form the mythical creations of the past. The poet finds the myths of conquering and conquered peoples, aborigines and immigrants, legends native and foreign, floating side by side, and these he shapes into the story he sings. The epic is thus a real, though perhaps unintentional, attempt to systematize mythology, so to combine and co-ordinate the conflicting positions and claims of the gods as to produce a credible and organized Polytheism.

But since the epic is a product of the reflective consciousness, since it attempts to combine heterogeneous elements into a homogeneous system, it marks the beginning of a new stage in the development of the idea of God—the reflective. The mythical faculty has exhausted its resources, ended its career, and further multiplication is now impossible. The reflective faculty now comes forward to develop the idea in another direction—that of unity. It does not begin by denying, but by assuming, the truth of the mythical creations. The gods are all true, have each their place and work in the universe. But it seeks behind and above the gods an abstract unifying principle, ascribing to it supreme power even over the gods. Characteristically the Indians developed their sacerdotal deity Brahman-aspati into Brahmā, the Supreme God, then into Brahmă, the Universal Soul; and quite as characteristically Greek thought started on its unifying course from

Μοῖρα, the Fate that controlled gods as well as men. The same dread power stands behind the German gods, Ragnarökr,* and works their destruction. These are the first steps of the reflective consciousness towards unity, more or less rude, more or less successful, according to the people's degree of culture and faculty of abstraction.

This touches a subject which cannot be even glanced at here and now. Along the path thus opened up philosophers and poets in India and Greece were to follow each other in quick succession, striving to find theistic unity, finding Monism often enough, never finding Monotheism. Into a subject so vast it would be mere impertinence to attempt to enter at the close of this essay. Enough to say, reason could neither discover nor create the true and exhaustive conception of God. The idea of order it reached, of unity, of a cause, of a supreme good, a principle that moved all things, but was itself unmoved, but the unity was abstract, impersonal, unity of a thought, not of a living Being capable of sustaining relations to every individual, personally governing the world, and interposing to save it when lost. Man can worship no other than a personal God, with qualities that appeal to the noblest and tenderest susceptibilities of his heart. But this God neither

* Pfleiderer, "Die Religion," ii. p. 101 ; Grimm, "Deut. Mythol.," p. 774.

poetry nor philosophy could create, and the brilliant thought of Greece, which started from the Fate of the Poet, landed in the Pantheism of the Stoic, the Atheism of the Epicurean, or the universal doubt of the Sceptic, while the speculative thought of India ended in the Atheism of Kapila, or the Akosmism of the Vedanta.* Without the God man needed, the religions of the West, smitten with hopeless incompetence and decay, perished amid general licence, under the indifference of the rulers, the antagonism of the philosophers, and the apathy of the people; while the more fervid spirits of the East forsook the religion of caste for the religion of despair, and plunged into the worship of annihilation. But in the fulness of time the idea the world needed was revealed. The Christian idea, which held in it the noblest elements of the Indo-European and Semitic conceptions, the pure Monotheism of the one blended with the Fatherhood of the other, unity yet plurality, distinction from the world, yet immanence in it, absolute divinity, yet not excluding union with humanity, was given as

* The terminology of our western philosophies can hardly be applied accurately to the Hindu systems. They are when most like ours always like with a difference. It depends very much on the interpretation given of the idea of God and the importance attached to it, whether the Sankhya philosophy be judged Atheistic, while the term Akosmism, applied first by Jacobi and afterwards by Hegel to the system of Spinoza, can be used of the Vedanta as a designation only approximatively correct. To it the world was an illusion; Brahma the only and absolute reality.

the most complete revelation of God man could receive. This idea, the only one that can at once commend itself to the speculative reason and maintain itself as a living power in the heart, abides amid all the fluctuations of thought "without variableness or shadow of turning."

THEISM AND SCIENTIFIC
SPECULATION.

THEISM AND SCIENTIFIC SPECULATION.

THE scientific and religious conceptions of the world seem to stand at this moment in the sharpest possible antagonism. Their conflict has, indeed, of late been too much of a mere platform and pulpit controversy to be a brave and fair facing of the questions and issues. Certain leaders in science, with a turn for metaphysics, certain leaders in theology, with a turn for science, have become almost intellectual knights-errant, always prancing about the country bellicose and armed, great in challenge and counter-challenge, retort, invective, and innuendo. These passages of arms may easily be overrated. The world's decisive battles have not been fought by careering and trumpeting errant knights. Thinking done in public and embodied in speech now scornful, now pitiful, now minatory, may, while very pat to the times, be deficient in every quality that can command conviction and win respect. But there is one fact we cannot well overrate,—the state of conflict or mental schism in which every devout man, who is also a man of culture, feels himself compelled more or less consciously to live. His mind is an arena in which two conceptions struggle for the mastery, and the struggle seems so deadly as to demand the death of the one for the life of the other, faith sacrificed to knowledge or knowledge to faith.

Our age is, perhaps, morbidly alive to the collisions and antitheses of Science and Religion. On the one side, science conceives a universe self-evolved, ruled by necessary laws, made up of forces inexhaustible, indestructible, convertible into infinitely varied modes of being and action. On the other side, religion conceives the world as a creation, the work of a voluntary Creator, regards Nature as the arena of a now ordinary, now extraordinary, but never still or ineffective divine operation. Science charges theology with setting up unverified and unverifiable notions, arbitrary will, supernatural interference, the fickle and irregular action upon Nature of a power without it. Theology reproaches science with seeking either to evolve an uncaused universe, or to reduce the divine connexion with it to the smallest possible point, making God as good as no-god, with hardly any part in the creation of the world, without active relation to it, or living concern in it, ever since. Conciliation by the division of their respective provinces is impossible, for the point contested belongs by equal right to both. The highest truth of religion is the ultimate problem of science; the one lives by faith in a Creator, the other lives to seek and discover a cause. Nor will peace be secured by conquest. Man cannot live either by religion or by science alone. Both are necessary to the perfection alike of the individual and society. The realities of science are as sacred as those of religion, ought to be as diligently sought by the intellect, as loyally served by conscience and heart. The truth that shall reconcile the two is to be found, not by silence or concealed convictions on either side, but by the frank criticism and co-operation of physicist and metaphysician. The discussion to be here attempted is meant simply as a humble contribution towards this most desirable end.

Our present controversies on this subject ought not to be deprecated. They are healthy and bracing, mark a clearer and more wholesome state of the mental atmosphere than existed twenty years since. Mind has proved too strong for the feeble and pretentious philosophy that then claimed to have defined the objects and limits of knowledge. Theism was ruled out of court on the plea of mental incompetence. M. Comte had banned the inquiry into causes, the very word cause. Phenomena and their laws were the only subjects of rational investigation. Mr. G. H. Lewes wrote his brilliant but inaccurate "Biographical History of Philosophy" to prove that philosophy, aspiring to the knowledge of causes, had endeavoured to compass the impossible, but positive science, recognizing the limits of human faculties, contented itself with the possible. And so, while the reign of the one had ceased, the empire of the other was established. Mr. J. S. Mill, in his most elaborate and influential work, pronounced "ultimate or efficient causes radically inaccessible to the human faculties,"* and based his judgment on what were thought irrefragable philosophic grounds. But now all is changed. The search after causes, both efficient and ultimate, is being conducted with the most daring and unwearied enthusiasm. Science has become as speculative, as prolific of physico-metaphysical theories as the most bewitched metaphysician could desire. On more than one occasion distinguished physicists have been seen to stray into a perfect wilderness of metaphysics, where, getting enchanted, they have become as enamoured of their physically named metaphysical entities as Titania of the illustrious weaver, only, unhappily, their disenchantment has not always been as complete as hers. The two men chiefly responsible for the change are Mr. Darwin and Mr. Herbert Spencer. Evolution, as a new creational theory, inevitably raised the old questions as to causes. While Mr. Darwin concerned himself with its scientific statement and relations, Mr. Spencer attempted to find it a basis in a metaphysical system compounded of certainly not too homogeneous philosophical and psychological principles.

* Logic, vol. i. p. 422, 1st ed.

The consequent crop of cosmic speculation has been of the most varied and extensive kind, ranging from theories as to the origin of species to theories as to the origin of the universe. Mr. Darwin, admirable in his caution, has held strictly to the scientific proofs of his, as compared with later developments, modest thesis, hardly ever adventuring into the exhausting atmosphere of pure speculation. Mr. Spencer, bolder and more speculative, has essayed the ambitious task of building a science of the universe on a philosophy of the Unknowable. Professor Haeckel, of Jena, has, in a work now translated, remarkable for its lucid eloquence, terse and intelligible exposition, easy and masterful movement of thought, expounded a system of the most thoroughgoing Monism, a "Natural History of Creation," which, as to the Becoming, alike of inorganic and organic nature, is meant to leave no room for a Creator. Professor Tyndall's presidential address is memorable enough, were it only as an instance of sweet simplicity in things historical, and the most high-flying metaphysics disguised in scientific terms. Recently there has come from the other side of the Atlantic a "Cosmic Philosophy," * which, while built on Mr. Spencer's, still more happily illustrates the aversion of our latest scientific speculation to Positivism. If the Becom-

---

* "Outlines of Cosmic Philosophy," by John Fiske, M.A., LL.B., —an admirable, though hardly a compendious, exposition of the philosophy of evolution.

ing of the universe is to be explained, the search into causes must be held not only possible, but necessary.

In these discussions, which touch its very being, Theism has a right to take part. If it and science stand opposed on many points, they ought to agree in their common love of truth and as common desire to find and confess it. We have come from a fresh point and along new lines face to face with the deepest questions, not simply of our, but of all time, and our common duty is to read as best we can the everlasting riddle. Theism has surely claims enough, even in the changed aspects old questions wear, to entitle it to a fair and patient hearing. But that is a thing hard to get. Our present controversies are cursed by our past. The quest after truth often turns into a hunt after fruitless and provoking error. Eminence ought to be above the meanness of mediocrity, science superior to the tactics of the secularist lecturer or pamphleteer. Distinguished scientists should leave it to obscurer men to make points against theology and the churches. But certain of them, though moving, as they believe, to victory, are ungenerous enough to confuse the battle by raising the ghosts of the dead, to exasperate the sons by fighting them with the bones of their fathers. They seldom forget that Rome burnt Bruno and tortured Galileo, that the Geneva Calvin ruled sent Servetus to the stake, and the synagogue of Amsterdam expelled and cursed Spinoza. They seldom remember that science has known, still knows, how to persecute, that cultured and pagan Athens could be as merciless to free inquiry and thought as Christian and Catholic Rome. If they become historians, they are eloquent over the "intellectual immobility" of the middle ages, but silent as to its daring and subtle and even sceptical thought. They praise Copernicus and Gassendi, but fail to indicate what relation religion and the Church had to their studies. They narrate the conquests of science as if they had been victories over theology, and not over ignorance. The antiquated and false views of Nature which old divines maintained, and, because old, could not but maintain, are gravely represented as essential to religion, almost identical with it, and are no less gravely classified and exhibited as exploded religious doctrines, rather than as what they really are, exploded conceptions of nature, necessarily, indeed, interwoven with the religious as with the other thought of the time, but as form, not as matter. These points are well illustrated in a recent book, an unworthy member of a generally worthy series, which professes to represent "the Conflict of Religion and Science,"* but succeeds in representing little else than an unscientific and shallow, perverse and untruthful, conception of their historical relations. Truth can never be served, or science promoted, by factional histories or sectarian polemics. Work done under these con-

---

* Draper's "History of the Conflict between Religion and Science," Henry S. King and Co., 1875, one of the international scientific series, though one can hardly see what right it has to be there.

ditions can never be done well. They tend to create and maintain a state of feud, with the jealousies and retaliations that interfere with honest husbandry, and raise on either side the borderland moss-troopers, not always careful whose cattle they lift or what happens to their owners.

This one-sided and ungenerous method of using the past against the present needs to be explicitly censured. It is, at best, but a caricature of the truth, not too sympathetically done, good, perhaps, as a caricature, but bad as a likeness. Theism has served science, and its services ought to be acknowledged. They might, indeed, be proved to be so many as to be more than the utmost generosity of speech and action could now repay. The belief that God created the world helped to make science religious, in the noblest sense, in her winsome and wondering childhood, reverent before Nature, as if it were the outer court of the great Temple, through which wandered veiled but beautiful light, the shadow of the God whose seat was the Holy of Holies. Inquiry was worship. To admire the work was to adore the Worker. To extend the knowledge of Nature was to enlarge the knowledge of God. The Moorish philosophers were devout Theists, religiously searched for more adequate modes of expressing the inexpressible greatness, the unresting activity, the unsearchable wisdom of Allah. Copernicus was as famous for his piety as for his genius, consecrated himself and his means to three services that were to him as one—God, man, and science.

The belief that the universe had been built, as it were, to divine music, and manifested divine purpose and action everywhere, in the minutest structures as in the splendid and harmonious whole, made the pious Kepler imagine, with Plato, that the Creator had geometrized, and that he, in discovering the laws of the creation, was but thinking the thoughts of God after Him. Bacon, too, the father of the modern Inductive Philosophy, not only thought Theology the crown and the queenliest of the sciences, but found his highest satisfaction in offering his great work as a sacrifice to the glory of the Immortal God. Galileo, victim of the Inquisition as he was, held that to despise his science was to despise "the Holy Scriptures, which teach us that the glory and greatness of Almighty God are admirably discerned in all His works, and divinely read in the open book of heaven." Newton thought every step in the knowledge of Nature a step nearer to the knowledge of God, and believed that the better we understood the systems, celestial and terrestrial, the more would "we admire Him on account of His perfections, venerate and worship Him on account of His government." To quote indeed every name illustrative of our position were to cite almost all the fathers of modern science. So far were they from thinking, like certain of their sons, that God was the last enemy to be destroyed, and religion a force that must not be "permitted to intrude on the region of knowledge," that they rather held with Plato—the farther they penetrated into the secrets of the universe the nearer they got to God. For they believed, as he did, that the world was "a perceptible God, image of the intelligible, greatest and best, the most beautiful and perfect, the one only-begotten universe." *

But there is no desire to speak as if men of science were alone to blame. They are not. Theologians are unreasonably jealous of scientists, given to ill-considered and ill-informed criticism, to rash and harsh judgments, to the words that now do the work once done by bell, and book, and candle. They are too fearful of free inquiry, confront science too much in the interests of the creeds, too little with the open sense that seeks God's truth everywhere. They well understand the sanctity of forms and doctrines, but not so well the sanctity of eternal fact. Yet the theologian has an apology for his failings on the ungenerous side that the scientist wants. Theology, by the very necessities of its nature, is more conservative and retrospective than science. Religion receives from the past the notional forms which seem to it the very truths by which it lives. But science reads the past simply as a history of mingled success and failure, written to stimulate the present to win by wiser methods more splendid triumphs. Religion builds on what it believes to be accomplished and explained facts, and so fears every change that touches its fundamental realities, or the forms which possess a sacramental

* "Timæus," iii. p. 92.

meaning and sanctity. But science, never satisfied with the old, ever seeking the new, welcomes every revolution that changes the lines of its thought and widens the circle of its knowledge.

Yet religion is in no proper sense the antithesis of science. Only confusion can come from so conceiving it. Constructive religious thought may be opposed to science, but only as one science to another, as distinct, or even contrary, but not as contradictory. In a sense quite other than the man who said it meant, we can say, "Theology is anthropology."* All science is anthropological, the creation of human faculties, the symbol of so much human culture, so many human ideas, the mirror of mind attempting to interpret itself and Nature. Man is the universe in little, but the universe idealized, become conscious mind. He can approach its interpretation from two sides, the real and the ideal, as it appears to thought or as it exists in thought, as it is revealed to mind or as it is unfolded by mind. The realist interpretation is science, but the idealist theology. Science is nature explained by man; theology is nature explained in and through him. But so understood, theology is a science, the science of the highest in the universe. Man, as the highest being in Nature, is the highest revelation of its secret, the Λόγος προφορικός, by

---

* Prof. Steinthal, of Berlin, in an article sadly significant in some respects, "Zur Religions-Philosophie, Zeitschrift für Völkerpsychol.," vol. viii. 271.

which knowledge of the eternal Λόγος ἐνδιάθετος is won. If, therefore, "theology is anthropology," it is because the ἄνθρωπος is the image of the Θεός, man the translucent manifestation of God.

But religion is not a science, or any constructive or reasoned system of thought that can be opposed to it. It is simply spirit expressing in symbol its consciousness of relations other and higher than physical and social. Religion is a permanent and universal characteristic of man, a normal and necessary product of his nature. He grows into religion, but works into theology, *feels* himself into the one, *thinks* himself into the other. He is religious by nature, theological by art. In a sense it can be said, there is only one religion, but there are many theologies, just as every human being knows he is a man, but not every human being knows what man is. The feelings of dependence, reverence, devotion, are universal, everywhere seek out and worship an appropriate object. And the object must be personal, a Being to love and command, be loved and obeyed. And only as the intellect begins to speculate on this Being, His relations to man and nature, does a theology arise. But these speculations, while right in the end to which they strive, may be wrong in the methods by which they work and the forms in which they are expressed. Imperfect and transitory doctrines in theology can as little disprove religion as provisional theories in science can discredit Nature.

An object of worship, a Being worthy of love and reverence, in other words, a God, is necessary to religion. But this religious idea is one thing, its scientific expression another. Man may conceive God and His relation to the world under forms the most varied. As a matter of fact he has done so, does so still. He borrows from Nature the symbols by which he tries to articulate his faith. Thought must, as it becomes abstract and metaphysical, refine the symbols, but cannot, save by the most violent revolution, break away from the ideas they represented, or the lines in which these ideas moved. The phenomena of generation have suggested an emanational relation of Deity to the world; those of organic life an immanent; those of adaptation an architectonic. Theism, both philosophical and religious, has conceived God under these and many other forms, and been still Theism and still religious. The theistic idea and the cosmic form may thus so grow together as to seem indissoluble, and even identical. But while this union may secure to the idea clearness and intelligibility, it may expose it to the greatest possible danger. In ages when science is active and progressive, it may so revolutionize our knowledge of natural processes and laws as to break up our cosmic conception, and change into antiquated errors the forms in which the theistic idea had been expressed. Men on both sides may think the old conception of Nature necessary to Theism, the notions of action and relation it supplied the only modes in which it is possible to conceive God and the world as related to each other, and so, an angry wail rising from the one side and a shout of defiance from the other, theology and science may join battle on the radically false issue, that a given cosmic conception is essential to faith in God. It is as if all the theistic words in a language had suddenly been lost or forgotten, and speech as to God made impossible. There would indeed be great temporary, in some respects permanent, loss. Words consecrated by tender memories, by holy associations, by sacred use, would no longer exercise their spell-like influence on the devout mind. Terms sharpened by centuries of definition and debate into watchwords of rival systems, would, by ceasing to be, cease to excite the enthusiasm of love on the one side or hate on the other. But theistic thought would not perish with its old verbal vehicles, would soon create a new and nobler speech, making the loss gain. The present, freed from the tyranny of the past, would speak its own thoughts in its own tongue. Religion, proved independent of its symbols, unweighted by a history of mingled good and ill, would win its way, not as letter to civil, but as spirit to moral supremacy. So the decay of old cosmic notions may involve the decay of theological formulæ, but need not touch the truth they provisionally expressed. It will survive the shock of dissolution, assume another body, and live through another of those epochs when men who "see through a glass darkly" strive towards the day when they shall "see face to face."

Now, our present theistic contests and perils rise, in great part, from changes effected, or being effected, in our cosmic conception. The old Theism is supposed to have been based on teleology. The world was an effect which implied a Cause, exhibited everywhere marks of design which proved a Designer. It was argued,—the more curious a contrivance the more certain a contriver; the world is the most curious of all contrivances; therefore, the being and intelligence of its Contriver the most certain of all conclusions. But evolution is said to have made an end of teleology. Design has vanished from the face of the earth; and with it the proofs of a Designer. Theism is represented as an anthropomorphic theory of creation, a "process of manufacture" by "a manlike Artificer." As Mr. Herbert Spencer, with happy assurance, generalizes,*—"Alike in the rudest creeds and the cosmogony long current among ourselves, it is assumed that the genesis of the heavens and the earth is effected somewhat after the manner in which a workman shapes a piece of furniture." And, of course, physicists who have every confidence in Mr. Spencer's metaphysics, cannot do less than follow him here, and set down the theistic theory as one which "converts the Power whose garment is seen in the visible universe into

* "First Principles," p. 33.

an Artificer, fashioned after the human model, and acting by broken efforts, as man is seen to act."* Theism and evolution thus become antitheses, the one exhibiting "the method of Nature," the other "the 'technic' of a manlike Artificer." The one is monistic, mechanical, causal; the other dualistic, vital, teleological.† But science knows nothing of final, knows only efficient, causes. And so it happens that we have, on the one side, men, for the sake of Theism, doing battle against a given cosmic conception; on the other, men, for the sake of a given cosmic conception, doing battle against Theism. The theologian, to save his evidences, denies a scientific theory; the scientist, to maintain his theory, denies a theological conception. Whether these are necessary issues is a not altogether unnecessary question.

The question, then, that here meets us is this—whether the theory of creation by the art or technic of a manlike Artificer be necessary to Theism. As the question has both an historical and a philosophical side, the historical had better come first. Our scientific speculation assumes that the belief in God was the product of an anthropomorphic

---

* Professor Tyndall, "Address," p. 58.

† Haeckel, "Natürliche Schöpfungs-Geschichte," p. 19. Professor Huxley, however, who has always been much more cautious and skilful in metaphysics than some of his scientific brethren, denies that there is any antagonism between evolution and teleology. In his review of Haeckel in the *Academy* he rebuked the distinguished German for his thorough-going denial of teleology, and now he has in his Glasgow lecture told us that evolution leaves the argument from design practically where it was.

interpretation of nature. Primitive man, superstitious, ignorant of the inductive method, and many other things, drew his creational theory not from the study of Nature, but the observation of himself. So he conceived God as a mechanic on a great scale, making the world as he made a machine. Now, how does the case actually stand? The earliest names of Deity show that men dreamed of nothing less than conceiving Him as an Artificer, or Architect, or Builder. The Hebrew was the purest monotheist of antiquity, the most strenuous believer in creation by God; but how did he conceive Him as acting? Not by a "process of manufacture," or like "a workman shaping a piece of furniture," but as an immanent yet intelligent Energy, Creator, Maker, if you like, but not mechanic. He created by speech, the symbol of thought; by a command, the symbol of will. The world was the expression of the divine thought, the creation of the divine will; and so came to be, not by an artificial constructive, but by a natural productive, process. In the Hebrew Scriptures there are indeed frequent anthropomorphisms of speech, but, allowing for the picturesque and sensuous orientalism of its form, little that is anthropomorphic in conception. Indeed, the fundamental relations of God and the world are conceived in a manner nearer Goethe's than Paley's. "The Spirit of God brooded upon the face of the waters." God is "covered with light as with a garment;" "clouds and darkness are round about Him." He is the Unseen, the Unsearchable, working unbeheld on the left hand, hiding unperceived on the right, yet knowing the way man takes, speaking to him out of the whirlwind, or by the sun, moon, and stars which He has ordained. He is in the heaven above, in the earth, in the abyss under it, and in the uttermost parts of the sea, no manlike Being, but an universal Presence, in moments of intense emotion realized by the attribution of human qualities, but not, therefore, conceived in his cosmic relations as a magnified mechanic. In the distinctive Hebrew Name of Deity there is nothing anthropomorphic; it is the very negation of anthropomorphism, as much so as the most abstract term of metaphysics, or the most generalized notion of science. Perhaps, it may be thought, that statement ought to be qualified by, except personality; but as the personality is not "manlike," does not individualize, it is more correct to leave the exception unmade. Hebrew Monotheism must, then, be allowed to stand as a Theism which did not know, therefore did not spring out of, the notion of creation by "the 'technic' of a manlike Artificer."

Where, then, did that notion rise? Not in Judæa, but in Greece, and in Greece, not as a religious, but as a scientific and philosophic dogma. It did not create the belief in God or gods, but was created by the endeavours of men anxious to explain the being and becoming of the world. Mr. Spencer says,* "A religious creed is definable as an *à priori* theory of the universe." The definition may be concise and positive enough, but whether it be correct is another matter. Certainly, the native religion of Greece was no theory as to the origin of the universe. The Greek gods were, in no proper sense, creators. They stood in the system of Nature, the children of the universal Mother, as real creatures as men, subject to all the limitations of the created, distinguished from men as immortals from mortals, but their very immortality derivative, not inherent, due to divine ambrosia, not to their own wills or natures. One of the Homeric poets, in a hymn to "Earth, the Mother of all things," can invoke her as "Mother of the gods."

Χαῖρε, θεῶν μήτηρ, ἄλοχ' Οὐρανοῦ ἀστερόεντος. †

Hesiod, too, brings out of Chaos first "the broad-bosomed Earth, the firm abode of all things;"‡ and then, from her union with "the starry Ouranos," makes the gods spring.§ A poet so devout as Pindar can attribute a common nature and parentage to gods and men:

Ἐν ἀνδρῶν, ἐν θεῶν γένος· ἐκ
μιᾶς δὲ πνέομεν
ματρὸς ἀμφότεροι.‖

Sophokles, too, can speak of the earth as "the all-nourishing, the mother of Zeus himself:"

Ὀρεστέρα παμβῶτι, Γᾶ,
μᾶτερ αὐτοῦ Διός,
ἃ τὸν μέγαν Πακτωλὸν εὔχρυσον νέμεις.¶

* "First Principles," p. 43.   † "In Tellurem Matrem Omnium," 17.
‡ "Theog.," 116, 117.   § Ib., 132—137.
‖ "Nemea," vi. 1—3.   ¶ Philoct., 391.

Hence the Hellenic mind, in its objective and spontaneous phase, did not conceive the gods as the architects of the world, but as stones of the great structure. Nature was living, self-existent, the all-fruitful mother; the gods her children. Certain oriental theosophies, with theological or pantheistic theories of creation, had indeed been introduced into Greece, but they had never been naturalized, or become even fairly intelligible to the native sunny naturalism. And so the earliest speculative and scientific thought was as remote as possible from anthropomorphism, or any conscious conflict with it. It rose to do what had hitherto been undone, find a rational theory of the origin and being of the universe. It never dreamt of utilizing the gods as creators, but turned to seek in Nature the secret of her existence, the common cause of the system which comprehended both gods and men. And so the earliest philosophic thought was physical and mathematical, looked for the universal cause successively in water, air, fire, number or harmony. Only as the conception of order became deeper did the necessity of assuming mind as its one adequate cause begin to appear. Anaxagoras was the first to see and state this necessity;[*] but so little did he understand his own principle that both Plato[†] and Aristotle[‡] had to complain of the imperfect and inconclusive way in which he applied it. Once the explanation had been suggested, it seemed

[*] "Diogenes Laert.," ii. 6.   [†] "Phædo," i. 97.   [‡] "Metaph.," lib. i. 4, 12

so obvious and sufficient, that Aristotle compared the appearance of Anaxagoras among the older philosophers to the rising up of a sober man to speak in a company of tipplers.* Plato, alive to the beauty and order of the world, made it in a still more eminent degree the work of mind, fashioned by divine handicraft after a divine archetype, the plan or idea of the eternal Artist.† And the end of creation was as divine as the idea, the diffusion of the goodness which is God's or God. In Aristotle, though his theology is much more fluid and less determinable than Plato's, yet mind, reason, is as necessary to the being of his universe, and the good as certainly its end. In one point his is the more scientific Theism—its conception of God's relation to the world and mode of action in it. He suggests, in a remarkable passage, that possibly the truth may lie in uniting the ideas of transcendent and immanent relation.‡ The general of an army represents the one, the order or discipline he creates the other, and as in the army, so in the world, the Supreme Good may be conceived as a distinct being and as the collective and inherent order, which secures the good of the whole. In that Aristotelian analogy there lay the germ of a Theism that might have saved religious thought from falling into the hard and shallow Dualism, which has caused much bewildered conflict in the past, and continues to cause no less in the present.

* Ib., lib. i. 3, 16.   † "Timæus," iii. 28.   ‡ "Metaph.," lib. xi. 10.

The Theism that thus emerged was philosophic and scientific, not religious, an attempt to explain the universe, not to create a religion. Its god was not Zeus. Plato's deity stood ethically far above the Olympian, was too good to be jealous of any being,* so good as to desire the perfect goodness of all. Aristotle's, as the causal and controlling principle, created order and happiness:

Οὐκ ἀγαθὸν πολυκοιρανίη· εἷς κοίρανος.†

Neither was victorious over the puzzle of personality. Plato came nearest victory, but he glides out of personal into impersonal modes of thought and speech with an ease and unconsciousness that greatly perplex a modern Theist. The theistic idea was in each case determined by the cosmic. Plato, ideal, artistic, conceived the world as a structure made after an eternal model, and so its creator was a Δημιουργός, a great artificer or mechanic. Aristotle, realistic, scientific, conceived the world as an organic whole, the realization of an immanent energy, and so his creator is the unmoved mover of all things. Both believed an ordered nature to be inexplicable without an ordering mind, and this mind became to later thought more personal, more capable therefore of religious use, and akin to the gods. Once this process was complete, the faith that had been so generated easily turned back to seek support in the very phenomena that had suggested it, and so in Cicero the Theism of

---

* "Timæus," iii. 29, 30.   † "Metaph.," lib. xi. 10; "Iliad," ii. 204.

antiquity claims the harmonies of earth and heaven as proving its right to be—"Quæ contuens animus, accipt ab his cognitionem deorum, ex qua oritur pietas; cum conjuncta justitia est, reliquæque virtutes." *

The technic or handicraft theory as to the origin of things, with its proof of a Maker, was thus no creation of religion, but of science. And the science had no religious proclivities, was not of the spurious apologetic sort, was simply doing its best to master the secret of the universe, and doing it with a cordial and unconcealed antagonism to the religion of the day that ought to delight certain modern scientists. This theory of pagan thought was passed on to Christianity. The culture of the early Apologists and Fathers was pagan, and their Theism, so far as scientific, Hellenic rather than Hebrew. Proofs of the Being of God were unnecessary things to the Jew, most necessary things to the Greek, and so men who had to prove His existence had no help but to apply to the latter. And with the technic proofs came the idea of a technic relation and action. They were the basis of such similes as—the creation suggests the Creator as a lyre both the man who made and the man who plays it.† This method of proof the more speculative Fathers and Schoolmen, like Augustine and Anselm, disdained; and preferred necessities of thought to probable inferences of reason, the ground of

---

* "De Nat. Deor.," ii. lxi.
† Gregory Nazianz., "Orat.," xxviii. 6, p. 499.

their preference being an entirely opposed conception of God's relation to the world. But the technic theory was too precise, intelligible, and useful to be allowed altogether to die out. And when modern science began to open its eyes to the wondrous mechanism of the heavens and the beautiful structures of earth, apologetic Theism, borrowing and developing the premisses, the theological and teleological conceptions of the "Timæus" and the "De Natura Deorum," defined and defended its position by a bewildering multitude of proofs. A divine law of compensation seemed to be at work. The science which with the one hand undermined the ancient faith, seemed with the other to clear for it a vaster and more stable foundation. The Royal Society of England contributed not only to develop science, but also to create a "Natural Theology" which once bade fair to be the rival of revealed. Boyle and Derham prepared the way for Paley, who reasoned from design to a Designer in terms and on principles which seemed those of invincible common sense. And since then Bridgewater and Burnett Treatises have appeared, and done the utmost that can be done on these lines to prove the Being, power, wisdom, and goodness of God.

The argument from design was valid enough so long as the old technic conception of Nature stood. If the world was a machine whose fittest analogue was a watch, then a maker was inevitable, construction impossible without a constructor. But the logical and popular excellences of the argument were its scientific defects. The premisses implied too much, required a cosmic theory too artificial to be true to "the method of Nature." The subtle and analytic intellect of Hume did much to turn the discussion back to first principles. He resolved mind into a succession of ideas and impressions, which could not transcend experience, being no more than its mirror. His analysis resolved causation into mere antecedence and sequence, eliminated the "idea of power or necessary connexion," which alone made any theistic inference possible. "Thought, design, intelligence, such as we discover in men and other animals," were made the parallels of "heat and cold, attraction and repulsion," and no more than one of the "springs and principles of the universe." Hume's scepticism explained nothing, made nothing certain, or it had not been Scepticism, made the world "a singular kind of effect," a product of blind custom, which had become what it is by chance or accident, rather than by any necessity of mind or nature. Thought could not stand where he left it, but it could not advance without solving the problems he had started. Man and Nature had to be interpreted anew, the thousand and one problems as to the nature, sources, and objects of knowledge reopened and re-discussed. The very subtlety of Hume's scepticism led his contemporaries astray, and allowed its full significance to dawn but slowly on the minds of men who, occupied with subsidiary points, missed cardinal principles. Kant headed the reaction against Hume, and it was characteristic of the new direction of thought that he was even more merciless to the old theistic argument. It was incompatible with his doctrine of the *Ding an Sich*. To reason from the phenomenal to the transcendental was illegitimate. For his system, God, though a moral, was no physical necessity. And here was its weakest point. Nature and God stood dissociated, the one lying, as it were, outside the other, capable of furnishing no evidence either to prove or disprove His Being. The old artificial dualism remained unvanquished, matter and mind standing over against each other in unreconciled antithesis. In physics his idea of the almost mutual inter-independence of Nature and God is well illustrated. His "cosmic gas hypothesis" is an attempt to explain the origin of the inorganic universe by mechanical law, and makes him the earliest and boldest of modern evolutionists. The unsolved problems that lay in his metaphysics forced his successors to try new speculative methods, to seek along various roads the reconciliation of matter and spirit, Nature and God. Hence arose the marvellous creations of the transcendental philosophy, Fichte's subjective Idealism, Jacobi's emotional Intuitionalism, Schelling's absolute Indifference and later kaleidoscopic Mysticism, and Hegel's absolute Idealism. The speculations started by his physics, carried along different but converging lines by La Place and Goethe, Lamarck and Oken, have become our now well-known theory of creation by evolution. It was perhaps fortunate, perhaps unfortunate, that the metaphysical and physical lines so diverged, but he who can so unite them as to evolve a conception of the universe that shall satisfy both science and religion, will be the greatest prophet of the Eternal modern times has known.

Here now we must pause and sum up the result of our historical discussion. The idea of creation by the art of a "manlike Artificer" did not produce the belief in God. That idea had a cosmic and scientific, not a theistic and religious origin. The world needed God to become intelligible; God did not need the world to become credible. Men were Theists before they were scientists, believed in the Being of God before they had thought of either a creator or a cause. And even where He was conceived as Creator, He was not conceived as a manufacturer or mechanic, but as a Maker by a process as natural and immanent as the thinking, the speech, and the volition of man. The technic theory is in no way essential to Theism, can as little destroy it as it could create it. Apologetic Theists have been its chief representatives and exponents, but the higher and profounder Theists have been as merciless to its shallow and contra-natural artificiality as the most audacious evolutionist. Our metaphysical physicists may, therefore, be allowed to handle said theory as severely as they like, only they must remember that it is neither the parent nor the child of Theism, nor in any degree necessary to its life, but an early ancestor of their own loved cosmic speculations—the first-born of adolescent Philosophy.

The way is now clear for the discussion of the next point—How ought the relation of God to the world to be conceived? The point is cardinal, and must be made prominent and luminous if Theism and science are ever to get honestly face to face, whether for contest or conciliation. Two things are clear. (1) Any interpretation of Nature that leaves out any creative and causal energy or force must be inadequate. (2) Any conception of God that leaves out His active qualities, His energies and their action, must be insufficient. But if every adequate interpretation of Nature must include its causal force, then the Theist cannot allow God and Nature to be conceived as divided, independent, mutually exclusive. Science seeks to explain Nature, but the What is remains inexplicable without the What caused to be. The *natura naturata* and the *natura naturans* are distinguishable in idea, but not divisible in reality, or the thought that represents it; and so, as science becomes more conscious of its problems and its goal, it struggles the more strenuously towards the region where physics melt into metaphysics. Scientist and Theist must, therefore, agree in this—neither can so distinguish as to disjoin Nature and its Cause. On the other hand, to conceive God as purely transcendental, as outside and apart from the universe, is to conceive the highest mental abstraction, a neuter absolute or infinite, but no real being, no positive entity, full of energies potential, actual, active. Nature realizes our idea of God, shows His energies in action, His life in contact with ours. But so to conceive the relation of God and Nature is to conceive the world not as outside or beside God, but as in Him; to conceive no *here* for it, no *there* for Him, but He everywhere in it, it everywhere living, moving, and existing in Him. Transcendence is not thus denied, but rather affirmed. God does not depend on the world for His being, but the world on Him. It is not the cause of His existence, but He of its. When so much is said, absolute, and therefore transcendental, being is predicated of God. But when He is conceived as a Creator, He must be conceived as related, and immanence in the creation not only expresses His mode of creative action, but is the only form of thought in which the antithetical notions of the absolute and the relative can be reconciled. Only as the Creator is conceived as immanent can the creation be *natura* as opposed to *factura*, or the region of things real the arena and manifestation of spirit.

But, if God and Nature stand so related to each other, His action and its action cannot be distinguished as respectively supernatural and natural. If He is represented as outside, a spectator, watching, like a mechanic, the movements of the enormous machine He has constructed and set agoing, then all His action must be "interference," the machine must be stopped, in whole or part, to let Him inside to repair, or change, or enlarge it. But so to conceive the matter is to deify Nature and undeify God, make it not only independent of its Cause, but able so to limit as to annul His omnipresence and omnipotence. The action of incorporate mind is not supernatural. It can express whatever it thinks, feels, wills, in and through its physical organism, and no one ever names the expression "interference." And the immanent action of God is as the action of incorporate mind, as natural and as necessary. The supernatural and the action of God are not identical. Wherever Nature works He works. There is no point in the universe, as there is no moment of time, without His presence, or shut to His energies. "What do I see in Nature?" asked Fénelon; "God—God everywhere—God alone." And a far greater theologian, who had allowed "pie hoc posse dici naturam esse Deum,"* only paraphrased Scripture when he said, "Spiritus divinus, qui ubique diffusus omnia sustinet, vegetat et vivificat in cœlo et in terra."†

But hitherto our argument has been concerned with points formal and preliminary; now it must essay hardier and more positive work. Theism needs to be made out not simply compatible with science, but necessary to the scientific interpretation of the universe. The false and inconclusive thinking that sets God and Nature in opposition and inter-independence has to be brushed aside, but only

---

* Calvin, "Instit.," lib. i. v. 5.   † Ib., lib. i. xiii. 14.

that Nature may the more evidently appear, as created, inexplicable, as creative, inconceivable, without God.

The world now is—once was not; man and his works are—once were not. How and why did they come to be? That question science rather delights to face than seeks to evade. Her search after the birth-time of the world has been so grandly victorious as to force her to attempt, from her own side and by her own methods, the perennial inquiry into its cause. Nature is uniform, works everywhere from within, grows, does not construct, bears and becomes, does not manufacture, and science, as her interpreter, expresses her method or process by development, evolution. The forms of inorganic nature have been developed by the operation of necessary mechanical laws; the forms of organic life have been evolved by the operation of natural forces. Variation, the struggle for existence, the survival of the fittest, explain the endless varieties of organized beings that have lived and are living upon the earth. The inter-active play of organism and environment, the creature and the medium in which it lives, has resulted in man and his works.

Now, there is no intention here of either questioning or denying evolution. Modern thought is too deeply penetrated with it to allow its exclusion from any scientific and speculative conception of the universe. Hegel lived before Darwin, and evolution was known to metaphysics long before it was adopted and naturalized by physics. Nature was construed from the ideal earlier than from the real side. And the construction was comprehensive too, aimed at expressing the laws of both matter and mind, at explicating the histories alike of nature and spirit. Evolution in science need not startle us any more than evolution in philosophy. But as it now appears in science, there is one question it inevitably suggests—What does it explain or mean? It is, we are told, a theory of creation. But in what sense? a modal or a causal theory? Does it simply explain the method by which things came to be, or does it express their cause? Process or method is one thing, cause another. Simplifying the process is not the same thing as simplifying the cause. Granted the old handicraft theory replaced by "the struggle for existence," in which, by "survival of the fittest," Nature evolves more perfect forms and creates new species—what then? Simply the old inevitable question—Whence the "existence" to struggle, the "fittest" to survive, the Nature which is the arena of contest, whose potencies, too, perform so many wonderful things? The new creational process simply makes us confront the old question of cause—does no more.

It is necessary to emphasize this distinction of a modal and a causal theory of creation. It is neither asserted nor assumed that our more distinguished evolutionists, philosophic and scientific, are blind to it; but it is often by their peculiar presentment subtly masked. The concluding sentence of the "Origin of Species" will be remembered:

"There is grandeur in this view of life, with its several powers, having been originally breathed by the Creator into a few forms or one; and that while this planet has gone cycling on according to the fixed law of gravity, from so simple a beginning endless forms, most beautiful and most wonderful, have been, and are being evolved."

But it depends on the sense read into "beginning" whether it can be called "simple." If the "few forms or one" be regarded in themselves, then they may be described as "simple;" but if they are regarded as the parents of the future, containing "the promise and potency" of the "endless forms" that have been and are to be, then they are exceedingly wonderful. They are simple as a beginning, but not as a cause. A process starts at the lowest point and culminates in the highest, begins with the least, ends with the most perfect. But the lowest does not explain the highest, is not the sufficient reason of its existence. The cause must be adequate, not only to the immediate, but to the ultimate effect, must continue active and operative to the end. If Nature is called in to qualify beginning, if the environment is made to co-operate with the organism, then we are but made to see a subtle complexity in the process, that exalts our sense of the infinite sufficiency, the universal activity and inexhaustible energy of the Cause. The method of Nature is but a creation or result of the forces that have made Nature—their way of working, and only as these fontal or creative forces are known can the veil be lifted from the mystery of being. Even "spontaneous generation" would not, were it proved, be an ultimate explanation. As "generation" it could not, though styled "spontaneous," be held uncaused, and the generative force would remain no less mysterious than the evolution of the organism from the seed. The genesis of a form is not explained when it is shown how it came to be, but only when what caused it to be is made evident. Evolution has done the one, but not the other; has simplified our notion of the creational method, but not of the creational cause.

Evolution, then, as simply a modal, cannot be used as if it were a causal theory of creation. It has proved that the cosmic cause does not work as a handicraftsman, but has not disproved its being—has rather made it, if no greater necessity, a greater certainty. A beginning is now indisputable, demonstrable fact. Nature is not eternal, is created, evolved,—but by what or whom? This problem has of late greatly exercised our scientific speculation. In dealing with it, it proceeds in a very extraordinary fashion. It builds on the psychological foundation of Hume a structure it was never meant to bear, and cannot possibly sustain. Hume saw that on the principles of his psychology no rational inference could be drawn as to the being of anything supra-sensible, and he drew none; that it warranted no coherent or constructive theory as to the becoming of the universe, and he attempted none. He was wise, understood his principles and his terms, and went no farther than they allowed him. But now a kindred psychology is made to do very different work. A theory of knowing, which affirms that we can never reach reality, never know more than appearance, is made the basis of a theory of being which claims to be a constructive cosmic philosophy. Mr. Herbert Spencer holds that our states of consciousness are symbols of an outside reality "utterly inscrutable in Nature, that all things known to us are manifestations of the Unknowable," of a "Power by which we are acted upon."* These manifestations, he thinks, divisible into two great classes, called by some "*impressions* and *ideas*," but by himself "*vivid* and *faint*" manifestations respectively. The vivid "occur under the conditions called those of perception;" the faint "occur under the conditions known as those of reflection, or memory, or imagination, or ideation."† This distinction corresponds to the division between subject and object, self and not-self.‡ The faint manifestations are the ego; the vivid manifestations the non-ego. The faint are the reflection or echo of the vivid, the ego the creation of the non-ego, which determines the order or succession of the manifestations.

* "First Principles," pp. 99, 143. † Ib., p. 144.
‡ Ib., p. 154.

Now, here is a very admirable basis for a philosophy either of nescience or scepticism, but for little else. If we are but "faint manifestations" of an ego created out of the "vivid manifestations" of an "inscrutable reality," an "incomprehensible power," then, as the creative manifestations are but appearances, the created can hardly be known reality, can certainly be no better known than what it reflects. The ego becoming thus as inscrutable and unknowable as the non-ego, there remain two, and only two, alternative conclusions—either philosophic ignorance or philosophic doubt—either man can never know the truth, or there is no truth for man to know. But Mr. Spencer accepts neither conclusion. He defies both his ontology and psychology. He translates his unknowable reality by a scientific term; he works his manifestations into scientific ideas. His absolute becomes "absolute force." "By the persistence of force we really mean the persistence of some cause which transcends our knowledge and conception. In other words, asserting the persistence of force is asserting an unconditioned reality, without beginning or end."* Now, here is a step such as was never taken by hero of fairy tale or Arabian Nights gifted with magic boots. The Unknowable is named, and made by its name to lose its nature, assume a new character and functions, and enter a circle of very exclusive, if not very definite ideas. A cause that "transcends our knowledge"

* "First Principles," p. 192.

is here transformed into a cause that does not. Mr. Spencer may mean only to assert an "unconditioned reality," but he does it in terms that change his meaning, that connote ideas that overpower and extinguish the one expressed by the original phrase. And the connotation proves too strong for Mr. Spencer himself. Just as the term force revolutionizes the conception of the Unknowable, so it, in turn, transmuted into forces, beguiles the physicist into the fancy that he is walking in the to him sober and certain paths of observation and experiment, while, in truth, he is soaring in the heaven of metaphysics. If Nature and man are alike the manifestations of an inscrutable Power, then Nature and man, interpreted in the terms of matter, motion, and force, are misinterpreted, and the attempt at a cosmic science but the delusive appearance of knowledge where only ignorance is possible.

Mr. Spencer's philosophy is by pre-eminence the philosophy of evolution; and has supplied both basis and material for almost all our recent scientific speculation. He has created the fashion, now so common among English men of science, of rounding off their inquiries and speculations with mysterious, perhaps mystifying allusions to the Unknowable, the inscrutable Power, the unconditioned Reality, the unknown Cause manifested in the universe. The fashion has its significance. Science is growingly conscious of the little it can do to explicate and solve our first and fundamental problem, and has found a formula in which it can either humbly or grandiloquently confess the same, without being inconveniently committed to anything. But for this very reason it is necessary to insist that the arch by which Mr. Spencer would span the gulf between the unknown Cause and the persistent Force wants its keystone. Capital letters play a great part in his philosophy. They help to reveal his inscrutable, personalize his force and forces, and allow the mind to glide into and out of meanings in the happiest and most unconscious ways. But these delicate and excellent ambiguities cannot be always victorious. The translation of the unknown into the known by the interpreters, matter, motion, and force, though a valiant and even audacious feat, can hardly be entirely successful if there are phenomena in the universe these terms fail to express.

What scientific speculation demands is a sufficient reason * for what is; but by an unreasonable adherence to its own terms, where they are utterly inapplicable, it misses what it demands. You cannot call that a reason which is by its very name placed outside the categories of thought, nor does it become one by being translated into a term which, while physical, denotes what is confessedly assumed and

---

* Our English philosophy has been since Hume so hopelessly bewildered and obfuscated in its notion of cause, that, perhaps, though for an opposite reason, it is better to follow M. Comte, and leave it in discussions of this kind unused.

indemonstrable. Professor Tyndall's "matter" ceased under his own analysis to be material, became "an outside entity" whose "real nature we can never know," which, while manifested in "the process of evolution," must remain "a power absolutely inscrutable to the intellect of man." He added, with most delightful naïveté, "there is, you will observe, no very rank materialism here." Of course not. The only material thing was the name, and perhaps the chivalrous faith that could believe it applicable and relevant. And the name in no way simplified the idea of creation, for the confession had to be made, "It is by the operation of an insoluble mystery that life is evolved, species differentiated, and mind unfolded from their prepotent elements in the immeasurable past." The mystery of creation is not vanquished by the attempt to express it in physical terms. The terms so break down as to foil the attempt. The unknown Being which science has first to postulate and then translate into its own terms, is a conception less coherent and rational than the theistic. For matter, in any sense that leaves it matter, can never be the sufficient reason of a universe like ours. That reason must be expressible in the forms and terms supplied by the last and highest rather than the first and lowest developments in Nature. In discussing a process—evolution—the beginning is the point of prime importance; but in determining the character of the cause—the creative power—it is the end. The beginning marks the process as a descent or ascent; but the end, by exhibiting the highest product, determines the kind and quality of the producing factors. This is peculiarly true in a case like the present. For evolution can allow no element to steal into the effect that cannot be traced to the cause. What is evolved in the one was involved in the other. What the method of Nature brings out in the conclusion, it must have found in the cause, the former being only the explication of the latter. On this principle, mind, as the latest and highest result of the creative process, cannot have been absent from the creative cause.

Man is the interpeter of Nature, but he is also its interpretation. That does not mean he is its final cause, but it means he is the highest revelation of its creative power. If we interpret the latter in "the terms of matter, motion, and force," we must interpret in the same terms the phenomena of mind and society. Now these are not interpreted when the possible or probable descent and development of man are traced. We have to do not simply with the becoming of a fact, but with the fact as become. And the fact is here a mind, the consciousness, in which both self and the universe are revealed. It therefore must be interrogated as to itself, as to what it knows, as to the sense in which it can be said to know at all, as to whether its powers, its thoughts, its emotions, its acts and their qualities, can be interpreted in the specified terms. Then the many minds in the present are heirs of the results achieved by the many minds of the past. Mind has a history—can it be written "in the terms of matter, motion, and force"? Whatever interprets it must interpret the systems it has built, the institutions it has created, the religions it has deposited and developed, the evil it has done, the good it has achieved, the progress it has made. These very words, "evil," "good," "progress," "done," "achieved," "made," start many questions that affect our interpretation of the cosmic cause. If man be the mere product of mechanical and necessary forces, they must rule him, but where they rule there may be a break-down, but can be no evil, an effective or resultful motion, but can be no good. Are the laws which have governed the development or education of humanity mechanical? If so, can moral terms be used to express results that must be as purely mechanical as any obtained in the earliest stages of the creative process? If so, how did evolution accomplish so extraordinary a revolution in the nature of the actor and the quality of his acts? Can the terms righteous, benevolent, wise, be applied to men and nations and be denied to the Power that has shaped human destinies? or, in other words, can man be in any sense a moral being without having his development governed by moral laws? Does the will count for anything in the sphere of action? If man is to any extent or in any real sense free, he cannot be the mere product of molecular action; if he is the pure creature of primordial molecules, his actions must be as much necessitated as the movements of the planets, or the ebb and flow of the tides, and all his thoughts, religions, institutions, achievements, nothing more than "the transferred activities of his molecules." But this is a point on which consciousness has a right to speak; and Mr. Spencer tells us that belief of it is a necessary condition of all knowledge. Scepticism on one point here involves scepticism on all. If a man doubted his own consciousness, he must doubt everything, and science is impossible. But if consciousness must be held veracious when it testifies to the existence of an outer world, the obligation to believe it is much greater when it speaks to what is known, not in symbol, but in itself. Now, if there is one point on which the consciousness of universal man as expressed in universal language has been more unanimous than another, it has been in testifying to his freedom, and because of it in judging as to the character and quality of his actions. One who believes the veracity of consciousness on other points cannot logically deny it here. But if man be free, he cannot be interpreted in "the terms of matter, motion, and force." Physical necessity can never be the equivalent of moral freedom. But if man cannot be so interpreted, neither can the Power that made him. Man is the image of his Maker. The lake may show the mountain hid in clouds, or the star sleeping in the silent heaven, and the shadow reveals the reality, known to be real were it only by its image.

Mind in interpreting the universe cannot escape from itself, must begin with thought, and what thought supplies and implies. The interpretation of Nature is the interpretation of thought by thought, the translation of ideas out of a mystic, unspoken, unwritten speech into the speech of men. The true and beautiful thought that lay at the basis of Berkeley's idealism was this—Nature is a visual language, its phenomena the visual words in which one mind speaks to another. So understood it is the expression and vehicle of intelligence, an orderly because a rational system. Science is a mirror held up to Nature, and the reason science exhibits but reflects the reason Nature embodies. The intelligible implies intelligence; what can be construed presupposes mind. So much every rationally conceivable theory as to the origin and being of the universe, even such as stand to each other as antithesis to thesis, must explicitly or implicitly recognise. The reasonable thing in the old artificial Theism was not its formal technic, but its recognition of reason as the source and end of the creation. The substance of Spinoza had thought to balance expansion as a mode of being. The *Natur* of Goethe, ever building and ever destroying, eternal life and eternal change, never permanent yet never fugitive, without speech yet creating the tongues by which she speaks and the hearts by which she feels, ever perfect yet never complete, is but Deity externalized and active. The *Universum* of Strauss, personal qualities working impersonally in Nature and man, is simply the cosmos invested with certain of the moral and intellectual attributes of the being men call God. The *Unbewusstes* of Hartmann is only a bad attempt to depersonalize a person, with the worst possible results as to the meaning and end of the world, the hopes and dignity of man. Darwin's evolution, too, lives and wins its way by the conception of a nature which, subtly penetrated by personal attributes, can in whole and in all her parts, contrive, struggle, preserve, develop, and do the million things possible only to perceiving intellect and active will. Thought cannot escape from mind in the universe, because the universe interpreted is thought interpreted and realized.

But it is time this discussion was ended. The conviction with which it was started has gone on deepening with every step, that the grand theistic problem of our time is, not how to prove the existence of God, but how to conceive His relation to the world. That problem demands earnest and honest thought as well as honest and earnest discussion. The discussion has turned hitherto on a false issue, because on a formal rather than a material question. There lies in all our scientific speculation a latent or blank conception of God only waiting to be drawn out or filled up. The Unknowable, the inscrutable Power, is like a dead mask concealing a living face, a ghastly eye-socket without the eye. Let the mask be removed that the face may be seen as the face of the living God. If we can rightly conceive Him, we shall see united into one the Architect of the atoms and the Parent of the minds that make up the universe, a Being that may complete and please science while satisfying religion. And with these reconciled and formed into a holy and ministrant sisterhood, man, happy in the possession of a wholly harmonized nature, the intellect no more harassing the heart, or the heart reproaching the intellect, will live untroubled under a heaven where the sun of knowledge shines in light, and the moon of faith walks in beauty. And when in those peaceful days man feels joy in God, he will read in it a response to God's complacency in man.

> "Freundlos war der Grosse Weltenmeister,
> Fühlte mangel, darum Schuf Er Geister,
> Sel'ge Spiegel seiner Seligkeit.
> Fand das höchste Wesen schon kein Gleiches
> Aus das Kelch des Ganzen Geisterreiches
> Schaümt ihm die Unendlichkeit."

THE BELIEF IN IMMORTALITY

*AN ESSAY IN THE COMPARATIVE HISTORY
OF RELIGIOUS THOUGHT.*

PART I. INTRODUCTORY.
    II. THE BELIEF IN INDIA.
    III. THE BELIEF IN GREECE.

PART I.

INTRODUCTORY.

I.

THE immortality of the soul, though a primary, can hardly be considered a primitive religious belief. It involves conceptions at once too abstract and positive to be intelligible to primitive man, and what he cannot conceive he cannot believe.

The belief in a life after death has, indeed, been coeval, or nearly so, with religion, but this differs from the belief in immortality as a Natural or Physical Polytheism differs from a Spiritual or Monotheistic faith. The belief grows up to satisfy a slowly evolved but deeply seated need of man, and marks a development in his religion almost equal to a revolution, or the creation of a new faith. The human mind then passes out of the mythical or creative into the metaphysical or deductive stage, and religion ceases to be a simple worship expressive of a people's instincts and impulses, and becomes a faith, shaping its institutions and manners, laws and literature, thoughts and hopes.

A religion never assumes or exercises its full authority, never awakens or satisfies the highest hopes of man, until it can command obedience here, and reward it with everlasting happiness hereafter. And this neither implies nor rests on any religious utilitarianism, in Leigh Hunt's phrase, *other-world*liness, but on the simple fact that the immortal nature of man demands a religion which can evoke and satisfy his aspirations after immortality.

It is not the design of this essay to discuss the question of Immortality either with or against our modern philosophies. Such a discussion would be in a great measure superfluous. Determine the fundamental conception or principle of any philosophy, and its relation to the belief in question is ascertained. But the discussion of a secondary or inferential position is useless while the primary is untouched. Scepticism can simply, with Hume, deny that there are any grounds to warrant the belief.* Materialism, resolving thought into a movement of matter, can only regard death as the destruction of the individual, and prefer everlasting annihilation to everlasting life.† Positivism,

---

* "Philosophical Works," vol. iv. pp. 547 ff. (ed. 1854).

† Büchner, "Kraft und Stoff," p. 212. Of course there was an older

allowing spirit no place in its system, denies immortality to man, but confers it on humanity.* Pantheism can grant no immortality to the individual, but promises to him either, as a mode of the divine thought or essence, eternity,† or an immortality which is realized by becoming in the midst of the finite one with the infinite and being in every moment eternal,‡ or a return from relative to absolute being through the knowledge that identifies subject and object. § Theism in all its forms can as little dispense with the immortality of man as with the personality of God. Both are as necessary to pure Deism as to orthodox

and less consistent materialism represented by Dr. Priestley, which tried to maintain itself alongside a belief in a future state of rewards and punishments. But it is now effete; its positions were too untenable to please these thoroughgoing days.

* Mill's "Comte and Positivism," pp. 135, 152.

† Spinoza, "Ethics," Part V., Prop. xxiii. See also Van der Linde, "Spinoza, Seine Lehre u. deren erste Nachwirkung in Holland," pp. 50 and 75.

‡ Schleiermacher, "Reden über Religion," Werke, i. p. 264 (ed. 1843). Schelling, "Philosophie u. Religion," pp. 71 ff.

§ Caro, "L'Idée de Dieu," pp. 370 ff. Hegel expressed himself very rarely and cautiously concerning the immortality of the soul, though he said very decisively, when charged by Schubart with denying it, that in his philosophy the spirit was raised above all the categories which comprehended decay, destruction, and death (Erdmann, "Gesch. der Philos.," ii. p. 650). The negative principles which lay in the Hegelian philosophy were held long in the background, but appeared distinctly enough in Richter's "Lehre von den Letzen Dingen" (1833), and his "Neue Unsterblichkeitslehre" (1833). Feuerbach's immortality of historical remembrance and Schopenhauer's nihilism were, so far as our belief is concerned, coarser and more positive in their negations.

Christianity—were, indeed, the articles in the creed of the older English Deism, by which it stood, with which it fell, when, in its exhausted old age, it had to confront at home the scepticism of Hume, abroad the full-grown sensualism of France and the highborn Transcendentalism of Germany.*

Philosophy did not create the belief in immortality, and acknowledges or denies its validity just as it is or is not involved in its own fundamental principles. Speculative thought has said all that it can say against the belief, and it still lives; has said, too, all that it can say for it, and it has not died. The old arguments, metaphysical, ethical, teleological, have been exhausted, advanced, answered, confirmed, repelled, in almost every possible form, and now thought must turn from the high road of abstract speculation, and study human belief as expressed in human religion. Religion, or rather its

* Erdmann remarks ("Gesch. der Philos.," ii. p. 650), with special reference to Fichte, in the first period of his philosophic thought, that the immortality of man was for the eighteenth century the dogma *par excellence*. It was so because philosophy was then pre-eminently theistic. From the rise of English Deism in Lord Herbert of Cherbury, to Rousseau in France, and Kant and Lessing in Germany, theistic thinkers as a rule held the immortality of man to be as necessary to a religion as the being of God. Kant reverses the argument of Warburton, and maintains the Legation of Moses to be un-divine, because without the doctrine of immortality ("Relig. innerh. d. Grenzen d. blos. Vernunft," Werke, vi. 301, Hartenstein's ed.). For Lessing's views, see "Die Erzich. d. Menschengesch.," §§ 22 ff. See also Wolfenbüt., "Frag. Viertes."

INTRODUCTORY.

philosophic theology, may now become a science as purely inductive as any of the physical sciences. The now possible analysis of the faiths of the world, if accompanied by a searching analysis of the faculties of the mind, will hand over to thought our primary and necessary religious ideas, which, as ultimate religious truths, constitute in their synthesis the foundation of the universal and ideal religion of man.

On this ground, not as a dogma of religion, or a doctrine of philosophy, but as a specifically human property* involved in the very nature of man, evolved in the evolution of that nature, the belief in immortality needs to be discussed. How does it arise, and why? What is its earliest form? What the law or principle of its evolution? What are the final forms it assumes? Why one rather than another? The materials for this discussion are, in one respect, ample enough. Scholars have supplied us with exhaustive and accurate expositions of the several cultured religions, ancient and modern, and so with the means of comparing their earlier and simpler with their later and more complex elements, and this comparison may help us to discover the principle of their growth, or the reason of their specific development. Then the several faiths can be compared with each other, and what is accidental and what essential in each may thus be determined. Ethno-

* Dr. Theodor Waitz, "Anthropologie der Natur-Völker," i. 325.

graphers, too, like the late Dr. Theodor Waitz, Mr. Tylor, and Sir John Lubbock,* have collected an immense mass of information as to the beliefs of savage and primitive peoples. But each of these authors is so absorbed in the search after superficial resemblances as often to miss fundamental differences, and the very comprehensiveness which they aim at forces them to overlook the course of genetic development in the cultured religions.† Now, it may perhaps throw some light upon the growth of religious thought in general, the formation of the cultured religions in particular, and the progress of a people in civilization, if we can trace, though but in outline, the origin and evolution of the belief in immortality among two kindred but very different peoples, the Hindus and the Greeks. On this point their religions, while starting from a common goal, reach the point of sharpest contrast, and so can be most instructively studied.

* The views of these ethnographers on our present subject will be found, "Anthropologie der Natur-Völker," i. 325, ii. 191 ff.; 411 ff., and very frequently; "Primitive Culture," chapp. xii. xiii. ; "Origin of Civilization," 138 ff.

† Mr. Tylor admits that the early Aryans did not believe in transmigration ("Prim. Cult.," ii. 8), and his theory of the origin of the belief (pp. 14, 15) certainly cannot apply to the Hindus. The men of the Vedic age had been long out of that savage stage of thought to which alone Mr. Tylor's theory is applicable.

II.

Perhaps it may be necessary to glance here at the origin and evolution of the Belief. Death as annihilation is a notion as little intelligible to a primitive or undeveloped mind as immortality. A child cannot understand death as loss of being, cannot imagine the dead as otherwise than still alive. It thinks of them as existing somewhere, as doing something; and neither the lifeless body, nor the grave, nor the burial, can break their simple faith. Wordsworth's "Little Maid" is a type of the child-mind the world over, and its belief translated into the language of man becomes a sublime "Ode to Immortality." To the instincts of a living man, who has not yet learned to reason either from the facts of experience or the data of consciousness, death cannot suggest annihilation, because annihilation is a thought too abstract and repugnant to these instincts to be either intelligible or credible. In such a man faith is stronger than sight; he can conceive and understand life, but not its utter negation. If he thinks of the dead, he thinks of them as living—the very attempt to represent them in thought is an attempt to represent living, not dead men.

But, while the instincts of primitive mind refuse to conceive the dead as non-existent, a double incapacity prescribes the limits and form of the only conception possible to it,—the incapacity to conceive other than embodied being, and the incapacity to comprehend unlimited duration. In other words, the undeveloped mind cannot conceive the abstract notion of spirit and the abstract notion of immortality, or endless duration of being. Hence the earliest notions of the future represent it as a shadowy copy of the present; and its duration is measured by memory, is not made measureless by hope—*i.e.*, the conception attaches itself to the recollection of the dead rather than to the expectations of the living. But notwithstanding these limitations, the belief is a real belief in immortality, so far as it is possible to a child-mind. The seed is here, as it ought to be; the natural and necessary growth of mind will transform the seed into both flower and fruit.

But, while the belief in the future life springs out of what we must call, for want of a better term, an instinct, its evolution, alike as to the time occupied and the order of thought observed, depends on the development of the mental faculties, as in their turn at once conditioning and conditioned by the history and situation of the people. In general, since the belief attaches itself to the past rather than to the future, it gathers round the persons of the fathers, and fancy, aided by memory, peoples the realm of the dead with the shades of renowned ancestors, whose society and fellowship become before long objects of intense desire to the living. Then, alongside the admiration rendered to the fathers, ethical ideas are evolved, and the conditions on which a man is granted or denied admittance to the circle of ancestral heroes, contain the germinal notion of a state of reward and retribution. Then, thought, gradually accustomed to conceive the dead as living, to see in nature life emerge uninjured from death, works out an abstract doctrine, a theory of form and life, body and soul, which, while committing the one to death and dissolution, assigns the other to independent and continued life. And these theories become in turn supports of the very belief which evoked them. The hope of a future life turns back for encouragement to the very metaphysic itself had created. And as the metaphysic is often fanciful and absurd, the evidence is as often weaker than the belief. The one is the creation of crude and premature speculation, the other the utterance of a great human instinct.

While the process of evolution is conditioned by the general development of the national mind, the specific form under which immortality is conceived is, on the other hand, conditioned by the idea of God. The idea formed of the divine nature determines that formed of the human. The two ideas develop side by side, constitute, indeed, the two poles or sides of the same thought. While the idea of God remains so inchoate as to admit the limitations and multiplicities of Polytheism, it does not and can not involve as a necessity, either of reason or faith, any specific form of the belief in immortality.

But as the religion generates a theology, as thought comes to conceive God as the One related to the Many, as the single source of the manifold creation, man is led at the same time and by the same principles to conceive and formulate his faith in his own immortal existence. This does not happen all at once, but is the result of slow and not always conscious movements of mind. Principles, struck out by single intellects or created by general tendencies, rise within every polytheism, lift it out of the physical stage, are made, either by conscious mental action or unconscious mental growth, to become inimical to it, and either abolish the ancient religion, or erect by its side a distinct and supplementary worship, under the form of mysteries, or, while sparing it as a mode of worship, substitute for the mythical creations, which were its original constituents, a body of reflective or speculative doctrines. If the prelusive thought had been tending to grasp a single universal and indestructible principle of the life manifested in nature and man, a pantheistic theory as to God, a theory of transmigration as to man, will emerge. But if its tendency had been to seek a Supreme Will and Authority, then the result will be a personal God, and the personal continuance of man. The first will thus have a metaphysical, but the second a moral, basis. Brahmanism may stand as an example of the one, Zoroastrism of the other.

Religious and philosophic thought on such questions as God and Immortality thus so run into each other in their respective beginnings as to be then indistinguishable. Philosophy springs out of religion—is the attempt of a devout reflective man to understand and explain himself and the universe. Hence the roots both of ancient and modern thought on our subject must be sought in the ancient religions.

Immortality is not a doctrine of the schools, but a faith of humanity, not based on the metaphysic or proved by the logic of a given system, but the utterance of an instinct common to the race, which has made itself heard wherever man has advanced from a religion of nature to a religion of faith. And there is no article of belief he so reluctantly surrenders even to the demands of system. One of the most daring critical and speculative spirits of our century rallied, with caustic irony, his transcendental countrymen on their tenderness for the ego—a tenderness which spared self, while Deity was sacrificed.* And he found the denial of personal immortality the last step of the inexorable logic which completed the cycle of Transcendental Philosophy.

* D. F. Strauss, "Die Christliche Glaubenslehre," ii. pp. 697 ff.

III.

The history of a great human belief ought to have some significance for modern thought. It exhibits mind in action, believing in obedience to its own necessary laws. What man has done by nature nature can justify. Certain beliefs are regarded as the results of art or accident or custom, and the source determines the quality and value of the stream. But the belief that can be proved to be native to mind has its right to exist vindicated, is a child of nature, not of art. What the intellect can best conceive it can best believe; the universal faith but articulates the universal thought.

To believe in immortality is not only more congenial to the heart, but more conformable to the reason than to believe in annihilation. Destruction is indemonstrable. It can never be proved that what makes the man a reasonable and moral being ceases to be when the pulse ceases to beat and the tongue to speak. The most that can be proved is, that certain signs interpretative of the man, expressive of his thoughts, emotions, and volitions, have ceased to be perceived. There is stillness, silence, the organ thrills no more with its living music, but there is nothing to show that the silence is due to the loss of the noble mind that touched its keys into harmony rather than to the failure of its pipes and breath. The senses are not the man. His eminence is not due to his organism, but to his moral and spiritual faculties. The savage is as a sensuous being often much more highly developed than the sage. The dog and the deer are keener in smell than man. The eagle excels him in strength and distance of vision; the game of the forest or jungle are quicker in hearing. The man is man by virtue of the mind that uses the senses, not by virtue of the senses used. Their loss is not the loss of him. Did he cease to be when they cease to act, then the accident were the essence, the sign the thing signified. The thinker who resolves thought into transfigured sensations may get rid of immortality, but he does so by getting rid of mind. And he does it by a suicidal process. He denies too much to be able to affirm anything, and where nothing can be affirmed nothing can be denied.

But if it is impossible, on the one hand, to prove that the dead have ceased to be real and living persons, it is as impossible, on the other, to conceive a state of absolute non-existence. Nonentity is a contradiction in terms. Its two parts annihilate each other. Nothing cannot be thought—must be by the very attempt to conceive it translated into something. If, then, death is imagined or defined, it is realized, becomes a state of real or positive being. What ceases to be ceases to be an object of thought; to think of the dead is to predicate existence in fact even where it is in form denied. And Being continued for ever is no harder to conceive than Being continued for a year or a century. Eternal is, indeed, more conceivable than temporal existence, the latter being only explicable through the former. Where spirit is concerned duration means growth, not decay. Mind does not count its being by seasons or suns, but by thought and action. Organized being has had a past, has a present, will have a future; but spiritual being simply exists, enjoys an everlasting Now. Thought is the life of the intellect. To think is to be. And thought creates time and space, is not created by them. To conceive personal being rightly is to conceive it as immortal.

Mind, then, has ever found it more easy to believe in its continued than in its interrupted and destroyed being. And it has done so by a necessity of its own nature, which we may name either an inability or an ability—the first, in so far as mind cannot conceive nonentity, the negation of reality, the second in so far as the conceived is the realized. Now, to trace the development of the Belief in India and Greece will be to show how mind, under the most dissimilar conditions and with the most opposed views of nature and man, has acted in relation to it; how the mental laws and necessities that create the Belief victoriously assert themselves under the most unfavourable circumstances, and in results whose differences are more significant than agreement had been.

PART II.

THE BELIEF IN INDIA.

THE limits of the discussion exclude any attempt, even were such possible, to discover by the analysis of words or legends, whether there are any traces of the belief before the Indo-European family divided into its several oriental and occidental branches. Our present inquiry has to do only with the Hindus and Greeks, and so must start, as regards both, with their earliest extant literature.

1. THE HYMNS OF THE RIG-VEDA.

In the earlier books of this Veda the indications of the belief are few, and, in some respects, indefinite.* This, indeed, was to be expected. The religion there revealed exists still in great part under the forms of the old nature-worship, though it moves in a circle of spiritual ideas, not, indeed, distinctly conceived, but

---

* Muir's "Original Sanskrit Texts," v. 284 ff.; Wilson's "Hymns of the Rig-Veda," i. xxv.; Max Müller's "Ancient Sans. Lit.," 19, note 2.

floating in the individual and general consciousness like shadows unrealized. The gods are conceived more or less under physical forms, and so thought is occupied with the visible manifestations of the gods and their present relations to man rather than with modes of being and relations invisible and future.

Thus intimations of a belief in a life after death could not be numerous, but though the intimations are few, it does not follow that the belief was uncertain. Agni,* Soma,† the Maruts,‡ Mitra and Varuna,§ are implored to grant immortality. By liberality∥ and sacrifice,¶ a man "attains immortality," "goes to the gods," meets in the highest heaven the recompense of the sacrifices he has offered. The Vedic notion of immortality was not, indeed, like ours, a positive abstract conception, but an indefinite concrete representation. Still it was as comprehensive and affirmative as was possible to those early Hindus,—the very immortality attributed to their gods.** Hence to

---

* R.-V., v. 4, 10; i. 31, 7.

† R.-V., ix. 113, 7 ff.; Muir's "Sans. Texts," v. 306; R.-V., i. 191, 18.

‡ R.-V., v. 55, 4. § R.-V., v. 63, 2.

∥ R.-V., i. 125, 5; x. 107, 2. ¶ x. 14, 8.

** In certain cases, as possibly R.-V., v. 4, 10, the immortality meant was to be realized on earth in offspring (Muir, "Sans. Texts," v. 285, note 415). But a comparison of the above texts with iv. 54, 2; vi. 7, 4; ix. 106, 8; x. 53, 10, &c., will bear out the statement of the text. In truth, Vedic thought had not yet learned to affirm an absolute immortality.

them it seemed a species of deification. The man who had been made immortal had become a minor deity. Thus, the Ribhus had "become gods," gone to the assemblage of the gods.* Hence, too, the belief is expressed less in the hopes of the living than in their thoughts touching the dead. "Our sage ancestors have obtained riches among the gods,"† as "companions of the gods"‡ they are implored to be "propitious,"§ to "protect,"|| not to injure.¶ The faith in the continued life of the fathers is thus so strong as to rise almost to apotheosis. Death had not annihilated the fathers, need not annihilate the sons, and so they pray to be "added to the people of eternity, the blessed."**

The belief in a life after death seems thus to have grown up round the thought of the fathers, or simply the dead. Primitive man conscious of "life in every limb," could know nothing of death—could only conceive the dead as still alive. And as the only notion of life outside and above nature was associated with the gods, a life akin to the Divine was attributed to the departed ancestors. Thus the belief stands enshrined in the heart of the Vedic religion, interwoven, on the one hand, with the idea of God, on the other, with

---

* R.-V., i. 161, 1—5; iv. 35, 3, and 8. Muir, "Sans. Texts," v. 226 and 284.   † R.-V., i. 91, 1; i. 179, 6.
‡ R.-V., vii. 76, 4.   § R.-V., vi. 75, 10; vii. 35, 12.
|| R.-V., vi. 52, 4.   ¶ iii. 55, 2.
** vii. 57, 6. Muir, "Sans. Texts," v. 28, 5.

the memory of the fathers. And that it had grown with the history of the people a primitive legend seems to show. In the later books of the Rig-Veda the future life stands impersonated, as it were, in Yama. Now Yama is the Iranian Yima. His father is in the Vedas Vivasvat, in the Zend Avesta Vivanghat. The names in each case are identical, and indicate that some legend connected with them must have existed prior to the separation of the Aryans.*

But the legend survives in the two branches under

---

* It is not possible to enter here in any satisfactory way into any of the many questions, critical, philosophical, mythological, historical, connected with this legend. As to its existence in the Aryan period, and its bearing on the relationship of the Iranian and Indian branches, see Dr Muir, "Sanskrit Texts," ii. 296, 469 f.; Spiegel, "Eränische Alterthumsk.," 439 f.; Lassen, "Ind. Alterthumsk.," i. 619 ff. (2nd ed.). For an exhaustive critical and philosophical discussion of the legend under its Iranian and Indian forms, see Prof. Roth's article, "Die Sage von Dschemschid," "Zeitsch. d. Deuts. Morganl. Gesel.," iv. 417, 433. Also, Duncker's "Geschichte der Arier," 453 ff. For a discussion as well as an annotated translation of the passages in the Rig-Veda referring to Yama, see Dr. Muir's "Sanskrit Texts," v. 287 ff.; 300 ff. Professor Max Müller, "Lectures on the Science of Language," ii. 481 ff., resolves the Yama legend as given in the Rig-Veda into one of the myths of the Dawn, Yama, the day, Yami, his sister, the night. Without attempting to discuss the question with the above distinguished scholar, I may simply say that his mythological theory seems to me to be too narrow and exclusive. It is so occupied with nature as to leave little or no room for the exercise of thought and imagination upon the condition and destiny of man. The tragic elements of human life, birth and death, must have touched primitive mind quite as profoundly as the rising and the setting sun; and the Yama legend appears to be pre-eminently one of those in which the thoughts of men concerning man found expression.

two different forms. The Iranian Yima is the founder and king of a golden age, during whose reign neither sickness nor age nor death, neither cold nor heat, neither hatred nor strife, existed. The Indian Yama is the king of the dead, the assembler of men who departed to the mighty streams and spied out the road for many.* But the legends, though different, are not contradictory. The tradition of the first man who lived might well include, or glide into, the tradition of the first man who died. In the ordinary course of nature the one would be the other; and so the legend, in its original form, might comprehend both the Iranian and Indian versions. And the division is explicable enough. The Iranic, as a reformed faith, seeking for itself a moral basis, clung to the picture of a golden past, where the antagonisms it hated were unknown. The Indian, less moral, more imaginative, caught in the toils of a nature-worship, sighed for relief, and sought it in the kingdom of light, into which the son of Vivasvat had been the first to return. And so, while the legend in the one case passed through a series of developments in which Yima and his golden age gradually deteriorated, it became in the other the centre round which the Hindu doctrine of the future life developed. The processes were similar, but the result different, because the

* R.-V., x. 14, 1; Muir's "Sans. Texts," v. 291 ff.

mythical faculty had its objects placed in different spheres.

Yama, then, is the highest expression of the later Vedic faith in a future life. He dwells in celestial light, in the innermost sanctuary of heaven.* He and the fathers are "in the highest heaven." He grants to the departed "an abode distinguished by days, and waters, and lights."† He grants a "long life among the gods."‡ He is associated with the god Varuna, worshipped as a god, and "feasts according to his desire on the oblations."§ "He shares his gratification with the eager Vasishthas, our ancient ancestors, who presented the Soma libation."‖ Yama and the fathers thus enjoy immortal blessedness in heaven. Such was the intense faith of the later Vedic poets. But as the faith was evolved so was the question— How can we be raised to the society of Yama and the fathers? Their ancestors, the men of the heroic age which lies always in the past, deserved to be made immortal, but how was immortality possible to their less worthy sons? And here a decisive and determinating peculiarity of the early Hindu faith emerged. Future happiness had a sacerdotal, as distinguished from a religious, or moral, or national basis—rested,

---

* R.-V., ix. 113, 7 and 8 ; Muir's "Sans. Texts," v. 302.
† R.-V., x. 14, 8 and 9.   ‡ R.-V., x. 14, 14.
§ R.-V., x. 14, 7 ; x. 15, 8.   ‖ R.-V., x. 15, 8.

not so much on virtue or heroism, as on the worship of sacerdotal deities and the practice of sacerdotal rites. The old natural deities, though now and then implored to grant immortality, are, as a rule, limited to action in the sphere of the present and the seen; but the sacerdotal deities, *i.e.*, gods formed from the deification of the instruments of worship, were the great distributors of future happiness. Thus, Agni is "made by the gods the centre of immortality;"* is its guardian; exalts mortals to it,† warms with his heat the unborn part and conveys it to the world of the righteous.‡ Soma "confers immortality on gods and men."§ He is implored to place his worshipper "in that everlasting and imperishable world where there is eternal light and glory."‖ Those who have drunk the Soma have "become immortal," "have entered into light."¶ Then sacerdotal rites like sacrifice, or virtues like liberality to the priests, purchase immortality.** So comprehensive and absolute is the supremacy of the sacerdotal element in the later Vedic religion, that the other gods are now and then represented as dependent for immor-

---

* R.-V., iii. 17, 4.   † R.-V., i. 31, 7 ; vii. 7, 7.
‡ R.-V., x. 16, 4.   See also passages from Atharva-Veda, in Dr. Muir's "Sans. Texts," v. 299 ff.
§ R.-V., i. 91, 1, 6, 18 ; ix. 108, 3; ix. 109, 3. See also the chapter on Indra's love of the Soma-juice, in Dr. Muir's "Sans. Texts," v. 88 ff.   ‖ R.-V., ix. 113, 7 f.
¶ R.-V., viii. 48, 3.   ** R.-V., x. 154, 3—5 ; x. 107, 2.

tality and enjoyment upon the sacerdotal deities or rites.*

The influence of this sacerdotalism on the development of the Hindu faith in general, and the belief in the future life of the soul in particular, must here be distinctly recognized. The question is not as to its origin, but as to its influence. Its source is psychological, and it forms an essential element in all religions —is represented in our Christian faith by the sacrifice and priesthood of Christ; but for reasons which cannot be stated here, it grew very early to portentous proportions and exercised a baneful influence among the Hindus. The Vedic religion may be described as a naturalism with a nascent sacerdotalism superinduced. In the earlier Vedic era the natural was the predominant element, but in the later the sacerdotal. When a religion is passing through such a phase of development, there runs beneath or within it a stream of what may be termed unconscious metaphysics—general tendencies understood at the time in whole by few, perhaps by none, understood in part by many, but felt by all. The new element has to assert and justify itself against the old by creating for the religion it seeks to transform a new basis, radically different from the old naturalism; and so the result is a twofold development—the

* Several illustrative passages will be found in Dr. Muir's "Sans. Texts," v. 14 ff.

growth of religious rites on the one hand, of abstract conceptions on the other. But while the former are manifested in the general constitution and practice of the religion, the latter can appear only in particular and partial utterances. Here and there an individual gathers into himself the dim and diffused consciousness of the people, expresses it in hymn or aphorism, and the expression, a mirror to the collective mind, seems the result of Divine inspiration. Hence, while the speculative and mystical hymns in the tenth book of the Rig-Veda form, in almost every respect, contrasts to the spontaneous and objective compositions of the earlier books, they are yet only concentrated utterances of thoughts which had been throughout the whole Vedic era slowly accumulating and assuming consistency and shape. They are like early spring flowers, at once manifestations of forces at work in the earth and prophecies of what is to come.

This double growth of sacerdotalism and abstract thought stands very clearly revealed in the tenth book of the Rig-Veda. The priesthood is professional, a priest necessary to worship. The sacrificial rites are numerous and minute. The value attached to prayers, hymns, sacrifices, excessive. The new sacerdotalism is superseding the old naturalism, and abstract thought is seen struggling to find a new basis and new forms for the changing religion. Creation is conceived as a sacrifice, either the self-immolation of a god, or the immolation of one god by others.* Sacrifice is the cause of human prosperity and the processes of nature.† The Brahman is the son of god, sprung from divine seed.‡ The Vedic poets are the organs and offspring of deity.§ The hymns are divine, god-generated, or given, and enter into the Rishis by sacrifice.‖ The speculative tendencies thus incline to assume sacerdotal forms. Now and then, indeed, an exceptional thinker, either above or outside priestly influence, asks and tries to answer the profoundest questions in simple but sublime words.¶ Speculation, partly the victim of the old naturalism as embalmed in language, partly the seer and exponent of the eternal truths there contained, finds in life ever emerging from death the principle that abides amid the decay and renewal of nature and man. This, indeed, is but guessed at, not explicitly developed; but the guess extends to the procession of gods and men from

---

* R.-V., x. 81, 5 ; x. 130, 3. But particularly the celebrated *Purusha Sûkta*, x. 90. See this hymn translated, explained, and illustrated at great length and on all sides in Dr. Muir's "Sans. Texts," vol. i. 8 ff. ; vol. v. 367 ff.

† R.-V., x. 62, 1—3, and very frequently.

‡ R.-V., vii. 33, 11—13 ; x. 62, 4, 5.

§ R.-V., x. 20, 10 ; x. 61, 7.

‖ x. 71, 3 ; x. 125, 3 ; x. 88, 8 ; x. 61, 7.

¶ See the extraordinary hymn, R.-V., x. 129, translated under the title, "The Thinker's Question," in Professor Max Müller's "Anc. Sans. Lit.," p. 564. Also by Dr. Muir, iv. 4, and v. 356 ff.; and by Mr. Colebrooke, "Essays," p. 17 (Williams and Norgate's edition).

a common source of life. The seeds of Hindu speculation lie like the germs of Brahmanism in the later Vedic hymns.

The belief in a life after death expressed in the later Vedic hymns must now be looked at in the light of these sacerdotal and speculative tendencies. Sacerdotalism held command over the future; it could reward and punish. The realms of light, the world of the righteous, the society of the fathers, a festive life with Yama, a life in the presence of the gods, immortality in a world where all the objects of gratification are attained, were in its gift. And it also knew an "abyss,"* a "bottomless" and "nethermost" "darkness"† for the wicked. Speculation has to seek a reason or ground for this sacerdotal power, and sees it, in a far-off sort of way, in the unity of human nature with the divine, broken by the earthly life, but restored by sacrifice. Thought had divined that unity in the source of life implied the creation and derivative immortality of the gods. It had deified the fathers, deified the rishis, and so had learned to conceive the permanent element in man as akin to the divine. On this ground pre- and post-existence become alike natural, complementary conceptions. And so Agni is implored in a funeral hymn to kindle with his heat the "unborn part" of the dead; to "give up again to the fathers him who comes

* R.-V., vii. 104, 3, 17; ix. 73, 8. † R.-V., x. 152, 4; x. 103, 12.

offered with oblations."* To the soul of the departed it is said, "Throwing off all imperfection again go to thy home."† Man has had a past, will have a future, has come from God and may to God return. And the thought has a side which indicates its ultimate anthropological form, as distinguished from its theological basis. The dead is told to "become united to a body and clothed in a shining form."‡ The varied constituents of the body are told to go to the elements to which they are akin.§ The like seeks the like. Without body or form individual life is inconceivable. And over all sacrifice presides, bringing the gods to receive the "unborn part," carrying it to the homes of Yama and the fathers.

In these Vedic Hymns, then, the belief in a life after death changes with the change in the religion. In the older Naturalism, it was a simple belief in the continued life of the fathers; in the later embryo-sacerdotalism, it is becoming related, on its material side, to the idea of God, on its formal, to the observance of religious rites. The older faith had as its objects persons, but the later is slowly refining its objects into abstractions. A Pantheism as to God, a theory of transmigration as to man,‖ had not yet been evolved, but the seeds of both

---

* R.-V., x. 16, 4, 5.   † R.-V., x. 14, 8.
‡ R.-V., x. 14, 8.   § R.-V., x. 16, 3.
‖ The only verse from the Rig-Veda ever quoted in proof of transmigration being believed when the hymns were composed is, i. 164, 32. Professor Wilson renders:—"He who has made (this state of things)

had been sown, and had even, under the forcing influences of the nascent sacerdotalism, begun to germinate. The seeds were still under the foot, still in the earth, while the Vedic Rishis lived, but in the centuries which followed those seeds grew into forests, in which their sons were inextricably entangled and hopelessly bewildered.

2. THE BRAHMANAS.*

These mark the next point at which the inquiry into the Hindu belief in the soul's life after death can be resumed, and its growth measured. Sacerdotalism is now "full-blown."† The Aryans have penetrated further into India. The consequent changes and conquests have contributed to the growth of Brahmanical

---

does not comprehend it; he who has beheld it, has it verily hidden (from him); he, whilst yet enveloped in his mother's womb, is subject to many births, and has entered upon evil." ("Hymns of the R.-V.," vol. ii. 137, 138.) But as the late Professor Goldstücker observed (Art. Transmigration, "Chambers's Cyclop."), "The word of the text, *bahu-prajah*, rendered by Wilson, according to the commentators, 'is subject to many births,' may, according to the same commentators, also mean, 'has many offsprings,' or 'has many children;' and as the latter is the more literal and usual sense of the word, whereas the former is artificial, no conclusion whatever regarding the doctrine of transmigration can safely be founded on it." Besides, such a doctrine is entirely alien to Vedic modes of thought.

* As to the date of the Brāhmanas, the place they occupy in Sanskrit literature, their design, relation to the Vedas, &c., see Max Müller's "Anc. Sans. Lit.," pp. 342 ff.; Muir's "Sans. Texts," ii. pp. 178 ff.

† Professor Roth, quoted in Dr. Muir's "Sans. Texts," ii. 183.

pretensions. The priest has extended and deepened his command over time and eternity. The number of the sacrifices has been increased, their efficacy heightened, their minutest details made essential. The supersession of the old Vedic naturalism is complete. The names of the old gods remain, but their natures are changed.

The speculative principles, which form the basis of this full-blown sacerdotalism, have also developed. Thought has changed the formal into the material element. It had made sacrifice first please, then command, then become greater than the gods, and now, finally, the source of gods, man, and the universe.

Prayer or devotion has risen by a similar process to be Brahma (Neuter), the supreme, the self-existent.

The gods became immortal by sacrifice.* Brahma produced out of himself the universe,† was, as to his essence, in the Brahman, pervaded and so made the once mortal gods immortal.‡ Sacerdotal thought, pursuing its career of abstraction, has thus deified its own conceptions. Brahmanical sacrifice is the source and basis and very substance of the universe. Brahmanical thought is eternal, its vehicle divine. The old worship still stands, only in more developed forms,

---

* S'atapatha Brāhmana, x. 4, 3, 1—8 ; xi. 1, 2, 12.
† Ib., xi. 2, 3, 1 ; xiii. 7, 1, 1.
‡ Ib., xi. 2, 3, 1 ff. See a variety of passages in Muir's "Sans. Texts," iv. 24 ff. ; v. 387 ff.

but sacerdotal thought, at once idealizing and abstractive, has explained into, or inserted beneath, it, a circle of ideas evolved from the old, but destructive of it.

In harmony with these general tendencies, the belief in a life after death has alike on its material and formal sides developed. There is the clear conception of another life conditioned, as to its nature and issues, by the present. The rewards received in it are determined by the sacrifices offered here. The greater the latter in number and value, the higher the former. These rewards are, indeed, on one side, continued individual life, proportioned in its felicity and duration to the quantity and quality of the sacrifices performed; but they point, on another side, to a union with Brahma, or a transmutation into other gods, which is hardly compatible with continued individuality. Thus it is said that he who sacrifices in a certain way "conquers for himself an union with these two gods (Aditya and Agni), and an abode in the same sphere."* Again, those who offer particular sacrifices "become Agni, Varuna, or Indra, attain to union and the same spheres with these gods respectively."† Again, "he who sacrifices with a burnt offering arrives by Agni as the door to Brahma, and, having so arrived, he attains to a union with Brahma, and abides in the same sphere with him."‡ And he

* S'atap. Brah., xi. 6, 2, 2, 3.   † Ib., ii. 6, 4, 8.   ‡ Ib. xi. 4, 4, 1.

who reached this union was not, while he who did not reach it was, subject to repeated births and changes. Thus, a passage of the S'atapatha Brāhmana represents the gods as made immortal by certain sacrifices, and then proceeds:—"Death said to the gods, 'In the very same way, all men (also) shall become immortal, then what portion will remain for me?' The gods replied, 'Henceforward no other being shall become immortal with his body, when thou shalt have seized that part. Now, every one who is to become immortal through knowledge, or by work, shall become immortal after parting with his body.' This, which they said 'by knowledge or by work,' means that knowledge which is Agni, that work which is Agni. Those who so know this, or who perform this rite, *are born again after death*, and, by being so born, they attain immortality. Whilst those who do not so know, or who do not perform this rite, *are, indeed, born again after death, but become again and again his food.*"*

The first italicized clause plainly promises final emancipation from death; the second as plainly implies successive appearances in a bodily form, subject to mortality. And the same thought is, in another pas-

---

* x. 4, 3, 9. Translated in Dr. Muir's "Sans. Texts," iv. 49 f. ; v. 316 f. All the passages quoted in this section will be found in the sixth chapter of 18th section of latter volume.

sage, thus expressed :—"He who does so (studies the Veda) is freed from dying a second time, and attains to a union with Brahma."* The Brāhmaṇas, then, did not regard the state after death as necessarily final. It was so to the good who attained the abode of the gods, or union with Brahma, but was not so to the bad. Hence the balances in which a man's deeds are weighed may be either in this world or the next. If a man places himself in the balances here he escapes them hereafter, but if not, then he must be weighed there, and follow the result;† *i.e.*, the pious in this life escape all changes in the next, others shall be subjected to change, determined by the relative proportions of the good and evil deeds placed in the balances.

Again, the theory alike of reward and retribution is, that like seeks like, or, rather, that the reward is of the same nature as the merit, the punishment as the sin. "Hence they say that a man is born into the world which he has made."‡ "So many sacrifices as a man has performed when he departs from this world, with so many is he born in the other world after his death."§ Certain sacrifices "free from the mortal body" and raise to heaven, certain others "conquer" for the offerer much less.|| Certain sacrifices secure a more, others a less, spiritual body.¶ Some become the soul

---

* S'atap. Brah., xi. 5, 6, 9. † Ib., xi. 2, 7, 33. ‡ Ib., vi. 2, 2, 27.
§ Ib., x. 6, 3, 1. || Ib., xi. 2, 6, 13. ¶ Ib., x. 1, 5, 4.

of the sacrificer, and ensure his birth with his whole body in the next world, but others are of more limited efficacy.* On the other hand, the punishments of the wicked are akin in nature, and proportioned in degree, to their sins here. Thus a legend, which Professor Weber extracts from the S'atapatha Brāhmana,† gives, while illustrating the difference between the old and the new belief, quite a Dantesque picture of their

---

* S'atap. Brah., iv. 6, 11 ; xi. 1, 8, 6; xii. 8, 3, 31.
† "Eine Legende des Satapatha-Brāhmana, über die Strafende Vergeltung nach dem Tode," Indische Streifen, i. pp. 20—30. See an epitome, with ample and instructive illustrations, in Dr. Muir's "Sans. Texts," v. 314 ff. Professor Weber attempts, in his remarks on the above legend, to explain the origin of the belief in transmigration. He says:—"The Brāhmanas do not speak distinctly concerning the duration of their rewards and punishments, and here manifestly is the starting-point of the dogma of transmigration to be sought. To men of the mild disposition and thoughtful spirit of the Indians, an eternity of reward or punishment would not appear probable. To them it must have seemed possible to expiate by atonement and purification the punishment due to the sins committed in this short life. And, according to their opinion, the reward for virtues exercised in the same brief period could not endure for ever." (Loc. cit., p. 22.) But the roots of the doctrine are to be sought in the metaphysical, not in the moral, ideas of the Indians. The notion of everlasting reward, though not perhaps in a European or Christian sense, had been reached in the Brāhmanas, and was the result of sacerdotalism crudely conceiving its own efficacy. Everlasting punishment was not conceived under a final form, but there was what might stand as its equivalent. Sacerdotalism could not allow those who had despised its authority to pass for ever out of its power. Transmigration did for the Eastern priesthood what purgatory did for the Western, but the dominant sacerdotalism in each case only developed and translated into a form suitable to its own use the matter of the general belief.

sufferings. Bhrigu, the son of Varuna, is sent by his father to the four points of the compass to be instructed by what he sees there. He goes, and finds in each quarter men being either hacked in pieces or eaten by other men, who keep saying, "This to thee, this to me." Bhrigu asks why they do so, and is told, "These did so to us in the other world, we do so to them again here." This is the legend in its original and ethical form; the explanation shows it transmuted into the later or sacerdotal. The men are made to represent respectively the wood, milk, grass, and water used in the Agnihotra sacrifice. He who sacrifices conquers the powers of nature these typify. He who does not becomes, in the next world, their victim; is divided and eaten there by plants and animals as he divided and ate them here. The change significantly illustrates the tendencies of Brahmanical thought. There is a certain community of nature between man and the world; the one can suffer at the hands of the other. Sacrifice has power to unite man to God, or to deliver him to punitive material forces. He can be assimilated to the Highest or subordinated to the lowest.

The Brāhmanas thus show our belief in a much more developed state than the Vedas. Their future state is not necessarily final; it may and it may not be so. Its highest reward, union with Brahma, gives finality, but not its lower. A man may become again and again the food of death. Then, its punishments are received at the hands of Nature unconquered by sacrifice. And the ideas that form the roots of these representations are monistic. Speculation, more or less consciously, recognises the essence of all beings as one; sacerdotalism, quite consciously, determines under what mode man shall exist. Its being is so bound up with the faith in a future life that it cannot allow that faith to perish.

3. THE UPANISHADS.*

The sacerdotal, as the formal and sensible, can never be to thoughtful minds the ultimate and highest element of religion. Worship in any form is a mediator, a mode in which man tries by articulate or inarticulate expression to speak to God. Intense and subtle spirits always seek to dispense with this mediator, to get face to face with God, discover what He is, and what their ultimate relations to Him.

Worship, whether sacerdotal or devotional, reposes upon and expresses certain doctrinal or speculative principles, and the more clearly these are comprehended, the more does the worship seem, so far as the instructed or initiated are concerned, a circuitous and unnecessary medium of

---

* For the literary questions connected with the Upanishads, see Prof. Max Müller's "Anc. Sans. Lit.," pp. 316 ff.; Colebrooke's "Essays," "Essay on the Sacred Writings of the Hindus," particularly p. 55.

intercourse and what it may involve. Hence, within every sacerdotal religion, yet above it, its contradiction, yet its offspring, a mystical or theosophic tendency is sure to rise. On the other hand, a doctrinal religion, *i.e.*, one which consists of formulated principles, or propositions addressed to the intellect, is, as a rule, antagonistic to mysticism. Thus, Greek theosophic thought is found, as in the Orphici, Pythagoreans, and Neo-Platonists, allied with elaborate and symbolical worships. Thus, too, Roman Catholicism has been rich, Protestantism comparatively poor, in eminent mystics. Tauler and Eckhart, Saint Theresa and Saint Catherine, Fénelon and Madame Guion, are natural products of the former, hardly to be matched in the latter. Thus, too, Lutheranism as compared with Calvinism, has been prolific in mystics, and can boast of Jacob Behmen and Emanuel Swedenborg, two of the most eminent. The reason seems to be, that a doctrinal religion has, but a sacerdotal has not, the semblance of ultimate truth, and so an intense intellect, while it may be satisfied with the first, cannot rest in the second, but craves to pierce the temporal forms to the eternal God behind.

This theosophic phase of thought, inevitable in India from its peculiar religious development, receives distinct expression in the Upanishads. It had existed as a tendency even in the Rig-Veda. The tenth book contains, not only the products of abstract thought, but praises of (tapas) austerity, rigorous abstraction. Right and truth are represented as springing from kindled austerity.* The sages of a thousand songs become by austere fervour invincible, went by it to heaven.† And in the speculative hymns its influence is indicated. That one which breathed breathless, while as yet death was not, nor immortality, was developed by the power of fervour (tapas).‡ This was the first step in the path of pure theosophic speculation. By austerity a limit was put to sacerdotalism—it might avail for the many, not for the elect few. In austere fervour there was generated the thought which strove to find a footing on the Ultimate Reality, to stand face to face with the first and final cause. And so the rishi became ambitious to practise austere fervour, the Brahman to leave sacerdotalism for asceticism, to become a $ὑλόβιος$, absorbed in the study of the Veda or the contemplation of Brahma.§ Hence arose the theosophic speculation which stands expressed in the Upanishads.

These embody attempts of generic similarity, but with specific differences, to construct the universe on the basis of abstract thought. Ascetic speculation must always,

* R.-V., x. 190, 1.
† R.-V., x. 125, 2. In x. 167, 1, it is said of Indra, "By performing austerity thou didst conquer heaven.'
‡ R.-V., x. 129, 2, 3.
§ Lassen, "Ind. Alterthumsk." i. 693 (2nd. ed.).

indeed, have either an accepted premiss or a foregone conclusion, but it may so transform, as to change their meaning, the formulæ in which these are expressed. Thus Brahma remains in the Upanishads as the supreme, the self-existent, but has lost his sacerdotal extraction and relations, and been transmuted into the Soul of the World.* The metaphysical conception of life or soul has replaced the priestly conception of deified prayer or devotion. How then is this universal soul to be conceived? If as absolute, it becomes a congeries of contradictions, defined yet undefined, endowed with form, yet void of it, without limit yet limited.† This simply meant, as it always must mean, that you cannot think an object without thinking a quality, and predication is limitation. *Determinatio est negatio.* If conceived as relative, then the only relation possible was one of evolution. Brahma, the universal soul, could become the Universe—it could not exist over against Brahma. "As the spider casts out and draws in (his web), as on the earth the annual herbs are produced, as from living man the hairs of the

* The Atman, which was the offspring and finite individualization of the paramātman, belongs to the theosophic rather than sacerdotal thought of India. As to the relation between the two words, see Max Müller's "Anc. Sans. Lit.," pp. 19 ff.; Lassen, "Ind. Alterthumsk.," pp. 916 f.

† Taittariya Upanishad, ii. 6; Röer's translation, "Bibliotheca Indica," xv. p. 18; Katha Up., iii. 15; Ib., p. 108. And similarly often.

head and body spring forth, so is produced the universe from the indestructible (Brahma)."*

How, again, shall the relation of the many to the one, the individual soul to the universal, be conceived? As there was in reality only one Being, Brahma,† individual existence was but seeming, the result of ignorance. Those who knew Brahma became Brahma,‡ those who did not know him were, in the degree of their ignorance, miserable, of their (comparative) knowledge, exalted and blest.§ For this old intra-sacerdotal speculation had, like every similar phase of thought similarly developed, to evolve the distinction between esoterics and exoterics. There are two sciences, the higher and the lower, and for those incapable of either, there are works.|| Those who perform works, *i.e.*, the customary sacrifices, gain only a perishable and transient reward, and must "undergo again decay and death," "go round and round, oppressed by misery, like blind people led by blind."¶ The lower knowledge comprehends the several Vedas,

---

* Mundaka Up., i. 1, 7 ; Röer, *ut supra*, 151 ; Katha Up., vi. 1 ; Röer, 116.

† Ch'handogya Up., v., a dialogue from which is quoted by Colebrooke, "Essays," pp. 50—53 (Williams and Norgate's ed.); Vájasanéya Up., 5—7; Röer, p. 72.

‡ Mundaka Up., iii. 2, 4, 6, and 8; Röer, pp. 163, 164.

§ Vájasanéya Up., 9—14, with notes ; Röer, p. 73.

|| Mundaka Up., i. 1, 4, 5 ; Röer, p. 151. See also Kéna and Katha Ups., with Röer's introductions and notes.

¶ Mundaka Up., i. 2, 7, 8; Röer, 154.

accentuation, ritual, grammar, &c.; but this, while securing a higher reward than works, still leaves the individual soul the victim of birth and death. Knowledge of Brahma as the universal soul, of the individual soul as Brahma, can alone give rest. "Thus knowing, he (Vámadéva), after the destruction of this body, being elevated (from this world), *and* having obtained all desires in the place of heaven, became immortal."*
"Whoever knows this supreme Brahma becomes even Brahma, so overcomes grief, he overcomes sin, he becomes immortal."†

In the Upanishads the belief in immortality thus receives marked development. Theosophic, as distinguished from sacerdotal speculation, now brings it into clear and recognised relation with the idea of God. The former attempts to understand the Universe from its notion of the ultimate or highest Being; the latter from its own claims and modes of worship. The one, since it educes all beings from the absolute Unity, asserts the eternity of the soul; but the other, since mainly anxious to found and extend its own claims, asserts an immortality whose good or evil states it can command. Theosophic speculation, again, does not, like philosophic, construct its idea of God out of its idea of man, but conversely, its idea

---

* Aitaréya Up., ii. 4, 6 ; Röer, p. 32.
† Mundaka Up., iii. 2, 9 ; Röer, 164.

of man out of its idea of God. Hence, since it starts with the absolute, it loses the notion of personality both as regards God and man, and the only relations it can conceive are metaphysical, not moral, necessary and evolutional, not voluntary and creational. It is not concerned with the question of immortality as such—that is settled by its fundamental assumption. Nothing that has issued from the universal soul can perish. The only questions that can concern it touch the processes of evolution and involution, emanation from God and return into Him. The first process can admit indefinite gradations of being between God and man, as the Gnostic systems witness; the second can admit as many stages and transmutations of being, as Brahmanism can best exemplify. The Upanishads have thus developed the notion of immortality into that of eternity, and made individuality an evil and a privation, since the detention of the individual from return into the universal soul. And so, at this point, theosophic speculation and sacerdotalism join hands; both seeking union with Brahma, renounce the belief in a personal immortality.

The following dialogue well illustrates the doctrine and spirit of the Upanishads. Yājnavalkya, about to withdraw into the forest to meditate upon Brahma and attain immortality, wishes to take farewell of his wife Maitrēyi. She asks him "What my lord knoweth (of immortality) may he tell that to me?"

Yājnavalkya replied, "Thou who art truly dear to me, thou speakest dear words. Sit down, I will explain it to thee, and listen well to what I say." And he said, "A husband is loved, not because you love the husband, but because you love in him the Divine Spirit (ātma, the absolute self). A wife is loved, not because we love the wife, but because we love in her the Divine Spirit; children are loved, not because we love the children, but because we love the Divine Spirit in them. The spirit it is which we love when we seem to love wealth, Brahmans, Kshattriyas, this world, the gods, all beings, this universe. The Divine Spirit, O beloved wife, is to be seen, to be heard, to be perceived, and to be meditated upon. If we see, hear, perceive, and know him, O Maitrēyi, then this whole universe is known to us."*

"It is with us when we enter into the Divine

---

* This early Hindu mysticism is far nobler than the later mysticism of the Bhagavad-Gita, where the existence of all things in God is prostituted to the basest uses, to teach indifference to the character and results of all actions. The earlier mysticism, as exhibited in the dialogue quoted in the text, may be compared with the German mysticism of the fourteenth century, to which it bears in some respects a remarkable resemblance. The doctrine of love in the one paragraph may be compared with Eckhart's (Wackernagel's "Altdeutsches Lesebuch," p. 891). The doctrine of the other paragraph with Ruysbroek's, that all who are "raised above the creaturely condition into a contemplative life are one with the divine glory, yea, are that glory," become "one with the same light, by means of which they see, and which they see." (Ruysbroek's "Vier Schriften," p. 144.)

Spirit, as if a lump of salt was thrown into the sea: it becomes dissolved into the water from which it was produced, and is not to be taken out again. But wherever you take the water and taste it, it is salt. Thus is this great endless and boundless Being but one mass of knowledge. As the water becomes salt and the salt becomes water again, thus has the Divine Spirit appeared from out the elements and disappears again into them. When we have passed away there is no longer any name. This I tell thee, my wife," said Yājnavalkya.

Maitrēyi said, "My lord, here thou hast bewildered me, saying that there is no longer any name when we have passed away."

And Yājnavalkya replied, "My wife, what I say is not bewildering, it is sufficient for the highest knowledge. For if there be as it were two beings, then the one sees the other, the one hears, perceives, and knows the other. But if the one Divine Self be the whole of all this, whom, or through whom should he see, hear, perceive, or know? How should he know himself, by whom he knows everything (himself). How, my wife, should he know himself the knower? Thus thou hast been taught, Maitrēyi; this is immortality."

Having said this, Yājnavalkya left his wife for ever, and went into the solitude of the forests.*

* The above dialogue, extracted from the Brihadaranyaka, is abridged

4. THE LAWS OF MANU.*

Theosophic speculation elaborated the notion of God as the world-soul, from which, by necessary evolution, individual souls emanated, into which by knowledge, possible only after many changes of form, they returned. Sacerdotalism accepted and assimilated the notion, and made it the basis of its authority and claims. Of men, the Brahman stood nearest to Brahma, and was "the lord of the whole creation."† The other classes had their position and dignity determined by their several degrees of distance from the universal soul, and so the caste system was founded in the divine order of the universe.‡ Veritable divinity was made to hedge the Brahman. He was an incarnation of Dharma. He was born above the world, the chief of all creatures. The wealth of the universe was in fact, though not in form, his.§

from a translation in Professor Max Müller's "Anc. Sans. Lit.," pp. 22—25. See also Colebrooke's "Essays," p. 39 (W. & N.'s ed.).

* The Laws of Manu, as marking the last development of the earlier Brahmanical sacerdotalism, are here placed between the earlier speculations of the Upanishads and the later speculations of the philosophical systems. For questions connected with their date, &c., see Lassen, "Ind. Alterthumsk.," i. pp. 882 f.; Duncker's "Geschichte der Arier," pp. 134 f. (text and note).

† Laws of Manu, i. 93.

‡ Ib., i. 31 ; also same relation, though on different grounds, stated, xii. 40—50.

§ Ib., i. 98—101.

But the peculiar province of sacerdotalism is the future. Its sovereignty is possible only in an age of intense faith in a hereafter, whose graduated rewards and punishments are in the hands of the priesthood. The *Divina Commedia* is the creation of the same century and system as Innocent III. and Boniface VIII. The faith embodied in the detested Pope inspired the detesting poet. The same schoolmen who proved in detail the claims of the Papacy, painted in detail the horrors of hell. So while the Brahmans made the theosophic theory of emanation the basis of their claims, the sanctions which enforced them were drawn from the migrations of the soul before it could attain union with Brahma. Souls were seen everywhere and in everything. The generic difference between minerals and vegetables, animals and men, men and gods, was abolished. The present stood connected alike with past and future, determined by the one, determining the other. The theories of individual existence and transmigration were, in a manner, combined. There were heavens for the reward of merit, hells for the punishment of demerit, each with a graduated scale, glorious enough in the one case, horrible enough in the other. When the rewards of the one, or the punishments* of the other, had exhausted the merit or demerit contracted in a former state of being, a new birth had to be undergone, deter-

* Manu, iv. 87–90; xii. 75, 76.

mined by the previous life.* The sinner descended, the righteous ascended, in the scale of existence. The virtuous Sudra becomes a Vaisya, the Vaisya a Kshattriya, the Kshattriya a Brahman, and the Brahman, when a perfectly holy and sinless man, returns by knowledge into Brahma.† If a man steals a cow, he shall be re-born as a crocodile or lizard; if grain, as a rat; if fruit, as an ape.‡ He who attempts to murder a Brahman, or sheds his blood, or kills him, is punished a hundred or thousand years in the several hells, and then born again and again in animal forms degraded in proportion to his crime.§ And to these mutations and migrations hardly any limit was recognised. The soul might glide "through ten thousand millions" of births or more.‖ Absorption was the prize of the elect few; transmigration the doom of the many. Only the selected Brahmans attained the first; almost the whole world revolved in the dreary circle of the second.

Now, this point of the Brahmanical faith was exactly the point most intelligible, most credible, and most terrible to the people.¶ It had grown up in the bosom of the ancient worship, and unfolded itself with the unfolding national mind. Theosophic speculations as to the world-soul were too recondite to be generally

---

* Manu, xii. 55.   † Ib., ix. 335.   ‡ Ib., xii. 62, 64, 67.
§ Ib., xii. 55.   ‖ Ib., vi. 63.
¶ Duncker, "Gesch. der Arier," p. 102.

understood; but sacerdotalism, developing as society developed, had its claims and their sanctions unconsciously conceded. Transmigration had its roots in the Brahmanical conception of God; but the people had grown into it without knowing whence it had sprung, or that it differed in any way from the faith of their fathers. To the thinker, the theological is the distinctive side of a religion; but to the multitude, the eschatological. Hebraism was strong in the former, but weak in the latter, element, and hence so often broke down before fiercer faiths. Christianity has exercised a greater command over peoples, though not over individual minds, by its eschatology than by its theology. The speculative intellect seeks to stand face to face with the ultimate cause; the general intellect regards religion as regulating the present by its power to determine the future. Hence in India, while a new speculative faith as to God grew up and assumed shape among the Brahmans, its eschatology alone took root among the people. They still worshipped the old Vedic gods.* The deities of sacerdotal and theosophic speculation were to them unknown. The funeral ceremonies and sacrifices wore still the old forms. But instead of the old heaven of Yama and the fathers, absorption into Brahma had come; instead of the old "nethermost darkness," "glidings

---

* Lassen, "Ind. Alterthumsk.," i. pp. 911 f.; Duncker, "Gesch. der Arier," pp. 113 f.

THE BELIEF IN INDIA. 155

through ten thousand millions" of births, with between each almost as many hells. The new eschatology was the product of a new theology; but while the first became the people's, the second remained the priest's.

5. THE PHILOSOPHICAL SYSTEMS.

The laws of Manu exhibit the development of the belief on the sacerdotal side; but the philosophical systems its further evolution on the speculative. The Hindu philosophies were, as to form and end, religious, professed to be based on the Vedas, recognised these as their formal source and authority. Philosophy has, as a rule, lived outside the positive religions. No one associates the philosophy with the religion of Greece, save by way of contrast; and the Greek systems found their characteristic element, not in their relation to the national worship, but to the idea of virtue or the general conception of the universe. Modern philosophy from Bacon on the one side, and Descartes on the other, has stood and speculated and inquired outside revealed religion, and been its best friend because its greatest critic. But the Hindu philosophies stood in formal connection with revelation, although as to principle they might be Theistic, Auto-Theistic, Pantheistic, or Atheistic. They differed as to substance, but agreed as to formal source, and so find their proper parallels, not in the Platonic and

Aristotelian, Baconian and Cartesian, but in the Athanasian and Arian, Augustinian and Pelagian, Scotist and Thomist systems and methods. The Hindu spirit was speculative, not critical, deductive, not inductive, and so sought truth by the process of abstraction along a single line. Sacerdotalism gave to speculative thought its objects and end, and hence it did not so much raise the question, What is man? as, Given soul as an essence successively appearing under different forms, how did it arise, and how can it cease to be? In the West, except in the earlier phases of Greek thought, and certain later exceptional instances simply demonstrative of the rule, there was a generic idea of personality, which, while admitting many specific differences, excluded, without discussion, any theory of transmigration. In India, on the other hand, the notion of soul as one, but as transmigrating through many forms, had become so fundamental, that the very conception of separate disembodied existence after death was *à priori* excluded. The belief so pervaded thought and life, that the notion of the opposite was never entertained even as a possibility.

The Hindu philosophies, like the European, have thus generic similarities with only specific differences, and their generic features are the exact opposite of ours. They stand related on the speculative side to the earlier theosophic thought, on the practical to the sacerdotal. The one relation is seen in their notions as to the origin and cessation of personal existence, the other in their conception of its miserableness and hatefulness.

The Hindu philosophies thus intensify, instead of counteracting, the sacerdotal teaching and tendencies as to our belief. The Vedanta might assert that the world was an illusion, and Brahma the only reality; the Sankhya might affirm a dualism, under a Theistic or Atheistic form; the Nyāya, whether dialectic or atomistic as to form, might declare the existence of a supreme soul and propound the true method of discovering the nature of things; but each system held that souls are eternal,* that they transmigrate through countless bodies,† that the bondage to birth and death is due to ignorance and maintained by works, whether good or bad.‡ Life is thus a calamity, personal existence exposure to successive cycles of conscious miseries under multitudinous forms. The grand problem of all the systems is thus, how to attain final beatitude. The beatitude known to each is the loss of conscious personality. The means of attainment in each, knowledge or right apprehension.

* See on this point, "Aphorisms from the several Systems," in "A Rational Refutation of the Hindu Philos. Systems," by R. N. S. Gore, p. 35, Dr. F. E. Hall's translation.
† Colebrooke's "Essays," pp. 184, 229, 240, 155.
‡ "Rational Refutation," pp. 10 ff.

Good works and bad, virtue and vice, are, because of their consequences, undesirable, hinder, by creating merit or demerit, the final emancipation of the soul.* Virtue needs to be rewarded; when its reward is exhausted, birth into another form is necessary, and so new virtues can only prolong the miserable cycle of births and deaths. Vice needs to be punished; when its demerit is exhausted, birth must again happen, and more vice leads to more births *ad infinitum*. The aim of the soul therefore should be to get quit of works, whether good or bad; "the confinement of fetters is the same, whether the chain is of gold or iron."† And it can do so only by knowledge. It prevents actions from ripening into merit or demerit. "Past sin is annulled, future offence precluded." "As water wets not the leaf of the lotus, so sin touches not him who knows God; as the floss on the carding comb cast into the fire is consumed, so are his sins burnt away."‡ Merit and demerit being obliterated, final beatitude can be attained. The Vedantin is identified with Brahma; the Sankhya student ceases to be a self-conscious personality. The first "quitting his corporeal frame, ascends to the pure light which is Brahma, and comes forth identified

---

* Rational "Refutation," p. 19.
† Anonymous Commentator, in Colebrooke's "Essays," p. 232.
‡ Colebrooke, p. 232.

with him, conform and undivided;" "as pure water dropping into the limpid lake is such as that is,"* "or as a river at its confluence with the sea, merges therein altogether."† The second has reached the point where he can say, "neither I am, nor is aught mine, nor I exist;" "yet soul remains awhile invested with body, as the potter's wheel continues whirling after the pot has been fashioned, by force of the impulse previously given to it. When separation of the informed soul from its corporeal frame at length takes place, and nature in respect of it ceases, then is absolute and final deliverance accomplished." ‡

Such then was the terrible conclusion to which Hindu sacerdotalism and speculation had alike come. Individual existence was a curse; the only immortality known the ceaseless succession of births and deaths. Self-annihilation, conceived either as absorption or the cessation of self-conscious being, was the only salvation believed in or desired. Sacerdotalism had made religion a calamity. Its modes of worship could neither gladden the present nor gild with hope the future. The priesthood might stand proudly pre-eminent, but its pre-eminence was dangerous, because founded on dogmas which created despair. There is a limit to the burdens the human spirit can bear, and that limit had been reached. A religion which intensified the actual miseries

* Colebrooke, p. 236.   † Ib., p. 234.   ‡ Ib., p. 164.

of the present, and the possible miseries of the future, had abdicated its functions, and deserved only what it was sure soon to suffer, abolition or revolution.

6. BUDDHISM.

Buddhism, at once the offspring and the enemy of Brahmanism, can hardly be understood apart from the India in which it arose. It was essentially an anti-sacerdotal revolution, specifically Indian alike in what it affirmed and what it denied. The Brahmanical gods, sacrifices, ceremonies, and inspired books it rejected. The caste system, the very foundation of Hindu society, it recognised, but practically abolished in the religious sphere, a preliminary to its general abolition.* But without, perhaps, consciously building on any previous system, it appropriated and developed certain tendencies and doctrines familiar to Indian speculation and translated them into a faith and a religion for the people.†

Buddhism was an ethical, Brahmanism a sacerdotal, religion, and so were specifically different, but both had a metaphysical as distinguished from a personal basis, and so were generically alike. The generic similarity necessitated resemblances in their respective conceptions of the universe, the specific difference affected their views of life and the conditions which determined its happiness or misery. Buddhism like Brahmanism

* Lassen, "Ind. Alterthumsk.," ii. pp. 440 ff.   † Ib., i. pp. 996 f.

had its graduated system of future reward and punishment, its descending circles of hells, its ascending circles of heavens,* but unlike Brahmanism its principle of award in the one case was virtue, in the other vice. Hence the grand "arbiter of destiny" is Karman, moral action, the aggregate result of all previous acts.† Buddhism, indeed, is nothing else than the religion of mora action, metaphysically conceived.

While Buddhism is nominally atheistic, it is really more theistic than Brahmanism. There is more of deity in its moral order than in the metaphysical monism of its opponent. A system that makes high moral qualities efficient in the unit and in the universe, is theistic in a better sense than the pantheism which in its last analysis makes evil and good indifferent, and God inclusive of both. A recent writer on ethics has happily remarked the resemblance Mr. Matthew Arnold's stream or tendency which makes for righteousness bears to the moral action of Buddhism, both being attempts to express a moral government without a personal moral governor. And the ethical element is so strong in Buddhism because of the idea of humanity which lives at its heart. Indeed it has, like Christianity, an ideal human being as its centre, and this similarity in centre or root is the

---

* Burnouf, "Introduction à l'Hist. du Buddhisme Indien," pp. 320, 366 f. ; R. S. Hardy, "Manual of Buddhism," chap. ii.

† R. S. Hardy's "Manual," pp. 394 ff.

cause of the similarity in their ethical codes, which has been so often recognised and pointedly mentioned to the honour of Buddhism.

Buddha's great problem was the problem common to every Indian thinker,—How to be delivered from misery, from that greatest of evils, the everlasting succession of births and deaths. He accepted the Indian theory of man—never seems to have imagined any other as possible. The sight of the misery around, the thought of the misery behind and before, pained him. He inquired—what is the cause of age, of death, of all pain? Birth. What is the cause of birth? Existence. What is the cause of existence? Attachment to the existent. What the cause of attachment? Desire. Of desire? Perception. Of perception? The senses. What is the cause of the senses? Name and form, or individual existence. Of individual existence? Consciousness. Of consciousness? Ignorance. To annihilate birth, existence must be annihilated; to annihilate existence, the attachment to it. Attachment, again, can only be destroyed by destroying desire, desire by destroying perception, perception by destroying the senses, the senses by destroying the consciousness, and the consciousness by destroying the ignorance, which is its cause. If the ground of personal existence is annihilated, it cannot continue, birth and death cease.*

* Duncker, "Gesch. der Arier," pp. 237 f.

What Buddha conceived this final deliverance to be cannot be discussed here and now. Enough to say, a religion without a God could hardly promise a restful but conscious immortality. Nirvana cannot be absorption, for Buddhism knew no world-soul, no Brahma, into which the perfect man could enter, nor can it be any conscious state of being, for the loss of consciousness was the goal of Buddha's ambition. The oldest definitions describe Nirvana as "the cessation of thought, since its causes are removed," as a condition "in which nothing remains of that which constitutes existence."[*] When the soul enters Nirvana it is extinguished like a lamp blown out, and nothing remains but the void.[†] "The only asylum and the only reality is nothing, because from it there is no return, and once at rest in Nirvana, the soul has no longer anything to fear, nor anything to expect."[‡]

---

[*] Burnouf., "Introduction à l'Hist. du Bud. Ind.," pp. 73, 83, 589 f.
[†] Ib., 252.
[‡] M. Barthélemy S. Hilaire, "Le Bouddha et sa Religion," pp. vii. viii. See the interesting discussions as to the meaning of Nirvana, by Professor Max Müller, "Chips," i. 223 f.; 248 ff.; 279 ff. On the same side stand the late Eug. Burnouf, "Introduction," *ut supra*, and 153—155, 211, 521, &c. ; "Lotus de la bonne Loi," pp. 335, 339, 784, &c. ; Lassen, "Ind. Alterthumsk.," i. 996; ii. 462; iii. 385, 395; C. F. Köppen, "Die Religion des Buddha," i. pp. 306 f. M. Barthélemy S. Hilaire often, but particularly the Avertissement. On the other side, holding that Nirvana denotes a state of repose, "non-agitation," "calm without wind," stand Dr. Wilson of Bombay, Art. "The Buddhist Revolution in Ind.," "Brit. and For. Ev. Rev.," July 1871, p. 422; Colebrooke's

Buddhism is a proof of what a false theory of immortality may become—life after death, a thing so terrible that to escape it man will court annihilation. The Hindu spirit had got bewildered in the mazes of transmigration, and unable to find a way to a right conception of God, and a consequent right conception of immortality, it rose into an absolute denial of both, produced and propagated a religion founded on the abolition of what Western thinkers used to regard as the fundamental truths of every faith—the being of God and the immortality of man.

7. THE REFORMED BRAHMANISM.

A religion so ancient, so highly organized, so strong in the traditions and associations of many centuries as Brahmanism, could not be easily vanquished. An old faith which has the courage and skill to reform itself, will also have vitality and strength enough to engage

"Essays," 258; and J. B. F. Obry, in Du Nirvana Bouddhique, a formal reply to M. B. S. Hilaire. Perhaps the truth lies in very equal proportions on both sides. In Buddhism as a system, Nirvana can mean nothing but annihilation, or extinction, escape from our own personal existence without passing into any other being or form of personal being. In Buddhism as a religion, Nirvana may mean to the simple-hearted multitude "profound calm," undisturbed by successive births and deaths. Professor Max Müller, who has very greatly modified his earlier views, now maintains that while the metaphysic of Buddhism is both Atheistic and Nihilistic, Buddha himself was an Atheist, but not a Nihilist. See his Lecture, "Ueber den Buddhistischen Nihilismus."

and defeat its young opponent. The counter-Reformation in Europe is a feeble type of the Brahmanical reaction in India. Roman Catholicism, though it could not expel from the Continent, drove back its vigorous but unorganized enemy; but revived Brahmanism swept from India the once-victorious Buddhism. The old system expanded to receive new and popular elements. The people loved the old gods, never knew or worshipped the abstract deity of the priesthood. Of the old Vedic Gods, Vishnu and Rudra had become the chosen of the people.* They, joined with the sacerdotal Brahma, formed a new godhead, the famous Brahmanical *Trimurtti*. Then, if, according to the old mystical notion, the human could be absorbed in the divine, why not the divine manifested in the human? If man could become God, why not God man? Hence the Avatar-notion arose, and by a well-known mythical process the heroes of the old national epics, Rama and Krishna, were deified, and as at once incarnations of the popular deity and heroes of the popular songs, powerfully commended the old religion to the Hindu heart.† Thus, on both the divine and human sides, the old faith was so modified as to suit, even better than the new, the mind and condition of India.

Our belief so shared in the general modification as

* Lassen, "Ind. Alterthumsk.," i. 918 ff.; ii. 1087. But particularly Dr. Muir's "Sanskrit Texts," vol. iv., comparison of the Vedic with the after representations of the principal Indian deities.

† Duncker, "Gesch. der Arier," p. 322; Muir, *ut supra*, ch. ii. sect. v.

to be in some respects improved, in others deteriorated. It receives fullest expression in the Bhagavad-Gita. The general conception is a crude Pantheism, with, on the one side, a final absorption, conditioned on knowledge, into deity, on the other a hideous moral indifferentism, which abolishes good and evil and inculcates action without any regard to consequences. Krishna says, "Immortality and death, being and not being, am I, O Arjuna."* He is everything, its source, its goal, father and mother of this world, whence all things and beings come, whither all return.† The soul is immutable, impenetrable, incombustible, can neither be pierced by darts, nor burned by fire, nor drowned by water, nor dried by wind.‡ It can wear out and lay aside old and assume new bodies, as the body can change its garments.§ Souls are thus conceived as immortal, or, rather, eternal, without beginning or end, but as transmigrating through many bodies. Man can be born into nobler and happier forms of personal being,|| and between birth and death taste divine joys in the heaven of Indra.¶ Till final emancipation is obtained birth and death succeed each other, but when knowledge of the divine being is acquired, birth ceases, the soul attains deity.** Quiescence, the supreme beatitude, is realized, and to the Supreme the soul is joined.

---

* ix. 19 .   † ix. 7—10; 16—18.   ‡ ii. 23—25.   § ii. 22.
|| vi. 41, 42.   ¶ ix. 20.   ** ii. 51 ; iv. 9, 10.

Here, then, our inquiry into the Hindu belief in immortality may end. Its historical conclusion was the antithesis and contradiction of its historical beginning. Our purpose was to trace the several steps in this saddest, most extensive and injurious revolution of religious thought, and the lessons suggested the reader can best discover for himself. An exaggerated sacerdotalism turned the Hindu spirit from travelling along the only line on which it could have reached a right conception of God, and, without that, no right conception of man, as mortal or immortal, was possible. Our thoughts weave themselves more subtly than we imagine into consistency and form, and the unsystematized faith of a people will often be found more logical than any reasoned system. The belief in a personal immortality can live only when rooted in faith in a personal God.

> "Thou wilt not leave us in the dust:
> Thou madest man, he knows not why;
> He thinks he was not made to die;
> And Thou hast made him: Thou art just."

PART III.

THE BELIEF IN GREECE.

I. INTRODUCTORY.

THE belief in Immortality, while a pre-eminent product of Greek thought, was almost unknown to Greek religion. The gods of Olympos ruled the present; death was the limit of their dominion. Their worship neither awed by the fear, nor cheered with the hope, of a future life. In the later mythology which grew up within and around the mysteries, the gods of the underworld distributed rewards and punishments to the dead, but they exercised no actual government over the living. While of all ancient peoples the Greeks had the profoundest faith in the reign of moral Law, no ancient people seemed so little conscious of any religious connection between the present and a future life. Greece was in this respect a contrast to almost all the other Indo-European nations. The Iranians founded on their ethical dualism a positive and intelligible theory of immortality—a theory which, passing first into Judaism and then into Christianity, has played so great a part in the religious history of the world. The Teutonic tribes so conceived the future as to reduce death to a "home-going," "a return to the Father." The Kelts believed in a metempsychosis which made the future life as active as the present. The Indian Aryans evolved, as already seen, from their early naturalism a religion whose distinctive characteristic was the continued existence of the transmigrating soul. But the Greek, whose conception of life was the most ethical, whose religious faith was the most beautiful, believed a religion which left him to live and die without the hope of an immortal hereafter.

The causes of this peculiarity in the religious development of Greece can be fully ascertained only by a minute study of its successive phases. Here, however, two may be specified: (1) the national mythology crystallized into permanent form before the national mind attained to full religious consciousness; (2) religious thought did not develop within, but without, this mythology.

The Greek mind lived long in the mythical and imaginative stages. Centuries after the Indians and

Iranians had elaborated great religious systems, the Hellenes remained in the simplest nature-worship. Their manner of life had been unfavourable to the birth and growth of religious thought, but conducive to the formation of brave and resolute character. The hero was more to the Greek than to the Indian; the god more to the Indian than the Greek. In the Vedic hymns the theological side is the predominant, but in the Homeric poems, apart from the general idea of the whole, the subordinate *—the divine action the mere background of the human. The first are religious; the second secular. The Rishis composed their hymns to praise the gods; but Homer made his poems to glorify the heroes. The Vedic mythology is the younger, but the more religious; the Homeric the older, but the more mythical. The Hindu hymns show a dependence of man on God, an abasement of self, a need of priestly mediation and sacrifice such as the Hellenic epics do not reveal: yet these, as later, are more perfect expressions of the Greek than those are of the Indian mind. The latter are more individual, the former more national. Homer and Hesiod, as Preller says, are only "mythical collective names."† Behind them lie centuries of mythological development: in them the results are concentrated, co-ordinated, and combined. The Hellenic faith thus

---

* Welcker, "Griechis. Götterlehre," ii. p. 69.
† "Griechis. Mythologie," i. p. 14.

crystallized at the point where the mythical deposit was greatest. The natural elements in it were many; the subjective and spiritual were few. The myths of the instinctive had been translated into the mythology of the imaginative stage, but not into the beliefs of the reflective.

The Greek Theogony remained, on the whole, as Homer and Hesiod had made it;* received mythical developments or additions, but did not change its character. But while it stood still, mind grew, became conscious of many things that did not lie in the old naturalism, even as poetically transfigured. Religion degenerated into a beautiful accessory to a singularly rich and genial life; thought became the actual ethical and religious Teacher.† The separation or antagonism of religion and thought is, indeed, a misfortune, pre-eminently so for the religion; for when it ceases to lead the national thought, it falls behind the nation,— crystallizes only to be hopelessly pulverized. And so ancient Greece experienced. The myths delighted the fine fancy of the people, the religious festivals gave to the lighter side of the national character a sphere in which to play; but the higher functions of religion

---

* Herodotos, ii. 53.
† Bunsen, "Christianity and Mankind," iv. p. 195. For a profound and appreciative discussion of the relations of philosophy and religion, see Hegel's "Geschich. der Philos.," i. 76 ff., "Religionsphilos.," i. 20 ff.

passed to poetry and philosophy. If in the days of Pausanias the old faith still lived in quiet rural spots, it had died centuries before in the centres of intellectual activity. The Exegetæ might repeat and explain in the temples the old myths, but the true divines were poets, like Pindar, in whose odes the ancient mythology was exalted and transfigured.* Zeus might still in the popular traditions thunder from Olympos, or wage an unequal contest with his subtle and termagant Queen, but in the hands of Æschylos he had been raised into a diviner deity.† The people might believe that once "immortal gods and mortal men partook of a common table, and lived under a common roof;"‡ but philosophy had in Plato sublimed God into the Supreme Good, which only purified reason could apprehend.§ Priests and people might imagine the gods to be animated by passion and pleased by sacrifice, but speculation had resolved deity into the unmoved mover of all things.‖ The superstitious or the politic might consult the oracle at Delphi, but the sage sought within himself the only voice he could obey. Religion and religious thought had thus not only parted company,

---

* "Olymp.," i. 44—57; ix. 35—62; Bunsen's "God in Hist.," ii. p. 149; Grote's "Hist. of Greece," pp. 365 f. (ed. 1869).

† "Suppl.," 81—95, 518—521, 584—590; "Agamem." 1461, 1462 (Paley's ed. 1861).

‡ Aratus, "Phœn.," 91; Pausanias, viii. 2.

§ "Repub.," vi. vol. ii. 509. ‖ Aristotle, "Metaph.," xi. vii. 2 6.

but fallen into violent antagonism. Devout men, no longer able to be religious in the old sense, because religious in a deeper, had to distinguish between religion as mythical, civil, and philosophical.* The old religion, crystallized at the imaginative stage, could satisfy only those who remained there: those who had passed beyond it had to create in its stead a religion of religious thought.

The peculiar order and conditions of religious development in Greece thus made the belief in immortality not so much the property of its religion as of its thought. Had thought developed under the mythico-religious forms until it had changed their matter, in other words, had the religion grown with the mind of the nation and passed with it from the mythical into the reflective stage, then our belief would have risen as a religious doctrine, shaped and enforced by religious sanctions. But, as it was, the poets became the true priests of Greece,† embodying in Epic or Ode or Tragedy the ideas of Moral Law and Order and Judgment; the philosophers her true prophets, revealing mind in Nature, the Supreme Good within, above and before man. So our belief, ignored by the popular religion, sought recognition and development at the hands of the actual

---

* Plutarch, "De Plac. Philos.," i. 6; "Amator.," 18; M. Scævola apud Augus., "De Civit. Dei," iv. 27; Varro, ib. iv. 5.

† Welcker, "Griechis. Götterlehre," ii. 66.

priests and prophets. It rose in answer to the demand first of the religious and moral instincts, and then of the reason. The answer to the former was given at first crudely in the mysteries, then clearly and grandly in the lyrical and tragic poets; the answer to the latter in the nobler and more spiritual philosophies. The mysteries were attempts to supplement the deficiencies of the national religion; the philosophies to reach ultimate and universal truth. The belief, as expressed in the first, witnesses only to a need felt alike by Greek and barbarian, but as expressed in the second, to a demand made by the constructive reason at its best. The mysteries were in their use and meaning national, significant only for a land whose public religion knew no future state; but the philosophies and their results have a universal importance, have helped and still help to shape the faith of the Christian world.

Our belief thus unfolded in Greece under conditions precisely the reverse of those which existed in India, and as the conditions differed, so did the results. The principles which imply or lead to transmigration were alien to the Greek spirit. It had seized too firmly the notion of personality, alike as to gods and men, of freedom, of the ethical principles implied in the government of the world and in the nature of man, to allow metempsychosis to obtain a permanent foothold on Grecian soil. Then, too, the belief in immortality was never general in Greece.* A religion alone could have nationalized it. Beliefs which depend on a given moral or metaphysical conception of the universe can never be general. But while religion alone can give universality, thought alone can give perpetuity to a belief, adapt it to changed times, defend it against novel objections, reconcile it with new sciences or fresh discoveries. If the faith in immortality has lived into this nineteenth century, it is in great part because Christianity has been married to the spirit and many of the results of the higher Greek Philosophy. Our former paper led us to the study of a belief the antithesis of our own, but our present leads us to the study of one of its sources. While in Palestine the Messianic belief and hope, which blossomed into the Christ of Christianity, were putting forth their tender shoots, the faith in an immortal hereafter for man was seeking in Greece basis and form. The history of that search is what this paper attempts to give.

II. HOMER.

The Homeric poems form the natural starting-point of our inquiry. They are impersonal in the highest sense—mirror the faith, not of a man, but of an age.

* Blackie, "Four Phases of Morals," p. 255.

For the Greeks, even more than for us, the significant point was the nationality of the poems, not the individuality of the poet. The doctrine of a future state exhibited in the Iliad and Odyssey was the doctrine held by the then Hellenic peoples. It was not peculiar to the man Homer—the poet's own doctrine, "not only a defect in his system of mythology, but a striking eccentricity of his genius."* The picture he draws may be "for this world only, for the mortality, not for the immortality of man,"† but the picture is faithful alike in its minute details and general effect. Poems like the Homeric can fulfil their end only so far as faithful pictures of the men and the religion they portray. The heroes were always dear to the Hellenic heart, and had Homer given them a worse fate hereafter than the popular faith did, his songs would have awakened censure rather than applause. Certain distinguished thinkers, indeed, showed small mercy to the old blind poet. Pythagoras consigned him to punishment in Hades.‡ Herakleitos would have expelled him and his songs from the national games.§ Plato banished him from his ideal Republic,‖ in great part because of his sins

* Colonel Mure, "Crit. Hist. of Lang. and Lit. of Anc. Greece," i. p. 495.
† Gladstone, "Homer and the Homeric Age," ii. p. 393.
‡ Hieronymus the Peripatetic, in "Diogenes Laer.," viii. 21.
§ "Diog. Laer.," ix. 1.
‖ "Repub.," bk. ii. vol. ii. 379 ff. (Steph.); bk. x. vol. ii. 595 ff. See

THE BELIEF IN GREECE.

on this very point.* But, then, these men judged the popular faith as severely as they judged Homer. What had pleased his contemporaries offended the philosophers.

The first question to be discussed is this, Did the Homeric men believe that any part or element of man continued to exist after death? They believed that the soul, ψυχή, so soon as death loosened its bands,† quitted the body by the mouth,‡ or a mortal wound,§ and either, restless and unhappy while the body was unhonoured with funeral rites, haunted the earth, ‖ or, when it had been so honoured, descended to live a ghostly life in Hades.¶ But what was the ψυχή? Its meaning in Homer is peculiar, alike removed from the simple etymological** and the later refined philosophical

---

also the familiar lines of Xenophanes, which declare that what both Homer and Hesiod relate of the gods would be a disgrace to men, "Sext. Empir. adv. Math.," i. 289; ix. 193.

* "Repub.," bk. iii. vol. ii. 386 (Steph.). † "Iliad," viii. 123.
‡ Ib., ix. 409.   § Ib., xiv. 518; xvi. 505.
‖ Ib., xxiii. 65 ff.   ¶ Ib., xvi. 85 f.; xxii. 362.
** Curtius ("Griechis. Etymologie," pp. 463, 482, 654) derives ψύχω, whence ψυχή, from a root, *spu*, whence also φῦσα, φυσάω, &c.; Sansk., *pupphu-sa-s*, the lungs; *puppha-la-m*, wind. Latin, *pusula, pustula;* Lithuanian, *pús-te*, to blow, *pus-lé*, a bladder. Cf. Fick ("Vergleich. Wörterbuch," p. 626), who also derives φῦσα, &c., from the root *spu*, to breathe, without, however, making any reference to ψύχω. Though the words denotive of soul in the several Indo-European tongues differ as to root, yet they agree, more or less, as to idea. The etymology of the Sanscrit *atman* is, indeed, uncertain (Bopp, "Comp. Gram.," i. p. 152 (Eng. trans.); Müller's "Anc. Sansk. Lit.," p. 21, note 1); and the derivation which identifies its root with *an*, whence Gr. ἄνεμος, Latin,

M

sense. It means more than the breath, because a shadowy personality remains to it after death, but less than mind or spirit. Perhaps word and idea are alike untranslatable, escape our mental grasp as the shadowy Mother of Odysseus eluded his embrace. It may be said, as in a qualified sense true, that when $\psi v \chi \acute{\eta}$ denotes what a living man possesses, its etymological meaning is apparent; but when it denotes what lives after death, its philosophical meaning is latent.

A short glance at the Homeric psychology as a whole may help us to understand the meaning of $\psi v \chi \acute{\eta}$.*
There are two classes of psychological terms in Homer. The one does, the other does not, localize the mental faculties, or rather, the one does, the other does not, use the name of a physical organ to denote a mental faculty. To the first class belong such terms as $\phi \rho \acute{\epsilon} \nu \epsilon s$, $\mathring{\eta} \tau o \rho$, $\kappa a \rho \delta \acute{\iota} \eta$, $\kappa \mathring{\eta} \rho$, $\sigma \tau \mathring{\eta} \theta o s$; to the second, terms like $\theta v \mu \acute{o}s$,

---

animus, *anima* (Fick, "Vergleich. Wörterb.," pp. 19, 7. Cf. Curtius, "Griechis. Etym.," p. 286), is hardly possible. The word used in the Teutonic dialects, Goth., *sáivala*, O. H. G. *sëola*, *sela*; M. H. G., *sêle*; A. G. S., *saul*; our soul, Dan., *själ*, is related in root with the Goth. *saivs*, sea (Grimm, "Deuts. Mythol.," p. 786. Von Raumer in Delitzsch, "Bib. Pyschol.," p. 120), which is, of course, in certain respects air-like. But see Fick, p. 885.

* Nägelsbach, "Homerische Theologie," pp. 380—397 (2nd ed.), with the valuable notes of the editor; Völcker, $\psi v \chi \acute{\eta}$ und $\epsilon \mathring{\iota} \delta \omega \lambda o \nu$; Nitzsch, "Anmerkungen zu Homer's Odyssee," vol. iii. pp. 189 ff.; Welcker, "Griechis. Götterlehre," i. pp. 805 ff., may be consulted, especially the first two, for a fuller exposition of the Homeric pyschology than is here possible.

μένος, νόος.* An analytical exposition of these terms is here impossible, but it may be said of them generally that φρένες and θυμός are the more generic, the others the more specific. Sensation, perception, thought, memory, will, consciousness, are attributed to the two former.† They are often co-ordinate terms used to denote the entire mental nature of man.‡ Of the other and more restricted terms, νόος denotes the intellectual, μένος the active powers, while ἦτορ, καρδίη, κῆρ, are used, with specific differences, vaguely and extensively, like our heart, for the emotive nature of man, alike on its active and passive sides. But among these psychological terms ψυχή has no place. No intellectual function is ascribed to it, no mental or moral action, no faculty of

---

* The earliest psychological terms seem to have been formed either from the bodily organ affected by the mental act or emotion, or from the effect produced by mental states on the body as a whole. Hence the two classes of terms noticed in the text. The functional terms refer to the heart and breast rather than the head—naturally so with a people accustomed to act and feel rather than think. Of the other class of terms, θυμός comes from a root, *dhu*, to sound, to rush, to rage (Fick, "Vergleich. Wörterb.," p. 103 ; Curtius, "Griechis. Etym.," 243), and its use seems to have risen from the analogous effects of a storm on nature and strong feeling or passion on the body. Hence Plato ("Krat.," 419) is partially right in deriving θυμός from the rushing and boiling of the soul,—soul being understood in the later sense. Μένος, again, is from a root, *men*, or *man*, which possibly denoted the tense or strained state of the body seeking to grasp a thing desired. But see Curtius ("Gr. Etym.," 291 f.).

† "Il.," xi. 682, cf. vii. 189; "Il.," xv. 81, cf. "Od.," xviii. 228; "Il.," i. 193; v. 671; xv. 163.   ‡ "Il.," iv. 163, and often.

thinking, feeling, or willing. It is often the sign and synonyme of life, but never of spirit or any spiritual power. It is, indeed, joined with θυμός* and μένος,† but then these words, when thus connected, lose their psychological and take a mere physical sense. Just as in our popular speech certain terms, *e.g.*, "heart" or "head," have both a physical and psychological import, so was it in the strictly popular speech of Homer. And as it is often hard to tell whether "heart" and "head" be used in their material or spiritual sense, so now and then it can hardly be determined whether Homer means by a given term, *e.g.*, φρένες, a physical organ or a mental faculty, or, *e.g.*, μένος, a manifestation of spiritual or material life.‡ But while the psychological terms have also a physical sense, ψυχή has only the latter. They in their lower sense may be synonymous with ψυχή, but never in their higher. Death may be described with equal indifference as the θυμός or the ψυχή leaving the body,§ but the latter can never, like the former, know, or hesitate, or perceive. ψυχή, in short, is, in Homer, a physical term; denotes the bodily, not the spiritual, life.

The powers denoted by the psychological terms cease to be at death, but the ψυχή continues to exist.

---

* "Il.," xi. 334; "Od.," xxi. 154.   † "Il.," v. 296.
‡ Nägelsbach, "Hom. Theol.," p. 386.
§ "Il.," iv. 470; xii. 386, cf. v. 696; xiv. 518.

THE BELIEF IN GREECE. 181

The θυμός, used as the synonyme of ψυχή, is, indeed, said to descend to Hades,[*] but the assimilation of the terms is never carried so far as to allow the θυμός to reside there.[†] That is possible to the ψυχή alone. Then φρένες are denied to the dead. Achilles exclaims, when he sees the shade of Patroklos, "Oh, strange! in the house of Hades there is soul and shadow, but no mind" (φρένες).[‡] Teiresias, the Theban seer, has, indeed, a steadfast mind (φρένες ἔμπεδοι) and understanding (νόον), but in this he is alone among the dead; "the others flit like shadows,"[§] are but "the ghostly forms of deceased mortals," without consciousness or thought (ἀφραδέες).[||] They are ἀκήριοι,[¶] without κῆρ (cor, heart); ἀμενηνὰ κάρηνα,[**] beings without μένος. Homer thus seems careful to deny to the ψυχή the intellectual and active powers characteristic of the living man. It is out of the body, as it was in it, without any spiritual qualities.

How, then, does Homer conceive the ψυχή? What kind and degree of being does he attribute to the dead? The ψυχή is an εἴδωλον;[††] the ψυχαί dwelling in Hades are εἴδωλα καμόντων,[‡‡] the ghostly forms of deceased

---

[*] "Il.," vii. 131.
[†] "Od.," xi. 221, 222, where the θυμός and the ψυχή are expressly distinguished, the latter alone being in Hades.
[‡] "Il.," xxiii. 103, 104.   [§] "Od.," x. 493—495.
[||] "Od.," xi. 476.   [¶] "Il.," xxi. 466.   [**] "Od.," xi. 29, 49.
[††] "Il.," xxiii. 104.   [‡‡] "Od.," xi. 476; xxvi. 14.

or worn-out men. εἴδωλον thus does not mean in Homer, as in Pindar, the deathless and divinely derived part of man,* but only his phantom or image. The phantom of Æneas which Apollo creates to deceive Trojans and Greeks, and round which they continued to fight;† the form Athene makes like Iphthima, and sends to visit the dreams of Penelope;‡ the semblance of Herakles which remains in Hades while he himself feasts with the immortal gods§ are εἴδωλα. The εἴδωλον thus stands opposed to the real person; is intangible, impotent —a shadow which can neither embrace nor be embraced. Odysseus in vain thrice attempts to clasp the shade of his mother,‖ and Agamemnon tries but fails to seize Odysseus.¶ They are compared to shadows (σκιαί)** or dreams.†† They "squeak and gibber,"‡‡ twitter like bats,§§ scream like frightened birds,‖‖ emit confused noises not at all to be compared with human speech.¶¶ But here Homer falls into curious and instructive inconsistencies. The shades of the dead are not mere illusions; are real after their kind. Odysseus fears that Persephone may have sent to him an εἴδωλον instead of his mother.*** The very attempt to conceive the shadow changed it into a substance.

---

* "Frag. ex Threnis," ii. 5. † "Il.," v. 449—451. ‡ "Od.," iv. 796.
§ "Od.," xi. 602.   ‖ "Od.," xi. 206—208.   ¶ "Od.," xi. 393, 394.
** "Od.," x. 495.   †† "Od.," xi. 207, 222.
‡‡ "Il.," xxiii. 101; "Od.," xxiv. 5.   §§ "Od.," xxiv. 7, 9.
‖‖ "Od.," xi. 605.   ¶¶ "Od.," xi. 633.   *** "Od.," xi. 213.

To attribute to it any action whatever was to attribute to it reality. And so while Homer denies φρένες, θυμός, μένος, and κῆρ, to the εἴδωλα καμόντων, he yet represents them as self-conscious and self-determining. They see and fear the sword of Odysseus.* They refuse to the soul of the unburied Patroklos entrance into Hades.† The unburied can appear and speak to the living, asleep or awake;‡ but while the buried cannot do so of their own will, because in Hades, they can yet by drinking the blood shed at a sacrifice to the dead enjoy a temporary return to consciousness and semi-vitality. Thus in the Nekyia of the Odyssey, the ghosts crowd eagerly round the trench Odysseus has dug and filled with the blood of his sacrifice,§ and so soon as they taste it, can recognise and speak with him. His mother can describe her own death, what happened at Ithaka after his departure, and her dream-like life in Hades.‖ Agamemnon can tell the story of his murder, and mourn his wretched fate.¶ Achilles, while lamenting his own miserable lot, rejoices to hear of his son's heroism.** The blood can thus give back for the moment consciousness and speech to the soul, probably, because the blood and breath were considered as the causes and conditions in their union of life, in

---

* "Od.," xi. 231, 232. † "Il.," xxiii. 72—74.
‡ "Il.," xxiii. 65—67; "Od.," xi. 51, 52. § "Od.," xi. 148, 225—227.
‖ "Od.," xi. 152—224. ¶ "Od.," xi. 405—461.
** "Od.," xi. 488—540.

their separation of death.* But even before drinking the blood it could perceive, desire, and act. The Homeric conception was evidently transitional; thought had advanced beyond language. The soul had become, or was becoming, to the former a substance, while it remained to the latter a shadow.

Our next question is as to the relation of the ψυχὴ καὶ εἴδωλον to the actual man. Whether did he perish with the body, or continue to exist as soul? The question in this form was the product of an age later than the Homeric. To affirm that to Homer "the I, the human self-consciousness, ceased to be at death,"† or that to him "what continued to exist was the personal element of the body,"‡ is to affirm on either side too much. Now the body and now the soul is described as the person, but in such cases poetical necessity is the grand arbiter of terms. To an impassioned Achilles, flushed with victory and gratified revenge, a dead body is in one line the actual Hector, a soul in another the actual Patroklos.§ The poet about to sing the woes caused by the wrath of Achilles leaves the heroes a prey to dogs, while their souls

---

* But see Nitzsch ("Anmerk. z. Odys.," iii. p. 203), who maintains that the belief in the power of blood to restore consciousness arose from the custom of sacrificing to the dead. He seems, however, to reverse the true order, and substitute cause for effect.

† Nägelsbach, "Hom. Theol.," 380.

‡ Welcker, "Griechis. Götterl.," i. 811. § "Il.," xxiii. 19—21.

go to Hades;* but when he paints his hero's visit to Hades† personality is entirely detached from the body, and attached to the soul. Thus, if only death was regarded, it seemed the cessation of existence; if the soul was conceived, it seemed the continuance of the person. As a matter of fact neither was fully meant. The person was to Homer neither the body nor the soul, but the living man. At death the hero as such ceased to be. The body, the vehicle of the powers constitutive of the man, was dissolved; the soul, its mere shadow, alone remained. But the inevitable tendency of thought was to deny personality to the one and give it to the other. The tendency exists in Homer, and, in spite of the spirit and design of his poems, he tends to conceive the soul as the continued though attenuated person, but his thought, as transitional and so far unconscious, cannot be translated into the language of later metaphysics.

A life after death was thus in a certain sense affirmed by Homer. But in what relation did the life here stand to the life hereafter? The one had no religious connection with the other. Zeus, the supreme god of the living, had no authority over the dead.‡ Death was

---

* "Il.," i. 3, 4. † "Od.," xi.

‡ Mr. Gladstone, "Homer and the Homeric Age," ii. 210, claims for Zeus a limited power over the dead; but the lines to which he refers, "Od.," xi. 300—304, can be interpreted in harmony with the statement of the text.

departure from the realm he ruled. He can, indeed, translate mortals like Menelaos to the Elysian plain,* or raise others like Ganymedes to the society of the Immortals,† but with, not without, the body—before, not after, death. And like limitations bind the other Olympians. Athene alone seems an exception, as she claims to have saved Herakles from the Styx;‡ but Herakles was a living, not a dead man. Thus piety could not lighten, nor impiety deepen, the misery of Hades. Reverence of the gods was there unrewarded; contempt of them unpunished.

The underworld had, indeed, its own proper deities, Aides and Persephone;§ the former, the infernal or subterranean Zeus; the latter, not, as in the later mythology, the lost and lovely daughter of Demeter, but the veritable Queen of the Shades.‖ Teiresias owes to her his seership.¶ She gathers and disperses the shades of the women.** Odysseus suspects she has deluded him with a phantom instead of his mother,†† and flees in terror lest she send out to him the Gorgon's head.‡‡ The epithets applied to her, ἁγνή, ἀγαυή, ἐπαινή, express the awe with which the Queen of the Dead inspired the living. But neither

---

* "Od.," iv. 562.   † "Il.," xx. 233.
‡ "Il.," viii. 362—369.   § "Il.," ix. 457.
‖ Preller, "Demeter und Persephone," p. 9; Mr. Gladstone, "Homer and the Homeric Age," ii. pp. 218 ff.   ¶ "Od.," x. 494.
** "Od.," xi. 226.   †† "Od.," xi. 213.   ‡‡ "Od.," xi. 634, 635.

Aides nor Persephone ruled the future with any reference to the piety, properly so called, of the present. Religion was to the Homeric Greek profitable only to the life that now is. Sacrifices persuaded the Olympians to friendliness; but Aides, implacable and inexorable, the most hateful to mortals of all the gods,* remained almost without worship,† so little relation had he to the present.

But the religious was not to Homer the highest element. Behind and above Zeus Μοῖρα stands; beside Aides and Persephone 'Ερινύς. Μοῖρα embodied the idea of an order, 'Ερινύς of an authority, or moral law, above every personal will, divine or human.‡ The gods fear the Erinyes, who maintain even against the gods the established order of things.§ They dwell in the underworld, and so are associated with the Chthonian deities. In the curse pronounced upon Phœnix by his father the Erinyes are invoked, but Aides and dread Persephone hear and fulfil it.‖ Althea, in her imprecation on her son, calls upon the two deities, but Erinyes, who stalks in darkness, implacable of heart, hears from Erebos.¶ The ethical

---

* "Il.," ix. 158, 159.
† Pausanias, vi., xxv. 3; Mr. Gladstone, "Juv. Mundi," pp. 253 f.
‡ Nägelsbach, "Hom. Theol.," pp. 262 ff.; Gladstone, "Homer and the Homeric Age," ii. 306 ff. ; "Juv. Mundi," 350 ff.
§ "Il.," xv. 204 ; xix. 418 ; xxi. 410—414.
‖ "Il.," ix. 454—457.   ¶ "Il.," ix. 565—568.

idea of retribution stands thus impersonated in the Erinyes: the associates, perhaps rather ministers, of the Chthonian gods; but is it a retribution limited to the present, or extending to the future? Of the twelve places where they are mentioned in the Homeric poems, ten quite certainly refer to the present.* Their action or judgment is exhausted here. Of the other two, one is the poetic myth concerning the daughters of Pandareos, carried off by the Harpies, and given up to be ministers to the Erinyes.† But this is without reference to death or the state of the dead, and so to the retributions of a future life. The other text seems more explicit. Agamemnon, when protesting his innocence as to Briseis, invokes as witnesses "Zeus, highest and best of the gods, Gē, Helios, and Erinyes, who dwell beneath the earth, and punish men forsworn."‡ A similar text, in a similar invocation, appeals to the infernal pair "who punish dead men who break their oaths."§ Homeric man seems thus to have had a glimpse of a moral law operative against perjury alike here and hereafter, and so associated its action with the infernal powers. But texts like the above easily mean more to us than they did to the early Greeks. The most awful

---

* "Il.," ix. 454, 567; xv. 204; xix. 87, 418; xxi. 412; "Od.," ii. 135; xi. 279; xv. 234; xvii. 475. † "Od.," xx. 78.
‡ "Il.," xix. 258—260.   § "Il.," iii. 278, 279.

oath the gods could swear was by the Styx,* the symbol of death, even to the Immortals.† So man in his most solemn oaths invoked the powers under the earth, whose function it was to punish by death the man forsworn. And this is the more notable, as in Homer's picture of the underworld the Erinyes have no place. While Epicaste dies, her Erinyes remain behind to follow her husband-son.‡ The ghostly dead cannot suffer such punishments as they inflict; if any can, the perjured alone. Had Homer's idea of spirit been as vivid and definite as his idea of law, he would have placed the present and the future in more intimate relation to each other. The notion of spirit as such was strangely foreign to him. His very gods were material, and had a material immortality.§ Their relations to men, whether as parents or protectors, were conceived physically. Men who boasted a divine descent were divine only as to the body; their souls were ghostly, like other men's. The soul was not to Homer, as to Horace, "divinæ particula auræ,"‖ or as to Virgil, "est ollis cœlestis origo seminibus,"¶ but only " tenuis sine corpore vita, cava sub imagine formæ."** Later the spiritual similarity of gods and men was the

* "Il.," xiv. 271; xv. 37, 38. Hesiod, "Theog.," 775 (Paley's ed.).
† Nägelsbach, "Hom. Theol.," p. 40.   ‡ "Od.," xi. 279.
§ Nägelsbach, "Hom. Theol.," pp. 39 ff.   ‖ "Sat.," ii. 2, 79.
¶ "Æneid," vi. 730.   ** "Æneid," vi. 294.

basis of the faith in immortality, but without the premiss Homer could not reach the conclusion. Immortality was the distinctive attribute of the gods, communicable to a living, but not to a dead man. The ethical element, without the metaphysical, could not connect the present and the future. The Erinyes could not follow a soul which was but a shadow.

In Homer's notion of the future state, as in his conception of the ψυχή, incompatible and transitional elements existed.* The only home of the dead he knew was the House of Aides. Tartaros was the prison of defeated gods.† The Elysian plain the heaven of certain translated mortals.‡ But in the realm of Aides dwelt the souls of all the dead. It was the shadow of the upperworld, as the soul was the shadow of the man; had its rivers and mountains, meadows and flowers, &c.§ It was a region of cheerless gloom, abhorred of the gods.∥ It was not a scene of retribution, but of deprivation—the ghostly home of ghosts. In the original Homeric conception pious and impious were mingled together—a multitude of wailing souls, whose life was one of unrelieved misery.¶ The souls of the dead stand round Odysseus wailing, each one

* B. Constant, "De la Religion," vol. iii. pp. 377 ff.
† "Il.," xiv. 274; viii. 479; 12—16.
‡ "Od.," iv. 560. Preller, "Griechis. Mythol.," i. 507.
§ Welcker, "Griechis. Götterl.," i. 798 ff.; Preller, "Griechis. Mythol.," i. 501 ff.   ∥ "Il.," xx. 65.   ¶ "Od.," xi. 605.

telling his sorrows.* His mother comes to him lamenting,† Agamemnon "weeps shrilly," and sheds the big tear.‡ Achilles approaches sorrowing, and meets the gentle remonstrance, "Be not grieved at death," with the terrible words, "Do not, illustrious Odysseus, talk to me about death. Rather would I be alive upon the face of the earth and serve for hire a master, and a needy master too, than be lord of the whole world of the dead."§

But this primitive and purely negative conception could not maintain itself. In the Homeric theology the notions of merit and reward were strangely absent. Gods and men stood too near each other: the god became easily jealous of the prosperous man. The Erinyes exhibited law on its penal side. Hence such transitional elements as existed in the conception of the future state were retributive: the tendency was not to conceive the good as rewarded, but special sinners as punished. In three pictures the existence and growth of this tendency are indicated. Tityos lies stretched over nine acres, and two vultures tear his liver.‖ Tantalos stands up to the chin in a lake, ever stooping to drink, while the water ever escapes his lip.¶ Sisyphos ever rolls his stone to the hill-top only to

---

* "Od.," xi. 541, 542. † "Od.," xi. 154.
‡ "Od.," xi. 391. § "Od.," xi. 472, 486—491.
‖ "Od.," xi. 576—581. ¶ "Od.," xi. 582—592.

see it evermore return.* In these almost certainly post-Homeric pictures, the idea of retribution stands embodied.† In Tityos, lust is punished in its peculiar seat; in Tantalos, gluttony; in Sisyphos, the speculative curiosity that seeks to transcend the limits appointed to human reason.‡ Beside these stands another and no less significant set of pictures. Minos, the phantom judge of the phantom dead, Orion, the phantom hunter, and Herakles, whose shadow lives below while he himself feasts above.§ These mark the progress towards a more life-like and less miserable conception of the future. The souls are becoming more substantive; their home, their sufferings, and their acts more real.

Such, then, was the Homeric belief in the future life of the soul, a faltering, inconsistent, indistinct, yet

---

* "Od.," xi. 593—600.

† Into the *quæstio vexata* of the interpolations in the eleventh Odyssey it is, of course, not possible to enter here. The entire passage, 565—627, seems to me for many reasons certainly spurious, and marks, perhaps, two successive stages in the development of the belief,—the lines 567—575 and 601—626, the first stage, in which the soul and the underworld become less shadowy, more substantial; but the lines 576—600, the second stage, in which the ethical and retributive idea receives expression. But see Nitzsch, "Anmerk. z. Odys.," vol. iii. pp. 304 ff.; K. O. Müller's "Hist. of the Lit. of Anc. Greece," i. 81. Cf. on the other side, Colonel Mure, "Hist. Lang. and Lit. of Anc. Gr.," ii. 185 ff.

‡ See the elaborate discussion in Nitzsch, iii. 320 ff. Cf. Virgil, "Æneid," vi. 595—600; Lucretius, iii. 980—997 (Monro's ed.).

§ "Od.," xi. 568—575, 601—626.

veracious utterance of that great human instinct which demands for man continued existence. It stood in no relation to the idea of God, and so had no ground in reason; had no connection with religion, and so could address no appeal to hope or fear. Because thus isolated, the belief was indefinite, feeble, inconsistent—an uttered longing which had sought but not found stable footing. Apotheosis in its proper sense was unknown to Homer,[*] and was never as it existed in Greece promotive of the belief in Immortality. The exceptionality of the boon it gave only helped to deepen the dreariness of the common lot. Translation,[†] too, was so rare and so conditioned as only to tantalize ordinary mortals with examples of unattainable bliss. The hero and the coward, the wise man and the fool, alike died, became shadows, and lived lives of gloomy misery in Hades. Hence the despair that sits at the heart of Homeric man when he becomes conscious of the lot appointed him by a mocking and ironical destiny.[‡] Men are $\delta\epsilon\iota\lambda o\iota$ or $\dot{o}\ddot{\iota}\zeta\upsilon\rho o\grave{\iota}\ \beta\rho o\tau o\iota$, are short-lived,[§] and each generation like the leaves of spring, which perish before the winds of autumn.[||] In the eye of Zeus there is no more

---

[*] Nitzsch, "Anmerk. z. Odys.," iii. 182, 340 ff. On the other side, Colonel Mure, "Crit. Hist.," i. 500, 501.

[†] Mr. Gladstone, "Homer and the Homeric Age," ii. 313 f.

[‡] "Il.," xxiv. 521 ff. Cf. Nägelsbach, "Hom. Theol.," 371; Mr. Gladstone, "Homer and the Homeric Age," ii. 393.

[§] "Od.," xix. 328.   [||] "Il.," vi. 146—149.

wretched being than man of all that live and move upon the earth.* Bright and beautiful as was the life of the Homeric Greeks upon the surface, the agony was at its heart which was soon to be uttered in perhaps the most memorable of the many axioms of despair—"The best of all things to mortals is not to be born and see the rays of the bright sun, but when born to die as soon as possible and lie buried under a load of earth."†

III. HESIOD.

The Hesiodic poems are more specifically religious than the Homeric, pervaded by a humaner and more ethical spirit. Had the belief in immortality then existed in Greece, it would, as pregnant with the promise of a golden future, have been peculiarly attractive to a poet like Hesiod, with his intense love of the traditional happier past, and his almost morbid sense of the wrongs and miseries of the present. The men of the golden age had indeed died as if falling into a gentle sleep, and had become by the will of God good spirits, guardians of mortal men.‡ The silver race, less pious than the golden, had been engulfed in the earth,

---

* "Il.," xvii. 446. Cf. "Od.," xviii. 130.

† "Theognis," 425. Cf. the story of the captive Silenus, Plutarch, "Consolatio ad Apollonium," Opp. Moral. (Wyttenb. ed.), vol. i. pp. 483 f.; Cicero, "Tusc.," i. 48. Also Sophokles, "Oid. Kol.," 1225; "Oid. Tyr.," 1528—1530.

‡ Hesiod, "Opp. et Di.," 116—123 (Paley's ed.).

THE BELIEF IN GREECE.   195

and become the Blest of the underworld.* The brazen race, terrible as they were, black Death had seized, and, inglorious, they had descended to the dreary house of chilly Aides.† The men of the heroic age had either died before seven-gated Thebes, or in the war for fair-headed Helen, or been translated to the Isles of the Blest, where they lived, happy and careless, in a land which thrice a year bore fruit sweet as honey.‡ But no hope of an Elysium cheered the men of the fifth, the poet's own age.§ To them death was a dread god, inexorable, iron of heart, a ruthless soul of brass in his breast, hostile even to the immortal gods.‖ Aides, too, has a relentless heart,¶ and at death souls descend to his dark and cheerless domain.**

Hesiod, then, did little to modify or improve our belief. Yet there are signs of progress. The notion of spirit is clearer and firmer than in Homer. It can exist without body, can live as a dæmon upon or under the earth. The spiritual element in man approximates to the spiritual in God. The heroes are demi-gods. The selecter spirits are immortal.†† Ethical notions, too, are developed.

---

* Hesiod, "Opp. et Di.," 140—143.   † Ib., 153—155.

‡ Ib., 161—173. I adopt Welcker's ("Kleine Schriften," i. 23) interpretation of 166, 167, which is also Grote's ("History," i. 65), in preference to Heyne's, which makes all the heroes be translated to the Isles of the Blest.

§ Hesiod, "Opp. et Di.," 174—181.   ‖ "Theog.," 759—766.

¶ "Ib.," 455, 456.   ** "Scut. Her.," 151, 254.

†† Cf. Tacitus, "Agricola," 46: "Si quis piorum manibus locus; si, ut

Each age is rewarded according to its works. The belief is nascent. The first green shoots appear.

IV. THE MYSTERIES.

In the ghostly and gloomy future of the popular and epical faith the Greeks could not permanently believe. The wail of Achilles, the tears of Agamemnon, the contemptuous pity of Zeus, the plaintive sigh of Hesiod over his birth in the age of mortal men,* but give voice to the corrosive misery that lay at the heart of Greece. Every step forward taken by the Greek mind made higher notions of the future destiny of man the more necessary. With the growth of civilization nationality had waned, individuality had waxed. While pictures of a happier past had satisfied the imaginative age, nothing but belief in a conscious future could satisfy the reflective, and save the Greek mind from the epicurean despair that made man festive in life because in death like a voiceless stone.† Had religion developed with mind, the belief would have risen out of their sympathetic and concurrent inter-action; but as the religion had crystallized into a mythology and worship which regarded the present alone, it had as to

sapientibus placet, non cum corpore exstinguuntur magnæ animæ." Minds moving upwards to faith, or downwards to doubt, often strangely meet on the road.

    * " Opp. et Di.," 175.   † " Theognis," 567.

the future neither promise to utter nor truth to reveal. Hero-worship, the natural product of a heroic land like Greece, had led to Apotheosis. Elect men had been deified and so immortalized. But this, while helping to naturalize the thought of immortality, did not generalize it into a belief. Only the rarest spirits could be raised to the circle of the immortal gods. Their reward could not become the common inheritance of man. But the Greek mind, determined partly by its own instincts and aspirations interpreting the nature within and without man, and partly by foreign influences stimulating and supplementing native thought, found out a way to the faith that it craved. A new religion was developed, not as antagonistic, but only as supplementary, to the old. A Chthonian court was constructed over against the Olympian, and while from the latter the Greek by public worship craved present prosperity, by secret he craved from the former future happiness. Of the Mysteries thus formed, the Eleusinian are the product of the native Greek mind, the Orphic-Dionysian the fruit of foreign influence.

1. THE ELEUSINIAN MYSTERIES.

The worship of Father-Heaven had developed into the Olympian system, of Mother-Earth into the Chthonian. The gods of the first were the products of the creative and combining imagination, those of the second of the intuitive and reflective reason. To the mythical faculty Heaven was the symbol of the active and generative forces, earth of the passive and created. The one was perennial, unchanging, present; the other subject to ceaseless change, the scene of growth and decay, birth and death. Demeter, Aides, and Persephone were not originally gods of the underworld, but of the dying and reviving earth.* Their earliest worship had been festivals at seed-time and harvest. The earth-mother had mourned when the fruits and flowers she loved died, rejoiced when they revived. Aides had borne away from the face of earth and the light of Heaven the daughter Demeter loved, but only to restore her when the Sun bade spring return. Life in man and nature was to the early Greek allied, akin. Earth was to him a mirror—a hieroglyph into which he explained himself. So the God that ruled the growth and decay of earth ruled the coming and going of man, determined his future state. In his brilliant and heroic youth the bright gods of Olympos had charmed and satisfied the Greek: in his sadder and more reflective manhood the stern deities of the underworld occupied his thought. His love of those he had embodied in epic mythology and

* Welcker, "Griechis. Götterl.," i. 385 ff.; 392 ff. Preller, "Griechis. Mythol.," i. 464 ff.

worship, his awe of these in mystic sacrifice and ablution.*

This new faith and worship finds its earliest embodiment in the Homeric Hymn to Demeter.† The transition from the old earth-worship to a worship which gives a better hope in death, is just being accomplished. The deities which presided over growth and decay above now preside over the life below. Aides is no longer the shadowy king of the Shades known to Homer, but own brother of Zeus,‡ the all-receiver,§ the veritable king of the dead.‖ Worship of the infernal deities is necessary to future happiness. Persephone, as wife of Aides, shall be mistress of all, and enjoy the greatest honour among the immortals.¶ Vengeance shall follow those who do not propitiate her heart by sacrifices.** He of mortal men who beholds the mystic rites is blest: he who is uninitiated does not participate in felicity, has a very different lot in the murky kingdom of

---

* The controversy as to whether there was any dogmatic teaching connected with the Mysteries, and if so, what, may be regarded as at an end. The public and secret worship of Greece were in this respect very much on a level. Both were spectacular, neither doctrinal in almost any degree whatever. Of course, under the ceremonies and acts of worship certain distinct enough conceptions lay, and it is with these alone that we are now concerned.

† See J. H. Voss' "Hymne an Demeter," with an excellent translation and notes; or the Hymn as given in Baumeister's "Hymni Homerici" (1860).

‡ Hymn 80, 365. § Ib., 9, 17. ‖ Ib., 31, 84.
¶ Ib., 364. ** Ib., 369.

death.* And the mysteries, which thus supplied a religion for the next world, became dear to the heart of Greece. The Chthonian deities rivalled the Olympian. Demeter and Persephone were goddesses loved and revered, holy and august, the most sacred names by which men could swear.† Pindar sang that the man who had prior to death seen the mysteries was happy, knew the end of life and its god-given beginning.‡ Sophokles pronounced the initiated thrice happy: to them alone was there life in Hades; to others evil.§ Euripides makes Herakles say on his return from the underworld that he has succeeded in his struggle with Kerberos, because he had seen the mystic orgies.‖ The initiated sing in Aristophanes, "To us alone shines the glad sunlight there."¶ Isocrates praises Demeter because of her two gifts, the fruits of the field and the mysteries, those who participate in the latter having sweeter hopes for the end of life and for all eternity.** Diodorus says that the gods grant through initiation an eternal life, spent in pleasant devotion.†† Cicero says these Attic mysteries have

---

* Hymn 480—483. See Baumeister's note, "Hymni Hom.," p. 333; also Voss, 142 f.

† Welcker, "Griechis. Götterl.," ii. 532 f.; Grote's "History of Greece," i. 37—44.

‡ "Frag.," xcvi., vol. iii., pt. i., 128 (Heyne's ed., 1798).

§ Plutarch, "De Aud. Poetis," p. 27; "Frag.," vol. ii. p. 244; Brunkii Sophokles. ‖ "Herc. fur.," 612.

¶ "Ranæ," 455. Cf. also 324 ff. (Bekker's ed.).

** "Paneg.," vi. 59. †† "Exerc. Vatic. Maii Coll.," ii. 8.

taught men not only to live cheerfully, but also to die with a better hope.* Krinagoras sends men to Athens to see the solemnities of Demeter, that they may live without care and die with a lighter heart.†

The worship of the Chthonian deities thus furnished a religious basis to the belief in a future life. While prayer and sacrifice implored from Zeus a happy life here, the mystic rites implored from Aides a happy life hereafter. The initiated were to dwell with the gods; the uninitiated to live in slime, or bear water in a sieve.‡ The sound of the flute, sunlight beautiful as above, myrtle-groves, happy bands of men and women, delighted the initiated below.§ Death thus became the entrance on divine honours.‖ The dead were the blessed; the happy, the godlike.¶ Death ceased to

---

* "Legg.," ii. 14. Cf. "Verr.," v. 72.

† Ep. xxx. The varied and numerous allusions in Greek and Latin writers to the better hope in death derived from the Mysteries can neither be cited nor referred to in a short essay on a great subject. But see the scholarly discussions in Lobeck, "Aglaophamus," pp. 69 ff.; Welcker, "Griechis. Götterl.," ii. pp. 511 ff.; Preller, Art. "Eleusina," in Pauly's "Encyclop.;" Creuzer's "Symbolik und Mythol.," iv. pp. 227 ff. Of course, Creuzer's peculiar theory of esoteric doctrines is a pure imagination. No such doctrines are needed to explain the better hope created by the Mysteries: worship of the Chthonian deities was enough.

‡ Plato, "Phæd.," i. 69 (Steph.); II., iii. 28 (Bek.). Cf. "Repub.," II., ii. 363; "Gorgias," i. 493; see notes in Bekker.

§ Aristophanes, "Ranæ," 154—157 (Bekker).

‖ Scholion on Ranæ, 158.

¶ Plato, "Legg.," bk. xii., vol. ii. p. 947; Æschylos, "Pers.," 63 f. (Paley).

be a descent into Hades, and became a departure to the blessed. Nor were the future rewards independent of ethical conditions. The mysteries known to the Christian fathers had degenerated,—shared in the corruption that had smitten the whole body of paganism. But at first initiation had bound to moral purity. To individuals, indeed, it became a substitute for virtue,* and an old man, haunted as Plato describes him by the fear of the death he had once mocked,† might wish, like the Trygaios of Aristophanes, to buy a little pig and get initiated before he died;‡ but to the representative Greek thinkers, it stood connected with piety and righteousness and improvement of life.§ The mysteries had helped to create and consecrate the noblest hope that can gladden the heart of man, and only in the most ignoble minds were made at once to pander to vice and promise future felicity.‖ In general the faith they both embodied and evolved saved the heart of Greece from despair, and inspired some of its noblest spirits to produce works immortal as the Odes of Pindar or the Philosophy of Plato.

* Plato, "Repub.," bk. ii., vol. ii. pp. 364—366.
† Ib., bk. i., vol. ii. 330.   ‡ Pax, 370, 371.
§ Isocrates, "Symmach.," xii.; cf. "Paneg.," vi.; Philem., "Frag.," xc.; Aristoph., "Ranæ," 457—460; Epictetus, "Diss.," iii. 21, 15.
‖ *Ut supra* (*). This abuse of the Mysteries is well rebuked in the characteristic story of Diogenes the cynic in "Diog. L.," vi. 39: "It were laughable were Agesilaos and Epaminondas to lie in mud, while worthless fellows, because initiated, should dwell in the Isles of the Blest."

2. THE ORPHICI.

The Greeks, accustomed to a religion defective and cheerless in its eschatology, became in the seventh century B.C. acquainted with religions, Eastern and Egyptian, whose eschatology was peculiarly elaborate and full.* The Greek genius, always receptive and susceptible, was just then, as the budding mysteries of Eleusis witness, sensitively alive to the action on this point of foreign influence. The result was an extraordinary religious development; the rise, on the one hand, of the Dionysian worship and mythology, on the other, of the Orphic Theosophy. The former increased the tendency to establish a secret eschatological religion,† the latter helped to originate the speculative and theosophic thought of Greece.‡ It alone can be noticed here.

The Orphic Theology, so far as now decipherable, was an amalgam, with specific Greek modifications, of Oriental and Egyptian elements. Speculative principles, clothed in mythical forms, partly Grecian, partly foreign, were prefixed and appended to the native mythology,

---

* As to the time of the rise of the Orphic sects see Lobeck, "Aglaophamus," pp. 255 ff.; Brandis, "Geschich. der Griechis.-Rom. Philos.," i. 53 ff.; Grote's "Hist. of Greece," i. 28 ff.

† Preller, "Griechis. Mythol.," i. 436.

‡ Zeller, "Philos. der Griechen," i. 47.

and the whole made to embody a crude but elaborate Pantheism. The primordial principle was Chronos,* which generated chaos and ether,† by whom was produced a silver egg.‡ From this egg sprang Phanes,§ a being who bore in himself the seed of the gods,‖ generated night,¶ and formed the Kosmos.** Night bore to him Uranos and Gaea.†† The origin and succession of the other gods is then described very much as in the traditional mythology.‡‡ Zeus and his brothers are born of Kronos and Rhea.§§ Zeus, nursed by Eide and Adrasteia in the cave of Night,‖‖ dethrones Kronos, swallows and absorbs into himself the whole existing system of things,¶¶ and then generates a new one framed according to his own ideas.*** The Universe, all things and beings, have thus issued from Zeus. And so Zeus is all things, first and last, head and middle, foundation of the earth and the starry heavens, male and female, the breath of all beings, the heat of the fire, the source of the sea, the sun, the moon, the Being who is all things, and in whom all beings live.††† Zeus is thus transformed from the King

---

* Lobeck, "Aglaoph.," pp. 470—472.   † Ib., 422 f.
‡ Ib., 474—477.   § Ib., 478.   ‖ Ib., 486.
¶ Ib., 493.   ** Ib., 496.   †† Ib., 499.
‡‡ Ib., 501.   §§ Ib., 514.   ‖‖ Ib., 517.
¶¶ Ib., 519.   *** Ib., 526—534.

††† See the Orphic Fragments in Lobeck, "Aglaoph.," 519—525, Fragm. vi., Hermann's "Orphica," pp. 456—463. Also the excellent expositions

of Olympos into the generative principle of the universe, and, as the generator contains the generated, to the universe as well. This Orphic Pantheism is thus, in many things, curiously alien to the conceptions of religion and man hitherto entertained in Greece.

A crude Pantheism always involves metempsychosis. Creation is impossible: new forms of being may arise, but being itself remains the same. As to man, he may be conceived either as a transient individualization of the one substance, or as an embodiment of an individualized principle, which, emanating at first from the One, must, before returning into it, describe a given cycle of appearances. The latter was the Orphic conception. The spirit, separated from the whole and individualized,* had the cycle of necessity, κύκλος ἀνάγκης, or of birth, γενέσεως, to describe.† Man was still moving in the cycle, often returning to the same point, where the old relations returned exactly as before. The past life determined the present, the present the future. The body was a prison in which the soul was confined because of past sins.‡ At death

---

of the Orphic Theology in Brandis, "Geschich. d. Gr.-Rom. Philos.," i. 59—64; Nägelsbach, "Nach-Hom. Theol.," 401—404; Grote, "Hist. of Greece," i. 17—19.

* Aristotle, "De Anim.," i. 5; Lobeck, "Aglaoph.," 755 ff.

† Ib., 797 ff.; Herodotos, ii. 123.

‡ Plato, "Kratylos," p. 400; Philolaus, in Clem. Alex. "Strom.," bk. iii., c. iii., p. 433.

the soul entered Hades, to be punished or rewarded as it deserved, and returned again to earth.* Ablutions and rites were instituted to purify the soul and secure it a better lot hereafter.† And so the Orphic Theosophy led, partly, to the development and extension and, partly, to the perversion of the mysteries.‡ The first, because it greatly helped to awaken the Greek mind to a consciousness of its own immortality; the second, because it contributed to give an alien and artificial meaning to what had been a worship expressive of the natural religious ideas and instincts of the people.

In the Orphic Theology the belief in immortality enters upon a new and important phase of its development in Greece, begins to seek a basis scientific while religious. It enters into relation with the idea of God; stands related to it, indeed, as a mere element or implicate. The soul is to man what God is to the world, the vital and permanent and active element. Psychology is no longer seated in the body, but in the soul. Death destroys nothing but its prison. Yet, while the notion of continued being is seized, that of personal is lost. The soul is no longer an $\epsilon \H{\iota} \delta \omega \lambda o \nu$, but man is no longer an individual—only an emanation from a deified universe, revolving in a cycle of necessity.

---

* "Phædo," p. 70.
† Lobeck, "Aglaoph.," 806—810.   ‡ Ib., 810 ff.

The Greek mind has still a long way to travel before it can reach the belief in a positive personal immortality.

V. THE PRE-SOKRATIC PHILOSOPHY.

As the philosophy did not grow up within the religion of Greece, its earliest forms of thought and expression were not religious. The national faith was mythical, not reflective or doctrinal, and so its very nature made it unfit to be either the object or vehicle of philosophic thought. While, then, philosophy starts from a point which seems very remote from our belief, it yet inevitably tends towards it.

1. THE EARLIER IONIANS.

Thales depersonalized the ancient Okeanos—sought in water the source of life.* As the cause was material, so was the effect. Soul was not peculiar to man,† but the synonyme of life, or the cause of motion, and so was mixed with all things,‡ existed in the magnet,§ or the amber.|| In a system where soul was so crudely conceived, its immortality could have neither place nor meaning.¶ Anaximander and Anaximenes alike defined the soul as "air-like,"** but to both it was material, as

---

* Aristotle, "Metaph.," A, 3; "De Cœlo," ii. 13. † "Diog. L.," i. 27.
‡ Arist., "De Anim.," i. 5. § Ib., i. 2. || "Diog. L.," i. 24.
¶ Though Choirilos, in "Diog. L.," i. 24, makes him the first who taught it.
** Theodoret, Serm. v. p. 72.

was the unlimited (τὸ ἄπειρον), the self-moved beginning of the one, and the air, the creative force of the other.* Diogenes of Apollonia held a sort of dualism, a universal matter and an intelligent Being, its organizer. But this Being he identified with the air which pervaded all things, which animals and men breathed, and became, according to the quality of the air they inhaled, intelligent and conscious.† This, however, still left creative and created intelligence alike material and impersonal. And so to those early Ionians man was but a physical being, with no existence apart from the body. But their attempts to refine and unify the primal cause, while apparently inimical to our belief, were, in truth, rude and unconscious struggles towards it.

2. PYTHAGORAS AND THE PYTHAGOREANS.

This School introduced into Greek Philosophy a new and more spiritual class of conceptions. The Society Pythagoras founded, the philosophy that bears his name, the myths that, like parasites, have so overgrown as almost to conceal his actual personality, bear witness to his profoundly religious spirit.‡ His

---

* See the texts in Ritter and Preller's "Historia Philosophiæ," §§ 17—27.

† Zeller, "Philos. d. Griechen," i. 191 ff.

‡ Zeller, "Pythagoras und die Pythagorassage," Vorträge, p. 35.

significance for Greece was threefold, scientific, religious, political. His Society was the first that it might be the second, and because the second the third. Of the doctrines attributed to him, the one that can best be authenticated, metempsychosis, he almost certainly derived from the Orphic schools.* The age in which he lived, the constitution of his Society, the doctrines it professed, the ritual it observed, the traditions and theories associated with his name, all tend to show that he had intimate relations with the theosophic sects that had grown up in and round the mysteries. Pythagoras may thus be considered the inheritor and transmitter of the more spiritual results of the old Greek religion. Man meant more to him than to the early Ionians. His conception of nature was more spiritual. Their philosophy was but the national mythology naturalized; but his was, on its religious side, the Orphic theosophy philosophized. It is difficult, perhaps impossible, to ascertain what Pythagoras taught concerning the nature of the soul, whether a harmony,† a self-determining number,‡ &c. More to the purpose is it to notice that the soul must have been to him an entity, not a mere attribute; that he distinguished in it the higher and lower faculties, the rational and the irrational,§ or mind ($\phi\rho\acute{\epsilon}\nu\epsilon\varsigma$), reason ($\nu o\hat{u}\varsigma$), and passion ($\theta\nu\mu\acute{o}\varsigma$); the former

* Herod., ii. 81, cf. 123. † Arist., "De Anim.," i. 4.
‡ Plutarch, "Plac. Ph.," iv. 2. § Cicero, "Tusc.," iv. 5.

was peculiar to man, the two latter he had in common with the animals.* The soul, too, though a distinct entity, was invisible, to be sought in the motes floating in the sunbeam, or in what sets them in motion.† Certain disembodied souls existed under the earth, or in the air, as heroes or dæmons, and appeared to men in dreams.‡ The individual soul emanated from the world-soul, or central fire,§ and transmigrated through many bodies.‖ Each body was a prison in which the soul was confined because of former sins,¶ and to which it was bound by number and harmony.** The body, as the medium of perception and exercise, was loved by the soul,†† which, released by death, was, according to its deserts, either rewarded by an incorporeal life in a higher world, or punished, either by an abode in Tartaros, where thunders affrighted, or a return to other bodies.‡‡ Pythagoras thus affirmed the continued being of the soul. The traditional theosophic form of his thought was imperfect, untenable, but his thought

---

* "Diog. L.," viii. 30. Mr. Lewes makes νοῦς the element peculiar to man ("Hist. of Philos.," i. 34). Perhaps another text, given in Ritter and Preller ("Historia," § 120), was running in his mind with the above, but he has given neither correctly.

† Arist., "De Anim.," i. 2.

‡ Ritter, "Hist. of Anc. Philos.," i. 407.

§ But see Zeller, "Philos. d. Griechen," i. 304, 305, text and notes.

‖ Xenophanes, in "Diog. L.," viii. 36; Ovid, "Met.," xv. 165.

¶ Philolaus, in Clem. Alex., "Strom.," iii. c. iii.

** Claud. Mam., "De Stat. Anim.," ii. 7.   †† Ib.

‡‡ "Diog. L.," viii. 31, 32; Arist., "Anal. Post.," ii. 11.

itself of vital moment to Greece. While it did not solve, it framed more profoundly the problem as to the nature and destiny of man.*

3. THE ELEATICS.

Their relation to our belief is indirect. Their polemic against the popular Polytheism, their search after the permanent and indestructible amid the evanescent and perishable, brought into prominence the thought of unity and continuity in the government of the world, and the thought of the imperishableness of its constituent substances. The one contained the germs of a right idea of God, the other, those of a right idea of man, and so were full enough of promise. Thus while Eleaticism was monistic, did not intend to recognise any distinction between matter and spirit, it yet did not utterly deny existence to the dead; conceded to them perception, though only of the cold and the silent.†
But while the Eleatic idea of permanence was beautiful in the abstract, it was merciless to the individual. Birth was hateful ($\sigma\tau\upsilon\gamma\epsilon\rho\acute{o}\varsigma$).‡ Though souls were sent now

* Pherekydes of Syros is by Cicero reckoned the first who taught the immortality of the soul ("Tusc.," i. 16). The truth is, the belief had no single father in Greece, but was a national growth.

† Arist., "Met.," iii. 5; Theophrastus, "De Sensu," 3, 4.

‡ Parmenides, xv. 128—130. But see conflicting interpretations of Ritter ("Hist. of Philos.," i. 467) and Zeller ("Philos. der Griechen," i. 415, note 3).

from light to darkness, and now back again,* individual existence was evanescent. Thought was unable as yet to reconcile the conflicting elements of continuance and decay otherwise than by attaining the conception of an abstract unity, the One, or Being, and sacrificing to it every individual existence.

4. HERAKLEITOS.

In Herakleitos "war is the father of all things."† Becoming is the law of the universe: "All is and is not, for though it does in truth come into being, yet it forthwith ceases to be."‡ Hence, "no man can wade twice in the same stream."§ All phenomena result from a "perpetual flux and reflux." But the source or principle (αρχή) of this ceaseless change is fire. "Neither any god nor any man made this world, but it ever was and shall be an ever-living fire."‖ And in his thought "living" was more real than "fire," the αρχή was a ψυχή "immaterial and ever moving"—the regulative and intelligent as well as animating principle of the universe.¶ Of this fire the soul of man is a spark or portion, lives as fed by the fire, and has in it something

---

* "Simpl. Phys.," fol. 9 a, Ritter and Preller, "Historia," § 151.
† Plutarch, "Is. et Osir.," 45.
‡ Arist., "Metaph.," iv. 3, 7; Plato, "Thæat.," p. 152.
§ Plato, "Kratylos," p. 402.
‖ Herakl. in Clem. Alex., "Strom.," v. p. 599; R. & P., "Historia," § 34.   ¶ Arist. "De Anim.," i. 2, 16.

infinite.* The purer the fire, the more perfect is the soul. "The driest souls are the wisest and best."† The dead body is more despicable than a dunghill. According to the doctrine of becoming, there was in man a perishable element; but, according to the doctrine of the primal principle, an imperishable. Man as a corporeal phenomenon stood in the "perpetual flux and reflux;" man as an emanation of the ever-living fire stood above it. Hence "the very birth of man is a calamity—a birth into death."‡ "Death is in our life, and life in our death; for when we live our souls are dead and buried in us, but when we die our souls revive and live."§ And as all souls are akin, "men are mortal gods, the gods immortal men. Our life is the death of the gods; our death, their life."||

5. EMPEDOKLES.

Empedokles was an eclectic. On the one side he developed the permanent and unchangeable being of the Eleatics, and so maintained that nothing can begin to be which formerly was not, nothing of what exists

* Sext. Emp. adv. Math., vii. 127—130; Plut., "Is. et Osir.," 76, 77; R. & P., "Historia," § 39; "Diog. L." ix. 7.
† Zeller, "Philos. d. Griechen.," i. 480, n. 1.
‡ Clem. Alex. viii. 432—434; Ritter, "Hist. Anc. Philos.," i. 250.
§ Sext. Empir. Pyrrh. Hypotyp., iii. 230; R. & P., "Historia," § 44.
|| Herakl. in Hippolyt. ix. 10; Zeller, "Philos. d. Griechen," i. 483, n. 1.

perish. On the other, he evolved the Herakleitean strife into two rival forces, love and hate, from whose antagonism the world resulted. The former principle applied to man, gave both pre- and post-existence. Of mortal beings there was no natural birth, nor death's destruction final.* The latter principle traced the earthly existence to moral causes. The original state was sinless, happy; but man fell, and was doomed to wander thrice ten thousand years apart from the blessed, a fugitive from the gods, and an outcast, obedient to raging strife.† Hate rules below, and so motion is ceaseless, rest impossible. Impious souls suffer misery, and are driven unresting through all parts of the world. But the happy sphere of love exists still alongside the unblest sphere of hate, and pious men when they die become deathless gods, are no longer mortals.‡

6. ANAXAGORAS.

In Anaxagoras pre-Sokratic thought becomes distinctly theistic. Mind had formed the world, was the intelligent and constructive power which had shaped the primal elements in the Kosmos. This mind was infinite

---

* Ritter, "Hist. Anc. Philos.," i. 502.

† Emped. in "Plut. de Exilio," 17; Hippolyt., vii. 29; Plut., "de Is. et Osir.," 26; R. & P., "Historia," § 179.

‡ Cf. Ritter, "Hist. Anc. Philos.," i. 510 ff.; Zeller, "Philos. d. Griechen," i. 547 ff.; Karsten, "De Emped.," pp. 5—7.

(ἄπειρον), absolute (αὐτοκρατές), simple in essence (μέμικται οὐδενὶ χρήματι), subtlest and purest of things (λεπτότατον τε πάντων χρημάτων καὶ καθαρώτατον), the unmoved cause of motion, omniscient (πάντα ἔγνω νοῦς), unchangeable.* While mind can never mix with things, it yet rules whatever has a soul, is present in rational beings, whether great or small. All mind is similar, homogeneous; difference relates to degree, greater or less, not to kind.† And mind, as it existed in man, he did not distinguish from soul.‡ The two were substantially identical, and, as Aristotle understood, had the same attributes. While then to Anaxagoras man was mortal, mind was not. The σῶμα could, the νοῦς could not, perish.

The Atomists, on the one hand, and the Sophists, on the other, had for our belief peculiarly little significance. The materialism of the first and the scepticism of the second were alike inimical to it. Each only helped to render a new method necessary, and the new method yielded more certain results. Meanwhile, we can see the inevitable tendency of pre-Sokratic thought. The starting-point had been extra-, though not anti-religious. Greek religion was peculiarly destitute of theological ideas. The words God and Creator were not to the

---

* "Simpl. Phys.," i. fol. 33; R. & P., "Historia," § 53.
† Zeller, "Philos. d. Griechen," i. 680 ff.
‡ Arist., "De Anim.," i. 2; Zeller, i. 696.

Greek, as to the Hebrew, synonymous. To the Hellenic mind the creative process was Theogonic as well as Kosmogonic. Its primary question was not, How or why did God create the world? but, *What* created gods and men? Thus in no impious or atheistic spirit did the earlier thinkers attribute the creation to water, or air, or fire. They but obeyed the instinct or intuition which compelled them to seek what their religion did not offer—a cause for the world. But this search involved another. As in Mythology, the Chthonian court had to rise as a supplement to the Olympian, so in Philosophy the question as to man's whence involved the question as to his whither. The nature of the cause, too, determined the nature of the effect. The eschatological idea shared the fortunes of the theological, was with it materialized, spiritualized, impersonalized, validated, or dissolved. In the early physical philosophies soul is but life, inseparable from body, common to whatever can move or cause motion. As the cause is refined, so is the soul; as permanence, intelligence, feeling, volition, are attributed to the one, they are attributed to the other. The point where mind becomes the creator is also the point where soul becomes mind. Thought thus drives the thinker to connect the Highest in the universe with the highest in himself; degree, not kind, quantity, not quality, distinguishes the two. The faith which had resulted from the more or less unconscious and collective action of the religious instincts, resulted also from the conscious and deliberate deductions of the reason—the faith that, while the body dies, the man survives.

VI. THE LYRIC AND TRAGIC POETS.

While philosophy was pursuing its quest after ultimate and necessary truth, and succeeding by failure, poetry was giving the most perfect expression possible to the living and creative thought of the people. Each represented in a different way the Greek mind—the one its inquisitive and intellectual side, the other its ideal and ethical. Philosophy was more individual; poetry more national. The first was a search after elements above and behind the accepted faith; the second, a growth from seeds contained in it. While, then, philosophy was the beginning of a new, poetry was the continuation of the old, cycle of Greek spiritual development. The two cycles could not fail now and then to touch, and even to blend, but in general their course was parallel, not identical, the one using the mythology of the past as the vehicle of the religious and ethical thought of the present, the other seeking to frame for the future terms to express universal and necessary truth. Hence we must trace in this section the growth of thought in the poetic sphere, so as to bring it abreast of the philosophic.

1. THE LYRIC POETS.

The earlier and minor lyric poets need not be examined. Their significance is political rather than religious. In general, what Bunsen says of Solon may be said of the others. They by no means deny or call in question the punishment of the evil-doer after death, but they are silent on the point.* Otherwise is it with Pindar. He is the pre-eminent religious poet of Greece, penetrated by the sense of the divine in man and nature, inspired by the highest religious ideas of the past and present.† The Eleusinian mysteries, the Orphic theosophy, the new-born philosophy, have combined to purify and ennoble his faith. His theology is almost infinitely higher than the Homeric. Olympos has ceased to be in a state of chronic feud. The old names denote new deities. But our belief is the point where the contrast with Homer becomes sharpest.‡ While mortal man is but the dream of a shadow ($\sigma\kappa\iota\tilde{a}s\ \check{o}\nu a\rho$),§ his soul, the εἴδωλον, lives in death, for it alone is from God.‖ "The soul of man is immortal, and at one time has an end, which is termed dying, and at another is

---

* "God in Hist.," ii. 133.
† See Bunsen's admirable chapter on Pindar, "God in Hist.," ii. 132 ff.; Nägelsbach, "Nach-Hom. Theol.," 405—407.
‡ K. O. Müller, "Hist. of Lit. of Anc. Gr.," i. 304.
§ "Pythia," viii. 136 (Heyne's ed., 1798).
‖ "Fragm. ex Threnis," ii. 5.

born again, but never perishes."* It was meant to attain progressive happiness through progressive holiness. The souls of the impious, remote from heaven, flit in murderous pain beneath the inevitable yoke of woe; but the souls of the pious dwell in heaven, chanting hymns.† Once sin is expiated, the soul returns to earth and becomes a king, or a man great in might or wisdom, a saint to after-ages;‡ and death is followed by a happy life in Hades with the honoured of the gods. Then once they have been thrice tried by birth and death and kept their souls free from sin, they "ascend the path of Zeus to the tower of Kronos, where the Islands of the Blest are refreshed by the breezes of ocean, and golden flowers glitter."§

2. THE TRAGIC POETS.

The Dramas of Æschylos are more distinctly national, *i.e.*, Homeric, than the odes of Pindar; mirror better the then faith of the people, unmodified by Orphic or other alien influences.‖ Yet to Æschylos the soul has ceased to be a shadow. The mighty jaws of fire cannot consume the spirit of the dead.¶ The dead are actual and potent

* Plato, "Meno," i. p. 81. † "Fragm. ex Threnis," iii.
‡ Ib., iv. See also Plato, "Meno," *ut supra*.
§ "Olymp.," ii. 123—130. But see also lines 103—144.
‖ See the beautiful essay of Mr. Westcott on "Æschylos as a Religious Teacher," *Contemporary Review*, vol. iii. pp. 351—373.
¶ "Choeph.," 316.

beings, can hear and answer prayers, receive sacrifices,* operate upon earth to bless or ban the living, or awake the Erinyes to the work of retribution.† The king retains the semblance of regal dignity, is godlike, ἰσοδαίμων, or divine, θεός,‡ is more miserable without than with the shadows of his ancient honours, before than after he has been revenged. § But though Æschylos attributes to the dead more reality of being than Homer, yet he describes their state as cold and dreary. The only light they have is coextensive or commensurate with darkness.‖ Though Dareios be still a king, μακαρίτας and θεός,¶ yet he bids the living enjoy life while they have it, "for the dead are shrouded in thick gloom, where wealth avails not."** Perhaps it were incorrect to say, that the only under- and afterworld Æschylos knew was retributive; but certainly in his idea of the future, as in his idea of the present, the penalties of guilt hide the rewards of righteousness.†† Hence Aides is to him another Zeus, who gives final judgment to the dead; a stern inquisitor of men, who views their deeds and writes them in the tablets of his mind; a god that destroyeth, an avenger

---

* "Choeph.," 475, 492, and often. † Eum., 114, 737.
‡ "Pers.," 635, 645. § "Choeph." 346 ff. ‖ Ib., 311.
¶ "Pers.," 635, 645, 687. ** Ib., 835.
†† See his doctrine as to the Erinyes, in such texts as Eum., 312, 322, 910—915.

terrible, whose sentence the lewd offender, when he dies, shall not escape.*

Sophokles, like Æschylos, recognises the continued existence of the soul after death. His picture of the future, as of the present, is, as to general effect, more calm and beautiful, more ideal and less mythical, than that of Æschylos, but each is in its ground-lines the same. The dead are conscious, know what transpires on the earth, remember what they suffered here, love or hate as in life, work good or ill to the living.† Their form and state resemble their earthly. Oidipous expects to enter Hades eyeless.‡ Kings still rule among the dead.§ But no happiness or reward can be enjoyed hereafter. The Fragment, which pronounces the initiated thrice happy, stands alone.|| Antigone, indeed, rejoices to join her beloved dead, but only because death was to her, as to familiar maxims the world over, the end of trouble.¶ Oidipous, the blameless king, the victim of a terrible destiny, purified from his unconscious crime, ennobled into saintliness by suffering, takes a touching farewell of the sunlight and beauty of earth.** The chorus begs for him a painless and easy death, an untroubled descent into Hades,†† but neither king nor

---

* "Suppl.," 226, 227, 408—410; "Eum.," 260—265.
† "Antig.," 65, 89; "Elec.," 449, 459, 482.
‡ "Oid. Tyr.," 1371. § "Elec.," 833. || *Supra*, p. 200, n. §.
¶ 895. Cf. "Oid. Kol.," 955. ** "Oid. Kol.," 1551. †† 1556 ff.

chorus anticipates other reward than the εὐθανασία. His very grave works good to the Athenians, ill to the Thebans, but to himself there is only a joyless life in Hades.

Our belief, like the other religious ideas of Greece, suffers in the hands of Euripides. The mythical side is indeed now and then exhibited, and prayers and worship offered to the dead heroes, or doubt or hope as to the state of the pious expressed. But the poet's own belief was hostile to a personal immortality.* He is indeed at times enigmatical, as in that sentence, which may mean much or little, according as it is understood, quoted in Plato's Gorgias,† "Who knows if life be not death, and death life?" but elsewhere he quite decisively expresses the impersonal view. The mind (ὁ νοῦς) of the dead does not live, but has immortal intelligence (γνώμην), falling back into the immortal æther.‡ And so he explains that, while what the earth produced returns to the earth, the offspring of the celestial æther returns to the vault of heaven.§

The attitude of the Greek mind to our belief had hitherto been progressively affirmative. Philosophy starting without any idea of spirit or permanent being, had been driven to affirm both. Poetry, the mirror of

---

* Nägelsbach, "Nach-Hom. Theol.," 459—460.
† P., 492.   ‡ "Hellen.," 1013.
§ "Chrysipp. Fr.," 833. See more to same purpose in Nägelsbach, 460 ff.

the ideal religion of Greece, had up to this point become more and more positive in its conception of the future and its relation to the present. But the Sophists in philosophy, and Euripides in poetry, were similar phenomena resulting from similar causes,—failure producing empiricism and scepticism. The ethical idea of righteousness, unqualified by the religious idea of goodness, had given to the intense and intuitive Greek spirit the conception of a universe ruled by Nemesis rather than by Eros. The active moral forces of the world were punitive. Their beneficent action had fallen into the back-, their retributive alone stood in the fore-ground. The old mythical forms were made by the stern spirit of Æschylos, the calm yet severe genius of Sophokles, to reflect, for here and hereafter, the action of those terrible forces. But to spirits more sceptical, less earnest, those stern ethical religious ideas seemed exaggerated, false as their mythical veil, and so, without the idea of divine goodness to lead to a platform of higher faith, the Greek spirit turned aside in Euripides to a feeble pantheistic materialism, which abolished the retributions of Hades by impersonalizing the soul.

VII. PLATO.

The relation of Sokrates to our belief is rather uncertain. The Memorabilia is silent, and it is perilous to base conjectures on any saying of the Platonic Sokrates. The Sokrates of the Apology, perhaps the nearest approximation to the reality, is dubious. While certain that "no evil can happen to a good man, either in life or after death," uncertain whether "death be a state of nothingness and utter unconsciousness, or a change and migration of the soul from this world to the next."* The reasons which Xenophon makes the dying Kyros adduce for the soul's possible continuance† have often been traced to Sokratic inspiration, but the point must always remain conjectural.

With Plato, however, it is different. He was the true Prophet of our belief, for the Greeks and for humanity. No man has contributed more to the culture and faith of the world. Augustine was a Christian Father, Plato a heathen Philosopher; but the heathen was more eminent as a religious thinker than the Christian. There is more of the essence and spirit of Christian theology in the Dialogues of the one than in the *De Civitate Dei* of the other. The Providence of God has reversed the order of History, and found for all that was noblest in the Greek a home within the Church of Christ.

Plato was in the realm of thought, in a more eminent sense than any other Greek, not excepting even Aristotle, the heir of the past and the creator of the future. He was, indeed, less cosmopolitan and more Grecian than

* i. 40, 41. † "Cyrop.," viii. 7, 17—23.

Aristotle, but simply because he was less extensive he was more intense. In him were concentrated all the hereditable elements of the Greek genius, but they were combined, sublimed, and complemented by a genius peculiarly his own. The sense of the divine presence and providence that lived in the old mythical poems, the faith in the likeness and intercourse of gods and men that inspired Homer and Hesiod, the aspiration after a happy hereafter embodied in the mysteries, the Orphic searchings after a system of the universe in which gods and men became emanations and manifestations of supreme deity, the philosophical attempts to reach a primal substance or first cause, the exalted faith of the Lyric Poets, the ethical conceptions which had received ideal expression in Tragedy,—these, and much more than these, Plato inherited, and his inheritance he harmonized and enlarged with the native wealth of his own splendid intellect. The old metaphysical abstractions ceased in his hands to be abstract; became personal, conscious, moral. The idea of the good qualified the old rigid ethical idea embodied in the Drama. Man ceased to be phenomenal and became real, theogony was sublimed into theology, and the world of eternal ideas made to transcend that of transient appearances.

Plato's doctrine of immortality is too integral to his entire system in all its phases to be separable from it, so lives like a subtle essence in all his modes of thought as to be hardly translatable into another language and other concatenations than his own. A philosophy may be analytically as a substance may be chemically dissolved, but in neither case have the elements, as single and distinct, the same qualities and force as they had when combined. Plato's arguments for immortality, isolated, modernized, may be feeble, even valueless, but allowed to stand where and as he himself puts them, they have an altogether different worth. The ratiocinative parts of the Phædo thrown into syllogisms may be easily demolished by a hostile logician; but in the dialogue as a whole there is a subtle spirit and cumulative force which logic can neither seize nor answer. Indeed, the belief belongs to the man rather than his philosophy. He holds it at every stage of his mental development, finds reasons for it in almost every principle he formulates. It is involved in his idea of God—the divine and therefore immortal part of man is derived from the supreme Creator;[*] in his theory of beauty—the beautiful beheld, not in image, but reality, makes man "the friend of God, and immortal."[†] His psychology in all its forms, whether it describes the individual soul as of the same nature and character as the universal,[‡] or as a simple, uncompounded, and so incorruptible principle,[§] or as in its own nature indestructible even

---

[*] "Tim.," iii. 34, 35, 41, 69.
[‡] "Tim.," iii. 69, 90.
[†] "Sympos.," iii. 207, 208, 212.
[§] "Phædo," i. 78 ff.

by its own evil,* or as self-moved and the cause of motion,† or as the divine and contemplative reason;‡ his theory of knowledge, whether as reminiscence§ or as identification of knowing and being, participation of the perceiver in the eternal ideas perceived,|| or as the intuition or vision of love and beauty, or things in their own immutable nature;¶ his moral conceptions, whether represented in the uneasy conscience of a dying man** or in the inevitable retribution which follows crime, or the reward which crowns virtue, or in the divine order and government of the universe††—are each, singly and collectively, made to imply and prove the immortality of man. It stands in the Phædo as the crown and complement of a wise and beautiful life; in the Republic, as the regulative end and realized idea of life in a perfect state. In the Symposium it rewards the inspired devotee of love; in the Phædros it consummates the pursuit of knowledge and virtue.

With deep regret that a worthier exposition of Plato's doctrine of immortality cannot now be attempted, this essay must close. In him our belief reached its culminating point in Greece. The Phædo " may be regarded as a

---

* "Repub.," bk. x., ii. 609 ff.   † "Phædr.," iii. 245.
‡ Ib., 249.   § "Meno," ii. 81, 86; "Phædo," i. 73 ff.
|| "Phædo," i. 65, 66.   ¶ "Sympos.," iii. 212.
** "Repub.," bk. i., ii. 330.
†† "Gorgias," i. 523—527; and the beautiful myth of Er, the son of Armenius, "Repub.," bk. x., ii. 614 ff.

dialectical approximation to the truth of immortality."*
But Plato's position was not simply the metaphysician's.
His conception was profoundly ethical, rested on the
moral nature of man and the divine moral government.
It was, too, profoundly religious, often in its form, almost
always in its matter. He outgrew as his thoughts ripened
the metempsychosis of his earlier dialogues. The same
tendencies and habits of thought which made the Greek
gods, and even the highest Platonic abstractions, anthropomorphic and anthropopathic, made the personality of
man too decided to allow a continued metempsychosis to
be conceived. The ethical idea defined, too, the personal.
Responsibility belonged to the individual, and was
everlasting in its issues. The man could never cease to be
himself, or to bear in himself the results of his actions.
Immortality was twofold—of souls and their acts.

The post-Platonic history of the doctrine need not be
here written. It lies upon the broad face of the successive
philosophies. Aristotle, true to his severe scientific spirit
and purpose, left the question undiscussed, or only
touched it with a hesitation which has made his utterances
standing puzzles to the student of his philosophy.†
Epicurean, Stoic, and Sceptic dealt with it as the spirit

---

* Jowett, "Plato," i. 391.

† See Sir Alexander Grant's scholarly discussion of the subject, "Ethics of Arist.," vol. i. pp. 294—302, 3rd ed. See also the vigorous but more limited and partial representation of Grote, "Aristotle," ii. 233—235.

and principles of their systems demanded. How Christianity found the belief, dead but with a name to live, unannihilated by the vehement denials of Lucretius, unproved by the balanced but unpersuasive periods of Cicero, ridiculed by the mocking descriptions of Lucian, impotent amid the dissolution of the old religions; what Christianity made it, a living and commanding faith, indissolubly bound up with the facts and doctrines she sent like a glorious constellation into the dark and almost starless heaven; its varied fortunes within and without the Church during the eighteen Christian centuries; its position to-day in the face of the science that threatens it from the side of matter and the philosophy from the side of mind; its claims upon life; its reasons against doubt and denial;—these, however inviting, are too extensive subjects to be handled here and now. For what is the inalienable property of humanity we need not fear. The revelation of God is coextensive with man, and though obscured in the individual, now by culture and now by barbarism, lives and lightens in the race. Meanwhile this essay cannot more fitly close than in the words of the great prophet of the belief whose history it has tried through two short cycles to follow*:—

'Ἀλλ' ἄν ἐμοὶ πειθώμεθα, νομίζοντες ἀθάνατον τὴν ψυχὴν καὶ δυνατὴν πάντα μὲν κακὰ ἀνέχεσθαι, πάντα δὲ

* "Repub.," bk. x., ii. 621.

ἀγαθά, τῆς ἄνω ὁδοῦ ἀεὶ ἑξόμεθα καὶ δικαιοσύνην μετὰ φρονήσεως παντὶ τρόπῳ ἐπιτηδεύσομεν, ἵνα καὶ ἡμῖν αὐτοῖς φίλοι ὦμεν καὶ τοῖς θεοῖς, αὐτοῦ τε μένοντες ἐνθάδε, καὶ ἐπειδὰν τὰ ἆθλα αὐτῆς κομιζώμεθα, ὥς περ οἱ νικηφόροι περιαγειρόμενοι, καὶ ἐθάδε καὶ ἐν τῇ χιλιετεῖ πορείᾳ, ἣν διεληλύθαμεν, εὖ πράττωμεν.

THE PLACE OF THE INDO-EUROPEAN AND SEMITIC RACES IN HISTORY.

> PART I. COMPARATIVE PSYCHOLOGY AND THE PHILOSOPHY OF HISTORY.
>
> II. THE RACES IN CIVILIZATION.
>
> III. THE RACES IN RELIGION.
>
> IV. THE RACES IN LITERATURE AND PHILOSOPHY.

PART I.

COMPARATIVE PSYCHOLOGY AND THE PHILOSOPHY OF HISTORY.

I.

MAN is, as it were, the condensed secret of the universe. As he is concerned with every science, every science is, directly or ultimately, concerned with him. The interpreter of Nature can fulfil his office only by the interpretation of himself. Man interpreted is Nature interpreted; and as he can realize manhood only in and through society, an adequate interpretation of man involves an adequate interpretation of society. But society is not simply present, contemporaneous, is the daughter of the past, the mother of the future, inheriting that she may augment and transmit the creative and plastic forces that find in men perishable, in their institutions and works permanent, forms. And so, as the product of many forces, manifest and subtle, physical, spiritual, and social, working through countless ages, man must be studied in his Becoming that he may be understood as Become. It is with humanity as with a great river, till its source be discovered and the streams and streamlets contributing to its volume numbered and distinguished, the river is a mystery, an unread riddle. And here the whence tells the whither. What lifts but a corner of the veil that conceals our past lets a ray of light fall on our future.

What is here called Comparative Psychology is one of the ways along which our age has been trying to reach a solution to the old problem—How has man become what he is? What forces have civilized him, determined his progress, made him man? It does not so much attempt to reach the source as to understand the conduct and the course of the majestic river whose drops are men. It regards the institutions and industries, literatures and arts, philosophies and religions of the world as phenomena needing to be explained and capable of a rational explanation. It asks, Why have those of Egypt and Greece, Assyria and China, India and England arisen, and been at once so like and so unlike? What was their relation, on the one hand, to man, on the other, to Nature? Our questions thus concern the origin not of man, but of his civilizations, not the creation, but the government of the world.

Yet the two classes of questions run into each other. The discussions concerned with the history of man are but a continuation, on a higher and broader field, of those concerned with his creation.

Comparative Psychology ought to imply, by its very name, that to it the causes of the above specified phenomena are psychical, rational. As mind can alone explain the becoming of the universe, nothing less than mind can explain the course, achievements, and progress of humanity. The reason embodied and particularized in man is expressed in his works. He is their creator, but a creator whose power is limited and whose action is variously conditioned. Nature, by her direct or indirect action, may stimulate or stunt, develop or repress, what she finds in mind, but she must find mind before she can act on it. Physical influences may explain differences in the psychical creations of different peoples and times, but cannot explain the creations themselves, may determine their form, but cannot furnish their matter. Here Nature may be a necessary occasion, but mind is an essential cause. Without the occasion the cause may be inoperative, but without the cause the occasion could not exist, can have no being apart from the activity it supplies with the condition and opportunity for exercise.

There exists at this moment, both in English and continental thought, a strong tendency to exaggerate and exalt the influence of Nature on man and society. The culture of our age is so strongly impregnated with the ideas and principles of physical science, that it can hardly conceive order without necessity, or law without invariable uniformity. The phenomena of mind and thought become, it is imagined, more intelligible when construed from the standpoint of Nature, or in the terms of matter and force. Law and order in history are conceived to involve the dominion of Nature and necessity over society and man. The theory of evolution has given new meaning and force to the brilliant, but unqualified and crude, generalizations of Mr. Buckle, and to the bald and inelastic theory of Dr. Draper.* The continuity of Nature can now be seen to be absolute and universal. The creative process is one throughout, operates along the whole line and in all its divisions, inorganic, organic, and super-organic. Society and civilization rise out of the interactive play of organism and environment; are but the last and most complex results of the great "struggle for existence."

* "History of Civilization in England," vol. i. cc. i. ii. "The Intellectual Development of Europe," vol. i. c. i. Dr. Draper holds strongly "the complete control of physical agents" over man and society; and believes that "the varied aspects he presents in different countries are the necessary consequences of these influences." "The origin, existence, and death of nations depend thus on physical influences, which are themselves the result of immutable laws." And he carries his doctrine so far as to hold that "an empire that lies east and west must be more powerful than one that lies north and south."

Now, we have here to do with only one point, the relation of Nature to the development of man and society. In the problem to be solved, whether is Nature or man the more influential factor? Suppose society does rise out of the interactive play of organism and environment, what is the worth of their respective parts in the interactive play? Organism, it is hardly necessary to note, here signifies no completed mechanical product, or structure capable of various modifications and degrees of growth, but a being full of many and immense potentialities, all struggling to become actual and active. It denotes no mere cluster of absorbent and assimilative vessels, but a centre of creative energies, intellectual, ethical, social, conscious and voluntary in its action. Environment can here mean, not simply climatic and geographical influences, but man, past, present, and to be. The plant is a thing of the soil, the animal the creature of its physical conditions, but man can make his own world, or be it. The more civilized he becomes society has the greater, Nature the less, influence on him. He, indeed, so acts on Nature as in course of time to change her very features and character, to transfigure, to idealize her, to make her the mirror of spirit, the consecrated home of mind. Historic events, heroic deeds, sublimed memories and beliefs, invest mountain, field, and flood with associations sacred to the present because significant of the past. The voices of the gods are heard in the thunders that wander round the brow of Olympos, in the breezes that murmur through the oaks of Dodona. The names of the heroes glorify and immortalize the places where they fought and fell. There shines on Thermopylæ and Salamis, Morgarten and Sempach, a light that never was on sea or shore, creative of "the inspiration and the poet's dream." Nature informed with mind helps to form it, lives in its life, receives that she may give ideas and images of beauty; but alone she is increative. Leave the physical, but change the psychical conditions, and the man is changed. Greece has still her Ionic heaven; her laughing sea, the crystal air through which her sons can lightly trip, but neither to Greek nor Turk does the Periclean age return. The occasion can never be the cause. Mind, not Nature, must explain the purpose and the progress of humanity.

Mind, then, has been the great creative and progressive force in society. With its progress, and because of it, society has progressed. And mind is progressive because free. It can innovate on the old, and initiate the new. Causation does not rule in spirit as in Nature. If it did, the circumstances of the one would change as little and as slowly as the condition of the other. Necessity excludes progress, unless, indeed, it be assumed as the means by which a Supreme Mind fulfils its ends. But then two things will follow, (1) the necessity will be relative, not absolute, in man, not in God, and (2) history will be the articulation of a great theological idea, the revelation of a single mind. It is not without significance that the theology which most strenuously denied human freedom most strenuously asserted the divine. Man was necessitated that the purposes of God might be assured. The infinite Mind freely decreed every event and act as necessary means to effect His final intention, which was the first thing designed, though the last executed. Men existed for the divine ends, and could not but fulfil them.

> ἀλλὰ μάλ' οὔ πως ἔστι Διὸς νόον αἰγιόχοιο
> οὔτε παρεξελθεῖν ἄλλον θεὸν οὔθ' ἁλιῶσαι.

But on this ground history may be theologically, cannot be philosophically, interpreted. If the interpretation is to be philosophical, then the reason and the cause of progress must be sought in the domain of philosophy, in mind. And to deny its freedom is to deny the only rational cause of progress. Where the will is caused the motives make the man, the man does not make the motives. As they find him, they keep him, leave him without the power because without the will to struggle against his destiny. And as the individuals are the generations must be. Each has its character determined by its predecessor, and determines its successor. If "the law of invariable causation holds true of human volitions,"* revolution or reproduction is possible, but not rational progress. The improvement of the race means the improvement of individuals by individual effort, but such effort can only be where there is the power to create new conditions in the heart of the old. The ability of man to control, to command, and to change circumstances, is the measure of his ability to advance, to create higher civilizations above the lower.

But, while man is free, his freedom is conditional. While motives do not necessitate our choices they are necessary to choice. A reasonable being can never act

---

* Mr. Mill, "Logic," vol. ii. p. 532. Mr. Mill imagined, incorrectly, I think, that unless "the doctrine of the causation of human actions was true," no science of history was possible. But he also saw that, were necessity absolute, progress were inexplicable, and fatalism inevitable. So he tried to lighten his doctrine of necessity in two ways, by reducing the idea of causation to "invariable, certain, and unconditional sequence" (*ib.* p. 423), and by allowing that man had to a certain extent power to alter his character (*ib.* 426). The first qualification served him but little. The causation was as absolute as Mr. Mill could allow anything to be. If a volition be "the invariable, certain, and unconditional" sequent of the strongest motive, it can only be because no other sequent is possible. But if no other sequent is possible, the actual must be a necessary sequent. The necessity which leaves us without choice is as absolute as the necessity which should overpower it. As to the second qualification, it had been much more important had it been consistently developed and applied, for then it would have modified Mr. Mill's position throughout. He says, "If they (the persons who formed our characters) could place us under the influence of certain circumstances, we, in like manner, can place ourselves under the influence of other circumstances. We are exactly as capable of making our own character, *if*

without a reason, but the reason can only be the condition and ground of his action,—he himself remains its cause. He selects the motive; the motive does not select him. His freedom is thus rational, not arbitrary, the freedom of a being both intelligent and moral. Then the motives, which are the occasions of his choices, are ever inviting and urging him to action; and as the occasions multiply the choices increase. Circumstances and the motives they supply have thus a great part to play in

we will, as others are of making it for us" (*ib.* p. 426). Hardly as capable, for, according to Mr. Mill, the two great factors of our volitions and actions are motives and the character and disposition. But before the character becomes a *factor*, it is *factus*, and the forces active in the process determine the product. If, then, we conceive the *factor* as first *factus*, it is clear that it cannot have, as made, as much power to make or re-make itself as the forces had which made it. The making is too nearly done before our wills can count for anything in the matter. But, again, the phrase, italicized by Mr. Mill, *if we will*, suggests the questions, What does *will* here mean ? Is it the synonyme of wish, desire, &c., or of choose ? Mr. Mill explained it as a wish or feeling formed for us by our experience, "experience of the painful consequences of the character we previously had ; or by some strong feeling of admiration or aspiration accidentally aroused." But the wish or desire is itself a sequent, the creature of experience, and so falls under the law of causation. To make the power to change dependent on the wish so formed is to deny that the will is any real power at all. The source of Mr. Mill's confused and imperfect argument was his false psychology. Will and wish, choice and desire, radically differ. Where they are identified, necessity is logically inevitable. Our desires are necessitated, but not our volitions. We may wish to modify our characters, and yet not choose to do it; but we can modify them if we choose. If the ability is made dependent on a wish which is necessitated, the ability is also necessitated, and the power conceded in word *is* in fact denied.

Q

human progress. Without them will could as little act as they without will could cause man to improve. Now, motives are of two kinds, real and ideal,—the real are the material, the sensuous, those created by the necessity of living and maintaining life; the ideal are the spiritual, the intellectual, those formed by the higher creations and aspirations of mind. In the earlier stages of civilization, the real, but in the later the ideal, are the more numerous and powerful. The struggle with the real necessities develop the ideal faculties, with their appropriate conditions; and as these are developed mind and society grow more complex, humane, universal. Ideal motives are either those of the heart, of the imagination, of the intellect, or of the conscience. Those of the heart come first. Home is loved. The parent becomes dear to the child, because the child has been dear to the parent. Brothers and sisters have been as playmates sources of joy, and so become objects of affection. Then the place where the home stands grows dear, the less depending for its being on the greater. And so the ideals of the heart are developed, home and country, father and fatherland, and whatever is necessary to their being and wellbeing, is loyally loved and revered. Then the ideals of the imagination are born. The loved is the glorified. Poetry, architecture, sculpture, painting, come to exalt and embalm sacred and gladsome memories. But the intellect grows curious, inquiring, asks after our Whence, our Whither, creates its ideal, the true, to stand beside the good, and the beautiful, the ideals of the heart and the imagination. But the life grows perplexing as it grows complex. The mind cannot always see clearly the path it ought to follow; and so has to inquire, What is the dutiful, the right? And the answer is the ideal of the conscience, virtue, righteousness. But though thus distinguished in thought they blend in reality. Patriotism, art, philosophy, religion, are objects the mind can study apart, but that subtly mingle in the minds that give them being and feel their influence. Religion penetrates patriotism, art, and philosophy; and art exalts the god while it glorifies the hero. Once his ideals have been created, man has become conscious mind, and discovered his affinities with the imperishable and universal, the spiritual and the divine.

But these two elements, freedom and the influence of ideals, explain one of the mightiest dynamic forces in society, the great man. The one explains his personality, the other his influence. Human freedom makes the great man possible; the ideals enable him to become an active and ubiquitous power. By his voluntary energy he can assert his individuality, control and change circumstances; by the forms his activity assumes he can shape or guide minds that are or are to be. Hero-worship is but a bad species of idolatry, heroes not being made for worship, but for the works that make and mark the ages. Persons are powers; great personalities are great creators. The lawgiver, like Moses or Solon, turns a struggling tribe or straggling city into a state, educes and educates the public conscience, lives throughout the centuries an active ethical and political power. The poet, like Homer or Chaucer, is not only the maker of a poem, but the father of a literature, influencing its whole course. The sculptor like Pheidias, or the painter like Raphael, wins by his genius dominion over the ages, creates not only objects of beauty, but ideals that form artists, preserve, develop, and perfect art. Individuals like Alexander or Cæsar have at critical moments determined the course of history. Our religions mostly run back into persons; those with the most distinctly personal source are the most powerful. Christianity had been impossible without Christ, and without Him could not live a single day. Buddhism is built on Buddha, owes to him its missionary successes and its ethical excellences. Islam had never been but for Mahomet, and to this day the Prophet is as necessary to the faith as his God. Without Confucius, China had been without a native religion; and the Parsee maintains a worship as ancient as Zoroaster. The world's great forces have thus been its great men. And they were great because they possessed, in the highest degree, free and creative activities. They may have incarnated what is called the spirit of their age or nation, but they did much more, became creators of a new order, did not remain simply creatures of the old. Historical analysis may discover many circumstances that constituted their opportunity, but cannot discover the circumstances that constituted their greatness. They were great by virtue of the indefeasible right given by genius, supreme because free, power sufficient to a work of everlasting significance. But to be so great is to have a will, a cause, not caused, the master, not the child, of circumstances.*

Comparative Psychology, then, regards the history of man as the history of mind, seeks by a Science of Mind to lay the basis for a Science of History. But it does not study the individual mind by itself and alone, That is the work of Psychology proper. Comparative Psychology is the psychology of peoples. Its aim is to explain the action of mind in the mass, to discover the distinctive mental qualities of different or related peoples, their rise, their causes, the laws and conditions of their development, their influence on society and history, national and universal. It does not seek to

* Mr. Mill has ("Logic," vol. ii. pp. 537 ff.) a very eloquent paragraph on the influence of great men on social progress. His opinions on the matter are in some respects very just, but involve more than he allowed to appear. He thinks "the volitions of exceptional persons may be indispensable links in the chain of causation by which even the general causes produce their effects." But what of the "exceptional persons" themselves. They are "exceptional" by virtue of their volitions; but how can the law of "invariable, certain and unconditional sequence" explain so extraordinary a result?

supersede the science of the individual mind, but assumes it, builds on its data, and applies its principles. Mind is everywhere akin, but kinship does not exclude difference. Psychology proper is concerned with what is essential, mind in the abstract, the universal, as it were, in the individual; but Comparative Psychology is concerned with what seems accidental, mind in the concrete, acting under the influence of place and time within a state or society, and embodying its action in works that are not so much individual as common and collective.

The science so named has thus a province, distinct, well defined, vast. It is a province, too, full of the most promising results. Until it be annexed to that of Psychology proper the science of mind must remain incomplete. Every man is not simply an individual, but a conscious and active atom in an immense organism. He is born into a society which gives to him before he can give to it; and its gifts are more than educative processes, are faculties that can be educated. A nation is an organic, not an artificial, unity, has a sort of corporate being. Inherited capacities which spring from a common descent, collective tendencies which flow from kindred natures formed under the same institutions, and existing under similar physical and geographical conditions, give to a homogeneous people a species of colossal individuality. The great men it produces are, as a rule, great after the distinctive genius of their race. The priest is characteristic of some nations, the soldier of others. In one land the prophet, in another the poet, is the great man. The Greeks had their Homer, the Hebrews their Moses. The Egyptians built temples, the Romans amphitheatres. The Phœnicians were merchants, the Assyrians conquerors. And this distinctive genius is ever and again concentrated in man or event, and thus quickened and sent forward with augmented volume in a deepened channel.

Now, this unity of character in a nation is the result of unity of mind, mental qualities possessed and mental processes performed in common. Where many minds live a kind of corporate existence they are certain to accomplish much that is at once individual and collective, work carried on by the units, but instituted and completed by the mass. Every day actions are performed by the whole, because by each of the conscious and voluntary persons composing it; yet, though the persons are conscious and voluntary, the products of their collective action are seldom the fruits of counsel and design. Indeed, the grandest structures of the world are structures that, like our languages and mythologies, have been built by builders that did not know they were building, or the glory of their work. And though no master mind conceived the design and secured unity in the workers who toiled at the strong foundation, or massive pillars, or stately dome, or tapering spire, or delicate tracery, yet the harmony has been more perfect than the genius of a Pheidias could give to the sculptures of the Parthenon, or an Angelo to St. Peter's. Humanity has been the great poet, the unconscious maker, and the creations of her blind Muse are more splendid than any epic, lyric, or tragedy, made by the consciously creative effort of " fancy's sweetest child." The undesigned is not always the accidental; where there is unity of mind evoked and exercised by common needs, interests, associations, and aims, there can hardly fail to be unity in its common work.

Now, these unconscious creations of the collective mind best reveal its distinctive qualities. What results from the voluntary efforts of so many conscious persons unconsciously combining to a common end, is certain to exhibit, in clear and distinct lines, their deepest idiosyncrasies, the finest aptitudes and capabilities of their spirit. Hence Comparative Psychology, in seeking to know the mind of a people, must study its most common, though, perhaps, least consciously designed, psychical creations. These enable it to regard the people as a unit, a subject possessed of qualities that can be analyzed and described.* Lan-

---

* "Zeitschrift für Völkerpsychologie und Sprachwissenschaft," vol. i. p. 28. In this Journal there are several papers of great worth to the comparative psychologist. While in some respects fundamentally differing

guage becomes to it embodied spirit, externalized and eternalized thought, the λόγος προφορικός, which shows the λόγος ἐνδιάθετος either potent and well-proportioned, able by delicate inflexional arts to weave its ideas into forms at once musical and variously significant and suggestive, or impotent and ill-balanced, able only to express its mind in rugged and unjointed speech. In mythology our science sees how a people, while still in its wondering and imaginative childhood, conceived Nature and man, articulated its thoughts of this mysterious, changing, yet permanent, universe, of the rising and the setting sun, of the living air, of the round ocean, now sleeping in calm radiance, now breaking into multitudinous laughter, now waking into thundrous music, and how those crude but glorious fancies were slowly sublimated into the beautiful forms of conscious poetry and the abstract theories of metaphysics. But these undesigned, yet not accidental, creations, are not alone incorporative of the collective mind; it exists no less in cases where the mental action may seem more conscious and individual. The polity which guards and defines the idea of the state and the person, his rights and his duties; the art which in its massive or graceful, beautiful or hideous forms incarnates the national taste; the industries by which the people

from the editors, Professors Lazarus and Steinthal, I wish to record in a general way my obligations to their Journal, and especially their own contributions to it.

lives, and which it either honours or despises; the manners and customs which declare its moral judgments and temper; the family life, the authority conferred on the husband, the place conceded to the wife; great personalities, the representative men that are in thought and action the vehicles of its governing ideas,—are all so many points through which we can approach our object—mind as it lives and acts in a nation or people. Only as the object is known can it be so studied as to be interpreted.

The object of Comparative is thus much more complex and vast than that of simple Psychology; and its methods are necessarily more indirect and intricate. It cannot interrogate consciousness, can only discover the mental qualities of its object by an analysis of its mental products. Its method has to be both historical and comparative. As historical it seeks to know the people, its institutions, arts, beliefs, speculations in philosophy and achievements in literature. As comparative, it examines the similarities and dissimilarities of different peoples, and of the same people at the various stages of its development and decay. It must be historical to get face to face with the facts, and must be comparative to discover their causes, meaning and tendency. Society evolves with the evolution of mind, and unless the evolution can be historically traced it cannot be scientifically explained. Existing peoples, savage as little as civilized, can be used as types or models of primitive.

Mr. Herbert Spencer's primitive man, physical, emotional, intellectual, is a purely imaginary being. He is built up by an inductive, but built upon a deductive, process. His deduction is by no means unassailable either as to principles or method, but we are not concerned with it meanwhile, only with the induction. And how does it proceed? Whence come the facts inducted? Mr. Spencer says,* "We must be content to fill out our general conception of primitive man, so far as we may, by studying those existing races of men, which, as judged by their physical characters and their implements, approach most nearly to primitive man." And as these races present him with a most bewildering multitude of differences, he has to select from these the features he considers primitive. And what is the principle of selection? "To conceive the primitive man as he existed when social aggregation commenced, we must generalize as well as we can this entangled and partially conflicting evidence (of the differences between the various savage races); led mainly by the traits common to the very lowest, and finding what guidance we may in the *à priori* conclusions set down above." †

Now, the method is bad, most unscientific, and the principle of selection is worse. The savage races are as old as the civilized, as distant, therefore, from primitive man. Change, too, has been as busy in them as in us— perhaps, busier. Their customs are less persistent, their

* "Principles of Sociology," p. 43.   † Ib., p. 62.

memories shorter, their past far less extended and powerful. The most distinctive features of the primitive man are exactly those least discoverable in the savage. His energy, his resolution, his inventiveness, his capacity for progress and discovery. The implements may be the same, but the skill is not. The physical characters may be alike, but what of the mental? If alike, how does the savage after so many ages happen to be savage, while we are civilized? Then, why select the traits common to the very lowest as the most primitive? Do the inferior members of a species best preserve the features of the primitive type? Does palæontology "fill out its conception" of an extinct plant or animal by combining the traits common to the members of the lowest and most degenerate species within the genus to which it belonged? Palæontology is one thing; zoology or botany another. If the development of life on the earth is to be studied, it must be through the once living forms preserved in its successive strata, not through the lowest and most degenerate forms of vegetable and animal life now on its surface. So if the growth of mind and the progress of man are to be understood, it must be by the method of palæontology—the comparative study of the peoples in the past who have made our present.

Such being the method of Comparative Psychology, it is evident that it must stand in the most intimate relations to the other Comparative Sciences concerned with the history of man. Comparative Philology seeks to discover the similarities and dissimilarities of cognate languages, to find out the words or roots of the mother tongue, to determine the laws of literal and structural change in the several dialects, so to analyze speech into its primitive elements as to exhibit the principles of its growth and decay. Comparative Mythology brings together the earliest lore and legends of related families, ascertains their coincidences and differences, aims at discovering their common element and determining by what process primitive belief grew into such varied and fantastic forms. Comparative Politics, to adopt Mr. Freeman's name, attempts to find out the rudimentary social organism of related peoples, and to trace thence the evolution of the many cognate but most divergent politics. Comparative Jurisprudence, in Sir Henry Maine's sense, studies the most ancient laws of kindred peoples, and the village communities of east and west, so as to discover the earlier modes in which the individual, the family, and the village or state, were related to each other, how property was held, the idea of legal right arose and law emerged. Now, Comparative Psychology employs the material supplied by these Comparative Sciences, using, too, though cautiously, such cognate sources as ethnography and anthropology, to get as near as possible to primæval man, to watch the origin of his ideas, their relation to, their action on, each other and on him, their growth, transmutation, dissolution, and re-combination under the influences exercised by changes of place, mode of life and social constitution. For peoples may not only vary from the original family type, but may branch into nations that move along the most divergent lines. Slips from the same stock may under dissimilar conditions grow into most dissimilar trees. The Hindu carried into India, the Teuton brought into Western Europe, similar types of the social state; but in India a caste system, iron, inflexible, hateful, has grown up, while in Western Europe society allows freedom of intercourse, an imperceptible blending of class into class, accords equal rights to citizens, equal worth to men. The Greek and the Slav possibly entered Europe together, though they soon parted, the one turning his face to the sunny south and its glorious sea, the other to the cold and barren north; but while the Greek centuries since began and ended the most joyous, brightest, and briefest career any people has known, the Slav is only now waking from his long sleep into a vast and terrible power. The warlike Assyrian and the commercial Phœnician, the nomadic Arab, the wandering child of the desert, and the modern Jew, truest child of the exchange, are sons of a common father and once dwelt in a common tent. Now, why these differences? What created these varieties of mind and history? And what worth have they possessed, do they still possess, for the world? If the comparative study of mind and its creations can bring us within sight of the answer to these questions, it will lead us nearer the immediate presence of the old and invincible problems, What is the meaning of man, of history? Whence, O Heaven! Whither? Does law or chance, order or accident, mind or mechanism, rule in the world? How do the earliest men and nations stand related to the latest? Did they come aimless and vanish trackless? or do they survive in us and find there the reward of their works?

Many questions in science and philosophy lie at this moment hot beneath the feet. But we must pass over the burning and blistering ground as softly and silently as possible. We must be innocently oblivious that—

$$\epsilon\pi\grave{\iota}\ \tilde{\epsilon}\theta\nu\epsilon'\ \dot{\alpha}\gamma\epsilon\acute{\iota}\rho\epsilon\tau o\ \mu\upsilon\rho\acute{\iota}\alpha\ \nu\epsilon\kappa\rho\hat{\omega}\nu$$
$$\dot{\eta}\chi\hat{\eta}\ \theta\epsilon\sigma\pi\epsilon\sigma\acute{\iota}\eta,$$

and, without word or nod of recognition, pass the ghosts of Kant and Herder, Buckle and Comte, Schelling and Hegel, Cousin and Guizot, Krause and Bunsen, fearful lest by the smell or taste of the blood sure to be shed in controversy they should grow so substantial as to forbid further search. Enough to say, it is here assumed that no Philosophy of History is possible without a patient and sufficient study of the facts and phenomena of mind, individual and collective. Speculation must build on the solid rock of reality if it is to build into heaven and for eternity. Man must be known before his being can be understood, or the laws that have governed his development formulated. So far as the Philosophy of History seeks to explain the becoming of civilization, or the past of man, Comparative Psychology helps it in two ways, by discovering the causes and conditions that created the distinct civilizations in the various ages and countries of the world; and by supplying the data that can determine the influence they respectively exercised on the progress of humanity, the value, number, and quality of the elements they severally contributed to the civilization, modern and permanent. For the nation exists for the race, as the individual for the nation. The best work of the unit is universal, lives longer and does more than its author designed. Genius, when it speaks the true in forms that are beautiful, speaks not to its own age and people simply, but to all peoples and times. And the nation that achieves a victory over barbarism, or ignorance, or wrong achieves it for the world. In solving the great problem humanity has been set to work out, every people with a history has had a share. None have lived or died in vain. If, indeed, in the life of humanity, as in our competitive examinations, many had fought, but only one had won, what should we say? That the unsuccessful had been useless competitors? or that it was better for them to fight and lose than never to win the skill and weapons necessary for the contest? If the many, whose non-success was no failure, not only contributed to the magnificence of the battle and the splendour of the victory, but made themselves in the struggle better than they otherwise could have been, shall we not say that as their being was good the conflict that so served it was not ill? And here the victory belongs to the many, not to the one. Whatever principle of order a people conquers, the conquest becomes in the long run that of the race. If history means progress, there has been in it, perhaps, many blunders, and follies, and crimes, but yet, in spite of all, victory for humanity. Civilization as it rises universalizes, and as it becomes universal unifies man, lifts the race to a higher level. When we look to the past man's progress seems marked only by the grave-yard, buried cities, fallen empires, civilizations decayed and dead. Of once wise and busy Egypt only broken water-courses, imperishable pyramids, waste temples and tombs survive. On the banks of the Euphrates and her sister stream, where once famed armies marched, are now only the shapeless and melancholy mounds, which have been made but of late to tell the story of the splendour and decadence of the empires whose sites they mark. Phœnicia, once Queen of the seas, is desolate, and her industrial, commercial, and colonizing genius gone down for ever. Greece, the beautiful, the land that sanctified by idealizing humanity; Rome, the once universal Mistress, the once Eternal City, of the world, are but names, loved, visited, studied for the memories they preserve, the shadows of the glorious past that sleep in their valleys and

R

on their hills. Does it not seem as if Nature, as careless of men and peoples as of "the fifty seeds," of which

> "She brings but one to bear,"

cried to us from the past,

> "I care for nothing, all shall go"?

But the carelessness is only in our eyes, not in her hands or heart. The less perfect dies that the more perfect may live. In man, as in nature, except the one die, it abideth alone; if it die, it bringeth forth much fruit. The conquests of humanity are permanent. As the mother-speech of our family died that her daughters might be born, died that she might impart herself equally to each, and descend into her remotest posterity, so the ancient civilizations died, that their ideal elements, universalized and immortalized, might build up and be built into the modern. The narrow spirit that in ancient Hellas divided men into Greeks and barbarians perished, but her bright genius lives and speaks in the language and art, the poetry and philosophy that must be beautiful for evermore. The ambition, the brutal pleasures, the exhausting exactions of Rome are buried under the ruins of her cities; but the sense of law, of order, of unity, she created has passed from expediency and policy into the very blood of our highest religious and philosophical thought. So men die that man may live; peoples perish that humanity may endure.

II.

Our discussion has tended to show the necessity of Comparative Psychology to the Philosophy of History. Our purpose can now be better served by an attempt to apply to history its principles and method. All that is possible is to present the subject in hurried and imperfect outline, but the outline may be meanwhile more significant than a more abstract and abstruse discussion.

What is intended is, by the analysis and exhibition, in forms more or less concrete, of their psychical qualities and capacities, to indicate the place and work in universal history of two great races, the Indo-European and Semitic. These qualities and capacities fitted each of the races for the part it has played in the development of man. Ever modifying, yet ever modified by, the rise of new conditions or changes in the old, weakened, or intensified by the generation of new forces, intellectual and religious, or the formation of new relations, social and political, they have never failed, at decisive moments, to embody themselves in distinctive acts, events, or works. The races form, therefore, a field where Comparative Psychology can be well enough tested alike as to principles, method, and results.

The Indo-European and Semitic races are two distinct families that have branched into many nations, and spread over a great portion of the earth's surface. The first extends north-westward from India, runs through Persia into Europe, includes almost all its peoples, excludes only such early Europeans as the Basques in the south-west, the Lapps and Finns in the north, and such recent invaders as the Huns and the Turks in the east. The second race had its ancient homes in the Mesopotamian valley, Syria, Canaan, Arabia, Æthiopia, and has more than once formed a fringe, here and there indeed pierced and patched by alien peoples, along the southern seaboard of the Mediterranean from Syria to the Atlantic. It embraces such peoples, ancient and modern, as the Assyrians, the Phœnicians, the Hebrews, and the Arabians. Each family has its unity sufficiently well established. Evidence of it need not be here adduced. It is conclusive enough to warrant us in assuming that the various branches of the above races are respectively branches of a common stock.

The names Indo-European and Semitic are unfortunately hopelessly incorrect. The first is geographical, the second genealogical, and neither is sufficiently either descriptive or comprehensive. The peoples named Indo-European have long since overflowed the limits of both India and Europe, and nations, like the Phœnician, though not reckoned sons of Sem, are yet Semitic. Indo-Germanic and Aryan are common but improper equivalents of Indo-European. Aryan is the proper name of the united Hindu and Iranian branches, and ought to be so limited and applied; Indo-Germanic leaves out peoples so important as the Slavs and Gauls, Italians and Greeks. Syro-Arabian has been proposed as a substitute for Semitic, but as it does not include certain main and subordinate branches, especially in Africa, it would be as incorrect as the term it seeks to supersede. Change is now, perhaps, hardly possible; the wrong must here be allowed to do the office of the right.

These races have furnished the most civilized and the most civilizing peoples of history. It is hardly too much to say that their history is the higher history of humanity. Were they subtracted, it would be the play without either Hamlet or Ophelia. They give to it unity, progress, purpose. Yet they stand related to each other as contrasts, often conflicting, but always complemental, helping humanity onward by the blending of their opposites, creating institutions and events, ideas and influences, that, imperfect in their isolation and independence, become by contact and combination increasingly perfect. The Semite has excelled as the creator of great propulsive forces, which he has relieved in crude but powerful forms; the Indo-European has been pre-eminent in the genius that could appropriate the new without losing the old, that could so interweave varied and dissimilar elements in his personal and social life as to give increasing variety and progress to both. To the Semite we owe the creation of commerce and maritime navigation, the diffusion of the alphabet, the Hebrew Scriptures, the Hebrew religion;

Christianity, the Mahommedanism that through the Moors in the West and the Turks in the East did so much to create the dawn that has broken into our modern day; to the Indo-European we owe the perfecting and permanence of the creative forces and ideas which had found in these great movements their vehicles, their victorious working out in all the regions of individual and collective life, in science and art, industry and commerce, polity and ethics, religion and philosophy. The Semite, unprogressive, though inventive, has soon exhausted his discovery and the enthusiasm it had awakened, but the Indo-European has made his inventions and acquisitions but deepen his resources and accelerate the march of his mind. The Semite has been intense but narrow, exclusive, limited in the range of his sympathies, violently hostile to every foreign influence that did not appeal to them; but the Indo-European, while of a stronger, has been of a sweeter and purer spirit, susceptible, assimilative, with force enough to naturalize and govern aliens coming to him from many lands. The great Semitic nations have been great along single lines, excelling in one thing, in commerce like the Phœnicians, religion like the Hebrews, war like the Arabs; but the great Indo-European peoples have excelled in many lines, in war and art, in thought and action, in religion and industries. These differences are not imaginary, but real, stand expressed in the achievements and fortunes of the two races. Minds produce fruit each after its kind, and kind is here co-extensive with kin.

The peculiar temptation of the comparative psychologist is to treat races like individuals, draw their characters with too great breadth of line, strength of colour, minuteness of detail.* Peoples are not persons. The most outstanding branches of the two races may be so interlaced as to be branches common to both, peculiar to neither; but interwound branches do not make two trunks one tree, especially where the trees differ as do the oak and the birch. Culture can never smooth into similarity minds so unlike as those of Shakspere and Milton, Goethe and Schiller, can only bring them to the polish and perfection needed in the creators of a perfect and varied literature. And so the course, the commerce, and the collisions of history do not abolish psychical types so distinct as the Indo-European

* It is as easy to exaggerate as to ignore racial peculiarities. Imaginary portraits are easily drawn, especially when the draughtsman has an imagination that commands his scholarship. M. Renan has painted the characteristic features of the two races in great detail, with remarkable brilliancy of colour, skill in grouping, sharpness of line and figure (" Histoire Génér. et Syst. Comp. des Langues Sémitiques," liv. i. ch. i.; liv. v. ch. ii. § vi. Also " Nouvel. Considérations sur le Caractère Génér. des Peup. Sémit.," "Journal Asiat.," xiii. 5th series, pp. 214-282 ; 417-460). But the picture is one of the imagination, represents only the brilliant scholar's own ideal ; and serves first as a vivid introduction, next as a graphic conclusion to a grave philological work. The late Professor Lassen, of Bonn, has sketched the races with much greater caution, truth, and masterliness, though at much shorter length. ("Indis. Alterthumsk.,"vol. i. pp. 494-497, 2nd ed.). Professor Spiegel, of Erlangen, less distinctly and in an almost purely imitative manner (" Erânische Alterthumsk.," vol. i. pp. 387-391).

and Semitic, only stimulate both to new enterprises and more perfect achievements. Our concern is not with the interlacing, but with the principal branches, standing out clear and strong from the parent stocks, and marked by their well-defined characters. What these are may be best seen by a study of the Races in Civilization, in Religion, and in Literature and Philosophy.

PART II.

THE RACES IN CIVILIZATION.

I.

CIVILIZATION is too complex a fact to be easily analyzed or described. As a term it denotes the degree of perfection realized, in its collective and organized life, by a given society or state. As a fact it is not the progress of humanity, but the point this progress has reached in a given community; and this point as the blossom of past, but as the seed-plot of future progress. Were it perfect we should have perfect citizens in a perfect state. The more civilized a state is the more will it endeavour to perfect all its citizens; the more perfect the citizens the more civilized will be the state. A society can never be better than its constituent members. One highly cultured class in a state does not make it highly civilized. Its civilization is determined both as to quality and degree by the extent to which it creates and distributes the conditions of social wellbeing, and the measure in which it secures their realization by the individual and the community. Civilization is to a state what culture is to a person, the harmony in being and action of the whole nature, the elaboration of the social organism into balanced and beautiful being by the full development of every social unit. There are as many varieties and degrees of civilization as of culture, but the one term like the other connotes an ideal element whose affinities are with the good and progressive rather than with the bad and decaying.*

The civilization of a given people and period stands expressed in the higher and more vital forms and forces of their social and national life. The forms—the laws, institutions, customs, wealth, arts—exhibit the good already achieved and realized; the forces are the ideal tendencies and aims that struggle in the persons and through the forms to still better things. What civilizes must humanize—create throughout the society a fuller manhood. If the civilized stands opposed to the savage state, every vice is a tendency to revert, a de-civilizing influence, alien, however apparently inevitable.

* Guizot's analysis of the idea and elements of civilization is well known to every student of history ("Hist. de la Civilisation en Europe," Prem. Leçon). Professor Flint's criticism ("Philos. of Hist." i. 233, 234) is searching, and in many respects just. It would equally apply to what is here said were not the reference to the idea of civilization rather than the fact.

Modern civilization stands related to ancient as its heir, but as an heir who must, to retain his estate, enlarge it, improve its fields, utilize its watercourses, dig out its minerals, ameliorate its homes, and throng its rivers with cities, that instead of polluting shall purify the waters, instead of defacing shall beautify the land. Modern is more complex, many-sided, universal than ancient civilization, has in it more elements of progress and permanence, more seeds of degeneracy and decay. The older the state the simpler the society, the earliest social structures being the most rudimentary. Egypt was a sacerdotal state, a kingdom which stiffened and died because it could not escape from the iron hand of caste. Phœnicia existed for and by commerce—its very religion was made to minister to trade. Assyria was a political state, but its laws were summarized in the king. The civilizations that succeeded these were more complex, made up of a greater variety of elements, partly native, partly foreign. Assyria was as ambitious as Persia, but the latter had a clearer idea of empire, of the relation the conquered countries ought to sustain to the conqueror. Greece was as commercial as Phœnicia, drove, indeed, her merchants from the Ægean and the Nile, but the mercantile was an element too little determinative to be distinctive of Greek culture. Into our own many past civilizations have been absorbed, and it has by the absorption been variously enriched. Our political constitution is a splendid, though complex, expansion of the old Teutonic norm. Our laws, judicial and civil, show everywhere the influence of Rome. Our literature, art, and philosophy are permeated with Greek ideals and ideas. Our religion has come to us from Judæa, but from Judæa as interpreted on the intellectual side by Greece, on the political by Rome. And these elements, while mixed in the great crucible of our collective being, are singly active, affecting every phase of our personal, social, and political life.

But modern civilization, as compared with ancient, is more universal as well as more complex. Our world has grown vaster, but it has also grown more accessible in all its parts. Distance does not now divide. Commerce has made east and west, north and south meet. Much as our telegraph would have surprised a Greek, what it signifies as to the relations of men and peoples would have surprised him still more. He might have been amazed at reading in the morning a debate he had heard overnight, and been still more amazed to know that it could at the same moment be read at what remains of his own Athens, and in lands he never dreamed of beyond the sea. But what would have amazed him most is the unity of interests, the affinities of feeling, the sympathies of thought and action between distant and different peoples such swift and ceaseless intercourse implies. The merchant seeks and finds a market everywhere. Everywhere the statesman sees a people with whom he has or ought to have relations, the student of nature or man an object he ought to study, the missionary a race he ought to evangelize. Thought and wealth circulate round the world. The ancient spirit was national, the modern is cosmopolitan. Where the idea of the state once stood the idea of humanity now stands. The influence of the present is thus becoming in every society so potent as to modify the influence of the past, and combine with it in shaping the future. And so our civilization, by what it consciously assimilates, as by what it unconciously inherits, is being made ever fuller, more varied and resourceful, less local as to position, more universal as to character.

And the individual grows with the society. Our culture is as varied, complex, manifold as our civilization. Its wealth does not burden the spirit, or its volume overflow the channel time has worn in it. Education is not so simple now as it was in ancient Greece, yet it is not, perhaps, any more difficult. The Dikaios Logos might despair of our youth who, though often familiar with the training ground, are not to be satisfied with the school of the harper and the ballads in praise of Pallas. His indeed was a glorious picture of the young man in his fresh and dewy spring-time, winsomely beautiful, gracefully exercising his energies as he ran with his comrade amid the sacred olive-trees of the academy, "crowned with white reeds, smelling of bindweed and careless hours and leaf-shedding poplar, rejoicing in the prime of spring, when the plane-tree whispers to the elm."* But, though there may be less grace there is more grandeur in our ideal of youth, making by hard work, which yet does not forbid bright play, the man that is to be. Our spirits may be without the open sense for the beautiful which made life in their land and under their sky so delightsome to the Greeks, but our world is a greater wonderland than theirs, our makrokosm is more immense, our mikrokosm more inexhaustible. The stars in heaven about the moon may look no more beautiful to us than they did to Homer, but they have a mightier meaning, speak to our imagination as they could not speak to his. Our nature may have less music, but it has more mystery, touches the spirit with a deeper and softer awe. Our earth has grown to us so old that its age has made our time widen into eternity. The very language we speak has its terms packed with the science of many ages and the wisdom born of many experiences. "Gravitation" is but a word, yet to learn it is to possess not only the great thought of Newton, but the many discoveries that made it possible. "God" does not simply translate the Hebrew *Elohim*, the Greek Θεός, or the Teutonic *Gutha*, but represents to us a Being in whom the might the

* Aristophanes, "Nubes," 989—995. See the beautiful paragraph in Mr. Symonds' "Studies of the Greek Poets," pp. 267—69, 1st series.

Hebrew adored, the beauty the Greek loved, and the paternity the Teuton revered, are unified, sublimed, and personalized. The vehicle has deepened with the thought it bears, yet has become no harder to acquire and carry. And the spirit which finds so much in its own speech can find as much in others. Greek has told to us more of its secrets, its parts, its roots, the past it embalms, than ever it told to Sokrates or Plato, subtle master as he was of its music. Everywhere has a deeper meaning come into Nature, and mind now sits in the shadow of immenser mysteries, now rejoices in the sunshine of a more glorious light. Yet with all it has to learn and to bear, the spirit of to-day may be as bright and gladsome as any that ever recited the measures of Homer or the wisdom of Hesiod ere sophists had begun to trouble or philosophers to teach. So does the individual grow with the society, less encumbered by a rich and varied than by a poor and narrow culture.

Now, the becoming of the civilization which has so enriched both the society and the individual is what we have here to understand. It is here regarded as a creation of man, the fruit of energies experience has educed, not created. It has, indeed, been a cause as well as an effect, has helped to develop the nature that developed it. The action has been reciprocal, the creation has educated the creator. But he has been the active and causal force, it the passive and occasional. The variety of the elements in civilization is thus due to the variety of the creative capabilities in man. It is at once the mirror and the fruit of mind. And as the minds concerned in its making were many, and were variously gifted and endowed, their qualities are reflected and reproduced in their work. Hence the creators must explain the creation, the peoples that have civilized the civilization they have made. These, then, must first be understood.

II.

As our work must be historical, while analytical, we must begin by attempting to form as clear and coherent a picture as is possible of the two races as they existed in what is the nearest point we can reach to the primitive and simply potential state. Our light is of the dim, but not altogether uncertain, sort supplied by Comparative Philology and Mythology; but such as it is, we must do our best to see by it. We begin with the Indo-Europeans.*

Centuries before the dawn of history, how many we need not attempt to guess, there lived in central and western

* The materials used in the following sketch of the pre-historic Indo-European civilization are derived from Max Müller's Essay on Comparative Mythology, "Chips," vol. ii.; Pictet's "Les Origines des Indo-Européennes," a most interesting work, but not too trustworthy; Fick's "Vergleichendes Wörterbuch der Indo-Germanischen Sprachen," and "Die Ehemalige Spracheinheit der Indo-Germanen Europas." My obligations are greatest to Fick. A very useful and readable essay on the same subject appears in the volume of Essays and Addresses by Professors of Owen's College—"Some Historical Results of the Science of Language," by Professor A. S. Wilkins.

Asia a tribe or clan still nomadic, yet not altogether without the rude beginnings of agriculture. They had a language rich in words and inflections, old enough to have lost and won much by the processes that have been termed phonetic decay and dialectical regeneration. Though without cities, they had what may be called a civilization, rudimentary indeed, but with rudiments plastic, expansive, generous. The man was named *vīra*, the desirer, the being laden with the instincts that made home and created society, and became in defence of the home he had made the strong, the hero. The woman was *ganā* and *gāni*, the fruitful, the childbearer. The man who had become a husband was *pati*, master, lord; the woman who was his wife was *patniā*, mistress, lady—through marriage the one realized manhood, the other womanhood, wife never being in the common speech of our family the synonyme of domestic slave. The man become a father was *pātar*, protector, provider; the woman become a mother was *mātar*, the measurer, the manager, who ruled home and distributed to old and young the food she cooked. The children were to the parents, the son *sūna*, the begetter, not the begotten, named from what he was to be, not from what he was; and the daughter *dhughtar*, the milker, so named, not because she was the primitive dairymaid, but because she was to be a giver of milk, a full-breasted nurse. To each other the children were not man and woman, or still worse, husband and wife, but *bhrātār*, brother, sustainer, defender,

s

at once winner of bread and guardian of the home treasures, and *svasar*, sister, one's own, the pre-eminently mine, child and light of the home. When marriage came to create new relations the daughter-in-law was *sunu-sā*, the son-ess, with as good a standing in the family as her husband, yet though a young wife, not a mistress, the father-in-law being *svasura*, my master, the mother-in-law *svasru*, my mistress. The grandchild was *napat*, the descendant; the widow, *vidhavā*, the bereft, the spoiled of Death, the great robber. The family lived in a house graced by a door, surrounded by a court, where, perhaps, the householder gathered his cattle for milking, his sheep for shearing, and where stood stalls for his horses. His flocks and herds constituted his wealth, which, by aid of his faithful dog, he drove and tended. He knew and had named fowls, wild and domestic, beasts of prey as well as of burden, plants noxious and nutritious; had, too, discovered the more common metals, and made himself weapons of offence and defence. He could kindle a fire and use it for cooking, could weave clothes for himself from the wool his sheep supplied. He knew how to make and use the boat and the oar; had observed and named the greater objects and the grander phenomena of Nature, had made the moon measure the month. He had distinguished his senses and knew their uses. He could count as high, at least, as a hundred, could compare, had a greater and less, a better and best. He had a polity, the notion of law he had formulated, the idea of right he honoured. He had a religion, believed in gods he was bound to worship, who loved sacrifice and incense, were not like man *marta*, mortal, but *anmarta*, immortal. And the name he gave to his god was borrowed from the brightest, most glorious, and unchangeable object he knew, the blue, beautiful, luminous, all-encompassing heaven, that abode for ever, looked unimpassioned, but never heedless on man's coming and going in his successive generations, that was often disturbed by storms or darkened by clouds, but yet ever broke into the clear shining that comes after rain. And, lest he should lose the god in the splendour of the name, he qualified it by the very word which marked the fulness of his own manhood, so confessing as his comfort in life and hope in death his faith in the great Heaven-Father.

Here, then, we have a picture, dim, indeed, compared with what it might be made, but still in its main lines distinct enough to give a clear image of our fathers as they lived a yet undivided family. One or two things here deserve notice. The family institution is loved and honoured. Polygamy and polyandry are alike unknown. The names that denote intimate and even remote relatives are many. The father supplies the thought that most exalts and the word that best defines God in heaven and the ruler on earth. Yet the woman has also her rights, and she would be as little likely then as now to leave them unclaimed and unexercised. The family is the source of dignity; the father is important, not as a man, but as its head. The state we see dimly through Cæsar, more clearly through Tacitus, as the state of our Teutonic fathers evidently exists here in germ. The community owns the land; the family its home and cattle; but the individual as such, nothing; holds only as standing within a family which stands within the state.

Now, this clan, wandering in its vast primitive home, gets broken into two great divisions, possibly either divided by the incursions of hostile tribes, or simply in search of new pastures. The one section retires south-eastward, and penetrates through the passes of the Hindukush to India; the other north-westward, and slowly finds its way into Europe. The southern or Aryan division, after a period of unity, again breaks up, the Hindus to press further into India, to sing their Vedic hymns, conquer the native tribes, and develop the most elaborate social and sacerdotal tyranny the world has ever known: the Iranians to seek and settle in the highlands of Iran, become a great, though evanescent empire, and evolve the most exalted religion of the race. The western or European division held together awhile, developed further their common speech, learned to make the plough, to ear the ground, divide the field, to attain greater complexity of domestic and social relations. Then a tribe parted from the rest, forced its way westward, absorbed or drove before it the aborigines, and did not pause till it had reached the sea and the islands that look out into the Atlantic, where it stayed to manifest in rude but magnificent monuments the architectural genius that has never deserted the Celt. The still united sister tribes by and by broke into northern and southern branches; each branch again dividing into an eastern and western—the northern into the Slav and the Teuton; the southern into the Greek and Italian, each carrying the portion of the common heritage he was to develop in his own way and time for the being of himself, but for the wellbeing of humanity.

There is something that strangely touches the imagination in those bands of brothers each going its own way to a near or distant, more or less glorious destiny. They were soon to forget their kinship, to become in some cases ignorant of each other's existence, to meet in others as civilized and barbarian, or as black and white, but almost always as deadly foemen. When Greek and Persian met in the war that decided for ever the supremacy of the West they despised each other as men of alien blood. Yet through the pride of race and of victory there seems to steal a faint feeling of the truth, when the old historian tells us that the Persians who fought at Platæa were in "bravery and warlike spirit no whit inferior to the Greeks."* The Romans that,

---

* Herodotos, lib. ix. c. 62. Æschylos, too, who had a soldier's love of courage, though an enemy's, styled the Persians a "valiant-hearted people" ("Pers.," 94).

under Cæsar or Agricola, Tiberius or Germanicus, in Gaul, Britain, or Germany, "made a solitude and called it peace," did not dream that the wild tribes they so curiously studied and so cruelly conquered were of their own kin, and on that wild day in the Teutoburger Wald when Varo and his legions perished before the heroism of Arminius and the revenge of his Germans, no man on either side imagined that the blood he shed was a brother's. And when fair-haired Saxon and tawny Hindu met on the sultry plains of India, with hate inspired by antagonistic religions and aims,—who could have believed that their fathers had once herded their flocks together, watched the rising and setting of the sun, "and the immeasurable heavens break open to their highest, and all the stars shine"? Yet so it is, on the great stage of the world as on the small stage of the family, brothers part in youth to meet strangers in age, the one a millionaire, the other a beggar.

But we must now glance at the other family, the Semitic. Comparative Semitic Philology, though it has proved the pre-historic unity of the family, is still too backward and on essential points too conjectural to supply the materials for a sketch of its pre-historic state. There is no language that can be used for the Semitic tongues as the Sanskrit has been for the Indo-European. The Assyrian discoveries promise, indeed, great things, linguistic, ethnographic, mythological, but the process is still too much one of analysis and verification to furnish data for synthesis and construction. Their value, too, is sectional rather than general, not so much for the whole family as for its northern branch. Much may also be hoped from the sub-Semitic dialects of Africa, especially in the way of throwing light on the earliest changes and migrations of Semitic speech. Meanwhile the best we can do is to use what is known cautiously and wait for further light.

What, then, can we know as to the primitive Semitic family? Its home was probably in Arabia, central and northern.* There it lived the nomadic life distinctive of the desert tribes to this day. Its polity was not, as in the sister family, communal, but patriarchal. The family was—the father. The woman was the servant, perhaps the slave. In the Semitic languages the nouns denotive of serviceable organs, instruments, and utensils, are mostly feminine; a fact which may allow the inference that the masculine was the served, the feminine the serving gender. Their religion was severe, stern. The Nature they knew was neither kindly nor fruitful. Their heaven was by day a consuming fire, by night more glorious and

---

* This, of course, is much more conjectural than the inference as to the primitive home of the Indo-European family. The opinion here ventured has recently been maintained with characteristic scholarship and ability by Professor Schrader ("Zeitschrift der Deuts. Morgenländ. Gesellschaft," xxvii. pp. 397 f.). See, on the other hand, Renan, "Hist. Gén. et Sys. Comp. des Langues Sémitiques," pp. 26 ff.

beneficent; and so their naturalism was on its better side astral rather than solar. Their deities were conceived as mighty, masterly, or sovereign, rather than as bright, genial, or paternal. Their life was a hard struggle against an unpropitious Nature; their religion a belief in gods who were the stern rulers of men.

The nomadic life is not favourable to political unity or progress. As the family grew it would tend to throw out and throw off branches, and so it seems to have divided very early into four, the southern, centro-southern, northern, and centro-northern. The southern broke into the Himyaritic, Sabean, Æthiopic peoples, and those advanced outposts which have left the sub-Semitic dialects as witnesses of their having been. The centro-southern branch was the Arabian, the most purely Semitic in growth and character. The northern was the Aramæan. The centro-northern became the Babylo-Assyrians, Phœnicians, and Hebrews. These, after breaking from the parent stem, seem to have lived long together, probably settling on the shores of the Persian Gulf, and extending up the Euphrates valley till they reached the ancient civilization that had grown up there. Of this the affinities of their tongues, mythologies, and traditions appear to furnish decisive evidence.* The Assyrian is more akin

---

* Schrader, *ut supra*, pp. 401 ff., and in the "Jahrbücher für Protestantische Theologie," No. 1, art. "Semitismus und Babylonismus." Sayce, "Assyrian Grammar," pp. 1—3. Duncker, "Geschichte des Alterthums," vol. i. pp. 194, 285 ff.

to the Hebrew and the Phœnician than to any other Semitic speech. The mythologies are in some respects startingly alike. The original home of the Hebrew patriarch was Ur of the Chaldees, and the Phœnicians represented themselves as having come from the Persian Gulf.* There are, too, similarities in their sciences, arts, and industries that imply their having learned together the rudiments of settled and civilized life.

Of the Semitic peoples those of the northern and two central branches alone became historical in the highest sense. Yet they did not alone become civilized. Those of the southern branch proved themselves capable of great things, achieved great things, have left the monuments of a very advanced civilization. But their opportunities were not equal to their energies. Their geographical position was unfavourable. There was no sister family they could at once stimulate and be stimulated by. And so our present purpose compels us to drop them out of sight.

III.

Here, then, we are face to face with our two races prepared to enter on the great stage of history. And in entering upon it they prove themselves possessed of one quality in common—extraordinary assimilative, imitative, and progressive power. Ever since 'the Spanish discovery and conquest of America we have been familiar enough with

---

* Gen. xi. 28, 31. Ur is the modern Mugheir. Strabo, i. 2, 35; xvi. 3, 4; 4, 27. Plin., "Nat. Hist.," iv. 36. Herod., i. 1; vii. 89.

the dismal tale of the less dying out before the more civilized races. But here we meet with a different story. The two branches of each of our two races that were the first to touch the ancient civilizations were the first to become in the higher, in one case, in the highest sense, civilized—the Assyrians and the Phœnicians on the Semitic side, the Iranians and the Greeks on the Indo-European. These names, indeed, mark the transition from pre-historic to historic, from Eastern to Western civilization. The Assyrian was the heir of the Accadian culture, but the Iranian of the Assyrian. Phœnicia was the scholar of Egypt and Babylon, but the teacher of Greece. The Semitic civilizations were much older than the Indo-European, but much younger than those of the Euphrates and Nile valleys. In the former, possibly centuries before the other family had entered either India or Europe, the Assyrians had met a Turanian or Ural-Altaic people, settled in cities, skilled in architecture, astrology, writing, the arts of peace and war. What they found they appropriated. Their culture terms are mostly Turanian, growths of the earlier soil. Their science, mythology, writing, arts, industries, are in root and essence Accadian.*
The children of the desert, vigorous, acquisitive, warlike,

* See an interesting paper by Mr. Sayce, "The Origin of Semitic Civilization," in "Transactions of Society of Bib. Archæology," vol. i. pp. 294 ff. Also his art. "Babylonia," "Encyclop. Brit." And Schrader's recent essay, "Ist das Akkadische der Keilinschriften eine Sprache oder eine Schrift?" "Zeitschrift der Morgenl. Gesellschaft," vol. xxix. pp. 6 ff.

imitated the arts and conquered the liberties of their more cultured but weaker neighbours. The Iranians stood related, though less intimately, to the Babylo-Assyrian as the latter to the Accadian. The architecture and sculptures, the cuneiform writing, the chariots and horsemen, the wicker shields we know so well from Herodotos,* all indicate the dependence of Persian art on that which had flourished for ages in the valleys between the two streams. Phœnicia, partly educated in Babylonia and early familiar with Egypt, transplanted their arts to Tyre and Sidon, and, urged by the love of gainful enterprise, carried them over the many-islanded sea to the men of Ionic and Doric blood, who, awakened by the light thus brought from the East, soon became the foremost runners in the race of progress and culture.

But these newer were not simply imitations of the older civilizations. The fresh people brought more than it received; faculties, aptitudes, latent energies, institutions and tendencies that variously modified, amplified, and developed what they found. The old people did not absorb the new: the new, stimulated by a civilization so far in advance of its own, started into fuller life, yet a life determined in all its material elements from within, not from without. The old culture was the suggestive cause, but the efficient was the new people. A people is too like a living organism, with all its parts in continual

* ix. 61. Also Xenophon, "Anab.," i. viii. 89.

interaction, to be capable of being assimilated by a full-bodied civilization. The people may assimilate the civilization; the civilization cannot assimilate the people.

We have then an efficient or real and a suggestive or formal cause. The first is the new people, the second the old cultures. Their relations may be illustrated, if not determined and defined. We have seen that each family had its distinctive political type; the Indo-European was communal, the Semitic was patriarchal. In the one case the family, in the other the father was the political unit. Now, there is nothing that so pervades and so commands a society as the idea latent in the germ from which it was developed. The idea may not be distinctly apprehended by any mind, but it lives a plastic power in all. So the primitive political idea went with the several branches of each family, and governed their development into nations and societies. In the one race monogamy,* in the other polygamy was common, which simply means,—while the one had equal respect to the person and rights of man and woman, the other gave rights to the male and only duties to the female. The communal principle extended from the family to the state becomes a commonwealth, but the patriarchal becomes an absolute monarchy. The common-

---

* Of course, this does not exclude exceptional cases, like that of ancient Persia, where polygamy existed. But even there traces of the original monogamy can be discovered, as in the monarch having only one queen, though several wives, and the authority of the queen-mother. Arrian, "Exped. Alex.," ii. 12; Herod., viii. 114; Plut., "Vitæ Artax.," c. 5.

wealth may exist as a kingdom, a republic, or a democracy, but in all its forms the people remains the fountain of authority. The monarchy may be an autocracy, where the authority is impersonated in one man, king by divine right, or a theocracy, where the authority is concentrated in a caste, priests by divine right. Now, the Indo-European states have been commonwealths, and even where, through the operation of exceptional forces, they have become empires, as in ancient Persia and in modern Russia, the communal has continued to modify the imperial idea; but the Semitic states have been absolute monarchies, quite as much so ideally when without as in reality when with a king. And so in the one family the state has existed for its citizens, but in the other for its head. In the one case the aim has been to perfect the ruled; in the other to glorify the ruler. Agamemnon might be the king of men, Hengest and Horsa the children of Wodin, but they were leaders that had to consult and obey the led. Rome might become imperial, but she was an empire that hardly ceased in form, however much in fact, to be a republic. Assyria, on the other hand, has no history but the history of her kings; theirs are the deeds that are glorified, theirs the fame and name that can never perish. The Hebrew monarchy at its highest point means but David and Solomon; and nowhere, perhaps, has the faith that sanctifies and the hopes that exalt a throne had such splendid expression as in those that gathered round David's. Islam is but faith in the one Prophet-King of the one God, Deity incarnate as truth, though not as essence, in Mahomet. A people works out its ideas with a daring, though with an unconscious, logic, and often achieves a consistency impossible to the subtlest dialectic.

But the very different parts played by the stimulating civilization and the stimulated people may be still better illustrated by the history of art. The illustration is the more appropriate that art exhibits the action of the political idea outside the political sphere. Assyria, Phœnicia, and Egypt contributed to the birth of architecture and sculpture in Greece. In her earliest attempts the influence of her masters is apparent enough. But nothing could well be more unlike than the creations of their respective primes. The sculptures that the chisel of Pheidias created subtly incorporated the mind of Greece, carved out in tangible yet idealized forms the genius of a free people, that loved beauty and activity, the city where the one lived for the many, and the many legislated for the one, the gods graceful, gracious yet majestic, who smiled in sunshine or wept in rain out of the blue and eternal heaven. But the pyramids, the magnificent temples and tombs that adorn the valley of the Nile, are monuments of a despotism that counted the toil and misery of millions nothing to the service of a priest or the memory of a king.* The palaces that have been unearthed on the

* Herodotos, ii. 124, 128.

THE RACES IN CIVILIZATION. 287

banks of the ancient streams that watered the Garden of the Lord, show a state which meant only the sovereign, where the thousands lived but to build the king's house, fight his battles, multiply his titles, and perpetuate his name; while the ruined amphitheatres which tell where Roman cities once stood, are significant of an empire which rose out of a republic, popular while imperial, living only as it pleased the permissive, if not creative, will of the people.

But the old cultures and the fresh peoples are not in themselves enough to explain the civilizations that now arose. These were varied in type, even when realized by the most nearly related branches of the same stock. To understand how and why these varieties emerge the action of two conditional or occasional causes must be considered —geographical position and ethnical relations. The effect of these can be seen in the two earliest Semitic civilizations, the Assyrian and the Phœnician.

The Assyrians settled in the upper region of the great Mesopotamian valley. The river valley is favourable to an early, but seldom to an expansive and generous civilization. The culture born on the banks of the Nile, shut in by its deserts, without the timber necessary to the building of ships that could brave the sea, tended to become, and became, monotonous, mummified, marking time, but not making history.* The Assyrian culture was also born in

* Curtius, "Hist. of Greece," i. 15.

a river valley, but was not affected like the Egyptian by its birth-place. Commercial indeed the Assyrians could not become. They were without the material for ships, and, besides, Babylon stood between them and the sea. Transit by land was expensive and difficult, and they could easily raise where they lived the necessaries of life. But the character of the people and their political relations modified the action of the position. They were surrounded by independent and alien tribes. They had to defend their city, and soon found that the best defence was the conquest of the enemy. The conquered enemy was made not only powerless, but tributary; his defeat at once protected and enriched the city. Soon ideas were formed which generated ambition, aptitudes which developed into martial genius. When conquest was found to be remunerative, a good reason was discovered why it should be carried outside the circle of hostile peoples. Every nation vanquished meant new wealth to the victor—the more numerous the tributaries the more splendid the sovereign state. And so their culture became eminently military and imperial. In literature and science they remained the pupils of Babylon. In architecture they were little more than imitators, though they so reflected their massiveness in their works as to be to a certain degree in size and expression, if not in design, original. In their age of greatest wealth and luxury their commerce was extensive, but it was a commerce made by their greatness, not making it. They lived by conquest, and when they ceased to conquer they ceased to live.*

Thus, then, on the banks of the Tigris, as later on the banks of the Tiber, a brave clan developed through its conflict with hostile tribes into a great world-empire. The Assyrians are for many reasons well entitled to be named "the Romans of Asia."† They were the first to conceive and realize the dream of universal dominion. The old cultured peoples were not ambitious as they were. And their ambition was a genuine growth of their spirit, inspired as it was by religious enthusiasm. They imagined that the being of their state was the glory of its god; as it was enlarged he was magnified. And he was represented by the king. The sovereign, indeed, epitomized the state. And it is significant that the strength of Assyria was its sovereigns. Perhaps no people ever had so many great kings. For almost seven centuries they maintained their empire. Their armies penetrated on the east to India, on the north to the Caspian Sea, on the west to the Nile and Isles of the Ægean. The wealth of Phœnicia, the ancient cultures of Egypt and Babylon, had to confess their supremacy. At first their ambition was satisfied with homage and tribute, but later they had so learned the art

---

* It is significant that in the time of Herodotos Nineveh was a thing of the past (i. 193). After its fall Assyria may be said to vanish from history, the only allusion to it showing its impotence.

† Rawlinson, "Ancient Monarchies." i. 2—39.

of rule as to appoint their own governers, and enforce their authority within the conquered province. The first empire was certainly not the least in energy, progressive intelligence, and capacity to deal with its subject peoples.

The Assyrian, then, marks an enormous advance on previous cultures. With it civilization enters on a new phase, becomes aggressive, missionary, as it were. By its conquests dissimilar peoples were made to touch and teach each other, the less were opened to the influence of the more civilized. Science was diffused, commerce extended, arts increased. The knowledge of Egypt was carried eastward; the science of Mesopotamia was planted among the tribes that had settled in the highlands of Iran. Palestine and Persia were introduced to each other, and by the introduction their religions, the highest evolved by the two races, mutually profited. Mind was everywhere stimulated by contact with fresh minds. The wealth, material and mental, that had been accumulating in isolated places was set in circulation, and so at once raised in value, increased in quantity, and made more variously productive. The very wars evoked heroism, the patriotism that fused scattered tribes into homogeneous peoples. The first world-empire made the others possible. Assyria created Persia, and Persia gave a powerful impulse to Greek, and through it to Western civilization. The Persian wars ennobled the Greek character, promoted

THE RACES IN CIVILIZATION. 291

the free development of the Greek states, quickened the Greek intellect on all its sides, helped to create the golden age of its poetry, philosophy, and art. So the Semitic spirit did splendid service to the cause of civilization when it created the first universal empire. It achieved a new thing in the history of the world, and made human progress easier, swifter, and more sure.

We come now to the Phœnicians. Their seats were on the Syrian seaboard. The land was fertile, and so was the sea. The fruits of the one and the fish of the other offered to industry and enterprise the stimulus they needed. The land did not exhaust their energies, while the sea afforded them an inexhaustible field. The wooded slopes of Lebanon supplied material for ships, and the coast was cut into safe and sheltered harbours. They had, too, when their culture was young, no dangerously hostile environment. The tribes that came pressing behind were kindred. The aborigines were not formidable foemen. The old civilized states, Egypt and Babylon, were too distant to be feared, yet near enough to be reached. The desert tribes, too, of Syria and Arabia, ever in need of the products of a fruitful land, invited to commerce. And as their ships ventured along the coast and out to sea, they came upon men of a whiter and simpler race, who looked with wonder and desire on the products of a civilization so much in advance of their own. Exchange was simple. The wares of Mesopotamia and the Nile could be hawked by the caravan or the ship,* and sold at such profits as can be realized when a more trades with a less cultured people. But the trader soon discovered that it was more profitable to be the manufacturer as well. So he began to cultivate the arts he had seen practised at Thebes and Babylon, and by practice he became more perfect than their inventors. Trade stimulated production; increased demands increased the supply, created new needs, new capacities, new arts. Phœnicia became celebrated for her own manufactures. Her purple, her ivory, the metals wrought by her sons, the coin circulated by her merchants, were known over the East. And so, while the Assyrians became "the Romans of Asia," the Phœnicians became the Englishmen of the ancient world, seeking everywhere a market, and seldom finding the search unprofitable.†

The Phœnicians were thorough men of business, followed commerce with the single-hearted devotion of the Semite. With an almost sublime genius, everything was subordinated to the supreme interests of

---

* Herod., i. 1, iii. 136, "Odys.," xv. 415 ff.

† As to Phœnician trade see Movers' " Das Phönizische Alterthum," pt. iii. Duncker gives an admirable summary of Movers' results, "Geschichte des Alterthums," ii. pp. 192 ff., 4th ed.

THE RACES IN CIVILIZATION. 293

trade. They were genuine Philistines, in the modern sense, devout as a matter and means of business, but merciless to ideal and unremunerative aims. They were wealthy in gods, did them all manner of service, clean and unclean, cruel, voluptuous, costly, built temples and altars, inscribed no end of votive tablets. They scrupulously carried their deities in their ships, spared no expense to propitiate the powers that promoted trade. Their colonies can be traced through the islands and along the coasts of Greece by the gods, myths, rites, and modes of worship they left behind. They turned, too, the arts and inventions of other lands to unexpected commercial uses. In Egypt and Babylon men had early learned to express and communicate their thoughts by rude pictures. In both the pictorial had grown into a symbolical writing, but had ceased in neither to be sacred or sacerdotal. Phœnicia adopted the Egyptian method, which was incomparably the more perfect, simplified it, and made it fit for general use.* The signs which priests had held sacred merchants made common, and employed on both their tariff and votive tablets. And so, when Tyre

---

* See De Rougé, "Mémoire sur l'Origine Egyptienne de l'Alphabet Phénicien," 1874. De Rougé (p. 108) supposes that the Phœnicians appropriated and developed their alphabet about the nineteenth century B.C. If so, they must have been long before in intimate relations with the Egyptians, and must by this time have had an extensive commerce and highly developed intelligence.

and Sidon had become the mothers of many cities, they could speak to their daughters in signs that, though inaudible, were as significant as spoken words. But the merchant needed a medium of exchange as well as of speech with the distant; measures, too, for his goods and weights for his wares. These he found in Babylon, and soon set in as extensive circulation as his alphabetic signs, and to as good purpose.* The Phœnician, indeed, devoted his energies to commerce with splendid persistence and success, and made the cultures and discoveries as well as the products and the needs of other lands contribute to his great end.

The Phœnician was no conscious benefactor of man. He was too good a Philistine to think of more than profit to himself. But he has none the less grandly served the cause of humanity. He awakened the Greeks to commerce; taught them the industrial arts, opened to their imaginations the wonderlands of the East, stimulated their intellects with strange thoughts and new problems, and enriched their mythology with some of the most poetic elements it contained. The Phœnician had no literary genius. He was wealthy in cosmogonies, in tablets inscribed to the honour of his gods, in the annals of his city or his trade, but a literature in the proper sense he had

* Duncker places the beginning of the trade with Babylon about 2000 B.C., basing his conjecture on the current use of the Babylonian weights and measures in Syria in the sixteenth century ("Geschichte des Alterthums," ii. 192, 4th ed.).

none,* certain suspicious fragments preserved in Eusebius but helping to show the shameful intellectual poverty of our ancient Philistine. Yet this illiterate people supplied the world with the few and simple but wonderful signs that made both ancient and modern literature possible.† Though the Phœnician had been a nomad, he was the first to become a mariner. Perhaps these two are not so great contrasts as they look. The child of the desert is by the very necessities of his life a wanderer, over vast plains, too, where unless he can guide his feet by the stars of heaven he cannot find his way to a place of life and rest. Place him on a rock by the sea, and the sea is sure to become to him in time like another desert, to be explored for wealth, to be traversed with goods and for profit, with the way

* But see Movers, "Phönizier," i. cc. iii. iv. Cf. Renan, "Hist. des Lang. Sémit.," 188 ff.

† Lenormant's "Essai sur la Propagation de l'Alphabet Phénicien" now enables us to trace, so far as it has been published, the diffusion of the Phœnician letters through the ancient world, and the many changes they underwent in their travels. M. L. thinks this great Phœnician invention branched almost simultaneously out in five directions, forming five currents of derivation, each with its special subdivisions. The five trunks are: 1. The Semitic, which divides into two families, Hebrew-Samaritan and Aramean. 2. The central trunk, embracing Greece, Asia Minor, and Italy. 3. The western trunk, the Spanish aborigines. 4. The northern, the German and Scandinavian runes. 5. The Indo-Homerite trunk, which has a greater number of derivations than any other. Antiquity was divided as to the nation which invented commerce, but not as to the inventor of the alphabet. Lucan, "Phars.," iii. v. 220, 224. Pliny, "H. Nat.," v. 12, 13. The purpose of a minuter account of the Phœnician trade, with its manifold agencies and extensive ramifications, has been abandoned with regret.

over it marked by the old lights that had guided his path across the great sand-ocean. And so the once nomadic but now seafaring Phœnicians, who had, too, been awhile among the famed astrologers of Babylon, turned with unerring instinct to the little star at the pole, and steered their course by it, while the Greeks, fascinated by the brilliance of the Great Bear, never reached the accuracy in nautical astronomy of their masters in navigation. And the people who conquered the secret of the sea made a conquest of the greatest moment for humanity. It marked the hour when man's victory over Nature, and his conscious fellowship with man the world over became not only possible, but sure. It prepared the way for a civilization which should make the wealth and intelligence of each land the common property of all. But the end was still distant. The conqueror was not the crowned. Phœnicia, indeed, prospered, but her prosperity was too commercial to live. She evoked the enterprise and genius of Greece,* and then could not live in their presence. She stimulated and then fell under the might of Rome. Her colonies grew up all along the shores of the Mediterranean, but only

---

* It is not possible to discuss here the question of Phœnician influence on Greece. Mr. Gladstone ("Juventus Mundi," pp. 118—144) has discussed it from his own peculiar standpoint. M. Lenormant has an interesting *étude* on the Phœnician settlements in Greece in his "Premières Civilisations," vol. ii. One thing is certain; while Egypt may on some sides have been much more influential—as in architecture—Phœnicia was more powerful on others, having been the means of introducing Greece to Egypt.

to fade before the richer civilizations they had fostered. Yet she did not die till she had proved how commerce could enrich, unify, refine, and civilize man. Her discoveries became the property of the race, so incorporated with its being as to make its thews brawnier, its life more persistent and extensive. If certain of them were lost, the memory of their existence did not perish, and their author remained for after ages a

"Pilot of the purple twilight, dropping down with costly bales."

But in spite of their differences, the Assyrian and the Phœnician civilizations were thoroughly Semitic. They were simple, sensuous, unideal, created by men of narrow aims, but intense purposes. Their good was material rather than spiritual. They were haunted by no visions of the beautiful, of a world too ideal to be realized. Nature was to them too dead to speak with the voices the poet can hear, to be full of the shapes the artist can see. And so in art as in poetry they were uncreative. In architecture the Assyrian seemed great, but it was as a builder rather than as an architect. The Phœnician, again, had no sculpture, no native architecture. Egypt and Babylon were eminent in architectural genius, and have left, especially the first, remains that excite in us a wonder akin to awe. But the Phœnicians could only imitate the works of their ancient neighbours,* and did not imitate them well. They

* Renan, "Mission de Phénicie," p. 825.

could be extravagant and gorgeous after the ostentatious manner of the genuine Philistine, but could not conceive or embody the beautiful. Herodotos admired and minutely described the monuments of Egypt and Babylon, but the only Phœnician temple he condescended to notice was that of Melkarth in Tyre, and the only thing about it he mentions is the number of rich offerings, especially two pillars, "one of pure gold, the other of emerald, shining with great brilliancy at night."* At first sight this poverty in art may appear strange. The Phœnician was a famed handicraftsman, a cunning worker in metals, woods, ivory, a maker of the ornaments the rude tribes loved to buy and he to sell. But he was too good an artisan to be a good artist. Art is work done for eternity; work for the most material things of time cannot be art. What is made for the market is not meant to embody ideal truth. And so the artisan is no artist, is imitative, not imaginative, a copyist, not a creator. The Phœnician, too industrial to be ideal, dreamed not of the art that could make the dumb stone the imperishable expression of things unseen.

The rise of the first Semitic civilizations, sensuous and unideal as they were, was a decisive event in the history of man. What the Turanian had begun the Semite carried forward, and passed on to the Indo-European. Greece received the ideal and spiritual elements the East had to

* ii. 44.

give, assimilated, transfigured, and then embodied them in the perfect forms she alone had the genius to create. Greece idealized, exalted the individual, made man conscious of the glory of manhood. She gave us our models and ideals of the beautiful, interpreted for us man and nature as they exist to the imagination. "In its poets and orators, its historians and philosophers," says Hegel,* "Greece cannot be conceived from a central point, unless one brings, as a key to the understanding of it, an insight into the ideal forms of sculpture, and regards the images of statesmen and philosophers, as well as epic and dramatic heroes, from the artistic point of view; for those who act, as well as those who create and think, have in those beautiful days of Greece this plastic character. They are great and free, and have grown up on the soil of their own individuality, creating themselves out of themselves, and moulding themselves to what they were and willed to be. The age of Pericles was rich in such characters: Perikles himself, Pheidias, Plato, above all Sophokles, Thukydides also, Xenophon and Sokrates, each in his own order, without the perfection of one being diminished by that of others. They are ideal artists of themselves, cast each in one flawless mould—works of art which stand before us as an immortal presentment of the gods."

While Greece perfected the free, individual, and ideal

* "Æsthetik," vol. ii. p. 377. The translation here given is Mr. Pater's "Studies in the Hist. of the Renaissance," 192.

elements in the ancient civilizations, Rome perfected the political. If the first was the heir of Egypt, Babylon, and Phœnicia, the second was the heir of Assyria. Rome deified law, embodied authority and justice, realized political unity. A Roman has described for us her mission, and great as he conceives it to have been we may well allow that it was still greater.

> " Excudent alii spirantia mollius æra,
> Credo equidem, vivos ducent de marmore voltus ;
> Orabunt causas melius, cœlique meatus
> Describent radio, et surgentia sidera dicent :
> Tu regere imperio populos, Romane, memento ;
> Hæ tibi erunt artes ; pacisque imponere morem,
> Parcere subjectis, et debellare superbos." *

We can follow our subject no further. Enough has been written to show the relation of ancient and modern civilization, of the people to the culture it creates. Here, as elsewhere, the first shall be last and the last first. The peoples earliest were not the most perfectly civilized. Many nations had to rise and fall before the elements of a rich and many-sided social being were evolved. And the more varied its elements the more permanent will be its existence. The early eminence of the Greeks had, perhaps, much to do with their premature decay. The greater strength of Rome might be due in part to her slower and more concentrated growth. The peoples most distant from the ancient cultures have not lost by having been the

* "Æneid," vi. 848—894.

last to be civilized. They were more mature when touched by the cultured peoples, and the culture that touched them was richer, more plastic and powerful. And now they, too, are working for the future, helping to form the men that are to be. "Generations are as the Days of toilsome mankind; Death and Birth are the vesper and the matin bells that summon Mankind to sleep, and to rise refreshed for new advancement. What the father has made the son can make and enjoy; but has also work of his own appointed him. Thus all things wax and roll onwards; arts, establishments, opinions, nothing is completed, but ever completing. . . . . Find Mankind where thou wilt, thou findest it in living movement, in progress faster or slower: the Phœnix soars aloft, hovers with outstretched wings, filling Earth with her music; or, as now, she sinks, and with spheral swan-song immolates herself in flame, that she may soar the higher and sing the clearer."*

* Carlyle, "Sartor Resartus," bk. iii. chap. vii.

PART III.

THE RACES IN RELIGION.

I.

WHILE the collective human race has been as a rule religious, Man has exhibited in his religions every variety of type and degree of difference lying between the rudest Fetichism and the most refined and abstract Monotheism. They have embodied ideas at once so antithetic and akin, that religion can be made a point specifically distinguishing savage from civilized races, or a generic characteristic of man as man. Here the object of worship is a stone, or tree, or rude charm; there, the high and holy One who inhabiteth eternity. In one place the worship has been glad and lightsome, has loved the festive garland, the mystic dance, and the exultant hymn; in another it has been fearful and sombre, seeking by pain and penance, by human or animal sacrifices, to propitiate angry deities. Now it has been a simple act of devotion which the patriarch or father could perform, and again, an extensive and burdensome ceremonial, sacred and significant in the minutest particulars, which an initiated and consecrated priest was needed to celebrate. Sometimes the simplicity has been carried so far as to seem Atheism to a foreigner accustomed to a more elaborate ritual. At others, the ceremonialism has determined the very social and political constitution, and made the nation appear not so much a people with a priesthood as a priesthood with a people. The varieties are so many, that classification is here peculiarly difficult, and the difficulty is increased by inquirers failing to agree on a principle of division. The theologian, ethnographer, comparative mythologist, historian of opinion, has each a classification suited to his own province, inapplicable to any other. Only one thing is clear—Religion is as universal as man, but as varied in type as the races and nations of men.*

The universality admits of but one explanation—the universal is the necessary. What man has everywhere done he could not but do. His nature is creative of religion, is possessed of faculties that make him religious. Religion is not an invention or discovery, but a product or deposit, a growth from roots fixed deep in human nature, springing up and expanding according to necessary laws. No one discovered sight or invented hearing. Man saw because he had eyes, heard because he had ears: the sense

* Waitz, "Anthropology," vol. i. pp. 277 ff. (Engl. trans.). Tylor's "Primitive Culture," vol. i. 378 ff.

created the sensations. Language, too, is neither a discovery nor an invention. It grew, and man was hardly conscious of its growth; grew out of the physical ability to utter sounds and the mental capacity to think thoughts which, as allied, we term the faculty of speech. And so religion is the fruit of faculties given in our nature, spontaneously acting. Hence man gets into religion as into other natural things, the use of his senses, his mother tongue, without conscious effort, but to get out of it he has to use art, to reason himself into an attitude of watchful antagonism at once to the tendencies and action of his own nature and to ancient and general beliefs. No man is an atheist by nature or birth, only by artifice and education, and art when it vanquishes nature is not always a victor. The world has before now seen a mind which had cast out religion as worship of God, introduce a religion which worshipped man, or rather idolized the memory of a woman.

Religion, then, as natural is universal—as universal as the natures which deposit and realize it. But the very reason of its universality explains its varieties. The creative natures are, while everywhere existing, everywhere varied. Minds, while akin as minds, are variously conditioned and endowed. Man, wherever he thinks and acts, must think and act as man, obedient to the laws built, as it were, into his very nature, but his power to think and act may exhibit the utmost differences of quality and degree.

What is true of the individuals composing a nation is also true of the nations composing the race. In the early ages, too, when states and religion were being formed, there was nothing to tone down, everything to emphasize, local or family peculiarities. Mind was not cosmopolitan, but national or tribal, and narrowed whatever it created or received to its own sphere. Hence the only religions it knew were, not like the modern, universal, but tribal or national, as distinctive of a people as its language or its laws. This limitation and isolation could not but produce variety in faith and worship, make the religion the mirror of the family mind in all its faculties and phases. The distinctive genius of a race is always, indeed, liable to be weakened or intensified by the rise of new or a change in the old conditions. The family or tribe may either absorb or be absorbed into other families or tribes, and the intermixture may result in a new correlation of faculties and ideas, acts and objects of worship, such as is shown us by the peoples who settled in the Mesopotamian valley, and founded the empires that successively rose there. A change in geographical position may modify the physical and psychical qualities of a people, and create a new order of thought and a new set of institutions, just as the Aryans in India developed as immigrants and conquerors religious and social systems, which, while originally like, were in their final form generically unlike, other Indo-European religions and polities. Intercourse with friendly peoples may introduce varieties of belief and worship, like those Bacchic and other frenzied rites the commerce with Phœnicia introduced into the calm and beautiful naturalism of Greece. But while such changes and relations may qualify and complicate, they do not nullify the action of the national mind. Its action, expulsive, assimilative, or evolutionary, goes on modifying the old, incorporating the foreign, educing or producing the new, and can cease only with the life of the people. The interaction of the living intellect and living faith is continual, every change in the one being answered by a corresponding change in the other.

What may be termed religious faculty or genius has been the characteristic endowment of certain peoples. The Semitic and Indo-European families have been in this as in every other respect highly, though not equally, gifted. The former has been in religion the more creative and conservative, the latter the more receptive and progressive race. The Hebrew faith in its earlier Mosaic and latter Judaic phases, Christianity and Islam, are of Semitic origin; Zoroastrism, Brahmanism, and Buddhism, of Indo-European. But however splendid these creations, they by no means exhaust the productive religious genius of the two families. Many other growths have lived and died, leaving in the successive strata that mark the rise and fall of nations remains, now gigantic and legible, and again, minute and hardly decipherable. But the very least of the dead have contributed to develop the living. The great religions of the world are like great rivers, springing from small and distant sources, swollen in their course by many a streamlet, sometimes enlarged by the confluence of another far-travelled river, and then flowing on in grander volume under a new name. No race can claim a true world-religion as its own exclusive creation. Though Christianity rose in the Semitic, it has been made what it is by the Indo-European family. The stream that eighteen centuries since started from its obscure source in Galilee was very unlike the river that now waters the many lands peopled by the Teutonic and Latin races. Every nation which has embraced Christianity has contributed to its growth. Race and religion have continued reciprocal in their action. Conversion has here been mutual, the mind modifying the very object which changed it.

The Hebrews may stand as the highest example of the Semitic religious genius, especially in its creative form. They were as a nation always insignificant, indeed almost politically impotent. Their country was small, little larger at its best than a fourth of England, and its sea-board was almost always held by tribes either hostile or independent. Their history was a perpetual struggle for national existence, first against the native tribes, then against foreign empires. Egypt, Chaldæa, Assyria,

Persia, Greece, and Rome, were successively either their masters or protectors, and their often threatened national existence was at last trampled out by the legions of Titus and Hadrian, and themselves sent to wander over the earth as a strange example of a destroyed nation but an indestructible people. Without the commercial or colonizing energy of their Phœnician kinsmen, without the architectural genius and patient industry which built the monuments and cities of Egypt, without the ambition and courage which raised their Assyrian brethren to empire and a sovereign civilization, without the poetic and speculative genius of the Greeks, without the martial and political capacity of the Romans, the politically unimportant and despised Hebrews have excelled these gifted nations, singly and combined, in religious faculty and in the power exercised through religion on mankind. The Book which has been incontestably the mightiest in the world for good is the Book which embodies the religious thoughts and aspirations, faith and hopes, of this ancient and in other respects almost despicable people. The Hindus are our own kinsmen. The blood in their veins was as pure Indo-European as ours, perhaps much purer, when on the banks of the Indus or the Sarasvati they sang their old Vedic hymns. But these hymns can never be to us or our sons what the Psalms of the Semitic Hebrews have been for centuries to the noblest Indo-European nations. No

Aryan faith was more spiritual or exalted than the Zoroastrian, but while Moses and the Prophets have been living religious forces, studied and revered alike by the simplest and most cultured intellects of the West, the Avesta ceased ages since to be a religious power, save to a scattered remnant of its ancient people, and is now only a study for a few scholars curious as to the religions and languages of mankind. In that Hebrew Literature, which has become the sacred literature of our most civilized races, and made the very blood and bone of their religious life, there must be something profoundly universal and quickening, which finds and satisfies the deepest spiritual wants of man. Perhaps the wheel of time never brought about a more ironical or more splendid revenge. Egypt is like her own sphinx, a broken and decaying riddle half buried in a wilderness of sand. The stately pride and power of Assyria lie buried under the mounds that mark where her cities once stood. Greece is living Greece no more, and Rome a strange scene of religious imbecility and confusion, political anarchy and incompleteness. But Israel, transformed indeed and re-named, but in all that constituted its essence and right to existence, Israel still lives in and guides the conscience of Christendom. So grandly have the weak things of the world confounded the things that were mighty.

There has been more variety of religious genius in the Indo-European than in the Semitic family. It has exhibited indeed a single generic type, but with many specific differences. As the finest example of religious genius this family affords, the Teutonic peoples may be selected, though their action in the religious province has been not so much creative as receptive. The Teuton has indeed been in some respects more religious than the Hebrew. His religious life has not been so concentrated and stern, has been more diffused and genial, but for this very reason it has blossomed into a broader and sweeter and more human culture. And so Teutonic has not been like Judaic religion, iconoclastic, but has loved the Fine Arts, Music and Poetry, Architecture and Painting, has not been conservative and race-bound, but progressive and missionary. The Teutonic peoples have in their energies and enterprises, wars and ambitions, been governed by ideals, have, because inspired by these, led the van of the world's intellectual progress, fought the battles of freedom, and carried light and culture and commerce to the savage races of the earth. And so, while they have not, like the Hebrews, created a religion, they have been created by one. The Christianity they received they have so assimilated as to become its noblest representatives.

The Chinese, again, may be selected as a contrast to the Hebrew and the Teuton. They stand, indeed, outside the two families with which we are here concerned, and are noticed simply as a people singularly deficient in religious faculty. Their country is extensive and rich, almost inexhaustible in fertility and mineral wealth. They are a gifted race, ingenious, inventive yet imitative, patient, industrious, frugal. Their civilization is ancient, their literary capacity considerable, their classics receive an almost religious reverence. But this people has a so attenuated religious faculty or genius, that it can hardly be said ever to have known religion, at least as Semitic and Indo-European peoples understand it. Their notions of deity are so formless and fluid that it can be argued, just as one interprets their speech, either that they are theists or atheists. They reverence humanity as typified, not in the endless promise and hope of the future, but in the completed characters and achievements of the past. Their piety is filial, their worship ancestral. There are, indeed, three established religions; but, not to speak of an advice to have nothing to do with any one of them given by a late emperor to his people, two would hardly be classed as such in any other country than China, while the third is a religion imported from India, and so depraved by the change that the Buddhism of the civilized Chinese stands beneath that of Tartary and Thibet. And so this gifted race, deprived of the ideals that could alone urge it forward, has for centuries moved in a cycle which gave movement without progress, and has, by turning back to a dead worship of a dead past, ceased to advance along the not always straight line which offers alike to the individual and the nation the only path to perfection.

The form under which the religious faculty or genius of a people works is twofold, the diffused and the concentrated, as a tendency common to the collective nation, or as a force embodied in a great personality. The one represents the faculty in its stationary and conservative, the other in its reformatory and progressive action. Religions are never changed or reformed by the collective and involuntary, but by the individual and conscious will. The people without a great religious personality is without distinctive religious genius, therefore, without a great religion, can only develop one relative, particular, exclusive, that may grow with the national greatness, but is certain to participate in its decay and death. Only where the genius is personalized can it become creative of a religion able to transcend the limits of race. The old sublime faith of Iran, which gave to Judaism some of its finest moral and spiritual elements, sprang from Zoroaster. The Hindu Sâkya Muni created the religion that seems like the blackness of despair to us, yet has helped so many millions of Aryan and Turanian men to struggle through self-denial to annihilation. At the source of Judaism stands the majestic form of Abraham, and the most splendid series of religious personalities known to history, some nameless, some named, like Moses and Elijah, Isaiah and Jeremiah, binds him to Jesus. Christianity has its Christ, Islam its Mahomet. Neither Jahveh nor Allah can live in human faith without his prophet. In lands where the prophet was unknown, or his voice unheard, the religions have been local, national, such as the genius of Greece might adorn but could not vivify, the power of Rome exalt but not universalize.

We are not here concerned with any question as to the origin of religion or religious ideas. Were we, our first work would be to analyze and define the religious faculty. To do so would be to raise some of the deepest philosophical and psychological questions. Is it a simple or complex faculty? Does it reach its object by intuition or does it proceed by induction? To what extent and in what order does it call into exercise or stand rooted in the conscience, or the emotions, or the intellect, severally or collectively? In other words, does religion proceed from the dictates of the practical reason, a feeling of dependence, or an act of the intellect searching after a first or final cause? These are, indeed, fundamental problems in the philosophy of religion, but they belong to an earlier stage than the one we are now concerned with. Our purpose is not to inquire as to the origin of our religious ideas, but to study the action and products of the religious faculty in our two races, to exhibit, on the one hand, their distinctive religious conceptions, and, on the other, the elements or principles they contribute to a Catholic and universal religion.

It is, perhaps, better in this connexion to discover and exhibit the differences than to inquire into their causes. These may become more apparent when our inquiry is further advanced, and is concerned with the interpretative and constructive thought of the two races. M. Renan tried, indeed, to solve the psychological problem by attributing to the Semites a monotheistic instinct, which a nomadic life in the monotonous Syrian and Arabian deserts had evoked in certain branches and intensified into a monotheistic enthusiasm. This instinct not only explained their character, but defined their mission. They existed to create monotheism. Their genius was monotonous as well as monotheistic, loved the simple, hated the manifold, was anti-mythological, intolerant, incurious, and therefore unscientific. Simplicity, the antithesis of the Indo-European variety, epitomized the Semitic character. Their instinct was not genius. Monotheism was as it were the minimum of religion, the creation of a people that had few religious needs.[*]

[*] M. Renan's "Histoire des Langues Sémitiques," liv. i. ch. i.; liv. v. ch. ii. § vi. Also "Nouvelles Considérations sur le Caractère Génér. des Peuples Sémit.," "Journal Asiatique," xiii., 5th series, pp. 214—232; 417—460.

Now, the word instinct explains nothing, needs to be itself explained. In a scientific discussion it is no reason, only an apology for one. And here the psychology was not simply bad, but useless, was used to explain a thing that did not exist. Scholars affirmed and proved polytheistic tendencies in all the branches of the race; so strong, indeed, in the very branch which gave monotheism to the world as to involve it in ceaseless conflicts. Yet there was this much truth in the picture—Monotheism was the creation of the Semitic genius, the finest blossom of its spirit. Nothing was more alien to the Indo-European mind. The unities it groped after and reached were not personal, but abstract conceptions, metaphysical like the Brahma of India, or ethical like the τὸ ἀγαθόν of Greece. Greek genius intensified would have produced more splendid tragedies than those of Æschylos or Sophokles, a sublimer philosophy than Plato's, not proclaimed a religion with "there is no God but God" as its Gospel.* The Hebrew genius enlarged, clarified, had only excelled on its own province, not invaded the Hellenic. The races are, indeed, contrasts, move in different orbits, yet each as complementary to the other, like lights made to rule the two sections of human thought. If the Greek has made our literary, the Hebrew has made

* Steinthal, "Zeitschrift für Völkerpsychol. und Sprachwissenschaft," vol. i. p. 343.

our religious classics, and the creators of works so different could hardly be similarly endowed.

II.

The discussion must now become historical, an inquiry into the fundamental differences in the religious ideas of the two races. The cardinal and fontal difference is this— the mode of conceiving and denoting deity. The distinctively Semitic names of God express, as is now well known, moral or metaphysical qualities and relations; the Indo-European denote natural objects, phenomena, and powers.* Language is here a faithful mirror of mind; the word speaks as the thought had conceived.

1.

The term for God common to all the Semitic family is *El*, the strong, the mighty. It often occurs in the Bible, and is applied both to Jahveh † and heathen deities.‡ It denoted the chief deity of Byblus,§ is found in the Babylonian‖ and Himyaritic¶ inscriptions, in Syria, Phœnicia,

---

* M. Müller, "Chips," vol. i. 359 ff. "Introduction to the Science of Religion," pp. 176 ff. Kuenen, "De Godsdienst van Israël," vol. i. pp. 224, 225.

† Josh. xxii. 22; Ps. l. 1; Gen. xxxi. 13; Dan. xi. 36.

‡ Exod. xv. 11; Isa. xliv. 10, 15; xlv. 20.

§ "Philo. Byb.," as explained by Bunsen, "Egypt," iv. 187 ff.

‖ Schrader, "Keilinschriften und das Alte Test.," pp. 41, 42.

¶ Osiander, "Zeitschr. der Deuts. Morgenl. Gesellschaft," x. 61.

Canaan, and North Arabia.* It is known in a simple or compound form to all the Semitic dialects, and is equally significant as an indication of their original unity and the conception the united family had of God. Alongside it may be placed the Hebrew *Eloah*, mostly used in the plural *Elohīm*, the Arabic *Ilāh*, with the article *Allāh*, which are not, indeed, etymologically connected with *El*, but derivatives from a root expressive of agitation, fear, and so denote the being who is feared.† Another very old Hebrew,‡ and possibly Phœnician,§ name was *Shaddai*, the powerful, which perhaps stood in some way connected with the Egyptian *Set* or *Seb*. In *Elyon*, the Most High, we have a name known alike to the Canaanites,‖ Phœnicians,¶ and Hebrews.** But one much more common is the Phœnician, Carthaginian, Canaanitish, Israelitish,†† *Baal*, the Assyrian *Bel*,‡‡ Lord, Master, Husband. Another name, *Adon*,

* Tiele, "Vergelijk. Geschied. van den Egypt. en Mesopot. Godsdiensten," pp. 460 ff. Gesenius, "Monum. Phœnic.," p. 406.

† Prof. Fleischer in Delitzsch, "Genesis," pp. 47 f., 4th ed. Kuenen, "Godsdienst van Israël," i. 45.

‡ Exod. vi. 3 ; Gen. xvii. 1 ; xxviii. 3, &c.

§ Bunsen explains the Agruēros of "Philo. Bybl." as a blundered rendering of *Shaddai*, "Egypt," iv. 221-1.   ‖ Gen. xiv. 18—22.

¶ "Philo. Bibl.," Bunsen, "Egypt," iv. 190, 231.

** Ps. xix. 2 ; xxi. 7, &c.

†† Movers, "Relig. der Phönizier," vol. i. 169 ff. The question raised in Professor Dozy's "Israeliten zu Mecca," and so exhaustively discussed of late in Holland, as to the ancient worship of Israel being one, not of Jahveh, but of Baal, cannot, of course, be touched here. Nor is it in any way of vital moment to our present discussion.

‡‡ Schrader's "Keilinschriften," 80, 81.

very similar in meaning, was used by the Canaanites,* Phœnicians,† Hebrews,‡ and in the form *Adonai* employed in the Old Testament, as Baal never was, to denote Jahveh.§ In the word *Molech*, possibly either an Ammonite‖ or earlier form of the Hebrew *Melech*, king, we have a name for God that appears in several Semitic dialects, as the Phœnician Melkarth, king of the city, Baalmelech,¶ and the Assyrian gods Malik, Adrommelech and Anammelech.** The national god of Assyria, *Assur*, was so named in all likelihood because his people conceived him as a good being, the deity giving his name to the land rather than the land to the deity.†† The specific and distinctive Hebrew name for God, *Jahveh*, means "he who is,"‡‡ and as it is etymologically explicable,

* Josh. x. 1 ; Judg. i. 5.
† Gesenius, "Monum. Phœnic.," p. 346.   ‡ Josh. iii. 13.
§ Exod. iv. 10, 13 ; Isa. xl. 10, &c. In Hosea ii. 16 (18), *Baali* is used not as a proper name, but as the synonym of husband, only with a sterner, less affectionate sense. Ewald ("Propheten," i. 194) translates *buhle*. Kuenen ("Godsdienst van Israël," i. 401—403) distinguishes thus, Baali *Mon mari*, Ishi *Mon époux*.
‖ Whose God Molech was said to be. 1 Kings xi. 27 ; Jer. xlix. 1—3. Movers' "Die Phönizier," i. 323.
¶ Movers, i. 419. Gesenius, "Monum. Phœn.," p. 292.
** Schrader's "Keilinschriften," 65, 168.   †† Ib., 7, 8.
‡‡ I confess to have great difficulty in deciding as to the meaning of Jahveh, whether it means "he who is," "he who causes to be," or "he who will be it,"—will possess a given character, or manifest a given quality, or sustain a given relation to the person who uses the name. This latter meaning is developed and defended in a paper of great learning and acuteness by Prof. W. Robertson Smith in the "British and Foreign Evangelical Review," xcv. Of course this latter view gives a much higher ethical and

so it remains religiously significant, only on Hebrew soil; can be traced as little to an Assyrian as to an Egyptian or Phœnician source.* These, then, common and distinctive Semitic names of deity show that though the tribal and national religions were distinguished by many and strongly marked differences, there was one point where they so met as to reveal their kinship—they conceived God similarly, attributed to what was divine the same qualities and powers.†

The distinctive Semitic conception of God determined the distinctive character of the Semitic religions. They are all *Theocratic*. The Being conceived as the Mighty Lord or King was regarded as the true Monarch of the State, its founder, lawgiver, guardian. The Assyrian kings reigned in the name of God, received from him "pre-eminence, exaltation, and warlike power." Their wars were "the wars of Assur," their enemies his

---

religious value to the name, and makes it still more specific and distinctive of the faith of the people who used it.

* The question as to the source of the name Jahveh has of late entered on a new, or rather returned upon an old, phase, and become of vital importance to the interpretation of the religion of Israel. Of course it is impossible to discuss it in a paper like the above. It must wait separate treatment. See, on the one side, Colenso, part v. pp. 269—284, app. iii.; Land, "Theologisch. Tijdschrift," ii. pp. 156—170. On the other, Kuenen, "Godsdienst van Israël," i. 274, 294, 394—401.

† The discovery that much of the Semitic mythology had a Babylonian origin does not involve a similar origin for the distinctively Semitic religious ideas. These, indeed, passed into the Babylonian myths, and inspired them with a new meaning. The Semitic mind read its own ideas into the Ural-Altaic forms.

enemies, their victories achieved by his might and for his glory, "to set up his emblems" in the conquered states. The king's acts in war or peace, council or chase, were under divine superintendence. His person, garments, ornaments, were sacred; he was priest while king, officiated at the great sacrifices, represented the people before God as well as God before the people.*
The same theocratic character can be discovered in the religion of the South Arabian Semites as revealed in the Himyaritic inscriptions. It was common to the Phœnician faiths both at home and in the colonies. Their deities bore such names as Baalmelech, Baal the King, and Melkarth, king of the City. Their high priest was often associated in government with the king, in certain cases exercised regal and judicial functions. The more eminent priests had to be of royal blood.† Theocracy was of the very essence of the Hebrew faith, attained in it, indeed, its highest and most spiritual form. Jahveh was Israel's king. Its wars were his. He owned everything, the lives of man and brute, the earth and the fulness thereof. The sublimity of the theocratic conception in Israel need not here be told. It rose with the idea of Jahveh, became transfigured,

---

* Rawlinson, "Five Great Monarchies," i. 200; ii. 106, 200, 311, 320, 321, 230, 274, 1st ed. Inscription, Tiglath-Pileser I., King of Assyria (London, 1854), 18—22, 64—72. Dr. C. P. Tiele, "Vergelijk. Geschied. der Oude Godsdiensten," 385—390.

† Movers, "Phönizier, Ersch und Gruber."

spiritualized in the minds of the Prophets, who, unheard at home, despised abroad, turned from the deaf and obdurate present to anticipate a time when their ideals should be realized, and the God whose spokesmen they were should reign as king over an enlightened and obedient earth.

As the inevitable result of the above characteristic, the Semitic religions stood in intimate connection with all the duties and concerns of life. They were, unlike the Indo-European faiths, pre-eminently ethical. The power of the deity to command, to reward or punish, seemed everywhere and always present alike to the individual and the state. Religious emblems were everywhere, on buildings, garments, ornaments, and signets, almost every weapon of war or the chase, every domestic or agricultural implement, had its sacred sign. Personal names had almost universally a religious meaning, contained as an element the name or title of a deity. Just as the Hebrew names had, in general, as a component part Jah, or El, or Adon, so Phœnician names were compounded with Baal or Il, Assyrian with Assur or Bel, Iva or Nebo.* This consciousness of the presence and power of God in the life and over the man was the cause of some of the noblest, and also some of the basest, qualities in the Semitic mind

---

* Layard, "Nineveh and its Remains," ii. 450—475. Rawlinson, "Five Great Monarchies," ii. App. A, on the meaning of the Assyrian Royal Names.

and its religion. From it came the exalted heroism of the Hebrew Prophets, their invincible faith, their sublime hopefulness, which even national apostasy, impotence, and annihilation could not quench. Hence, too, came the power which fused into unity and kindled into heroic enthusiasm the scattered Arab tribes when they emerged from their deserts to give Islam to the world. But from the same source came that awful dread of the Supreme Power which made so many men and women willing to offer the fruit of the body for the sin of the soul. Human sacrifices have, alas! been known to most religions, but no people at the same stage of culture ever had a religion so full of blood as the Phœnician. Subtract from the Semitic idea of God the merciful element, leave only the ideas of might and authority, and one can understand how a nation should come so to fear the very being it worshipped as to seek to appease him by burning its own firstborn. When deity is conceived simply as magnified ferocity, selfishness disguised as religious fear will rarely refuse to sacrifice to him the dearest possession.

But to the same source another peculiarity of the Semitic religions must also be traced—their extreme symbolism. Gods who had attributes so unique, powers so extensive, modes of operation so varied, who were so distinct from nature while acting through it, who were so high above while so intimately related to man, who thus held in them elements so apparently contradictory to thought and speech, needed symbols to express what language could not utter. Men, too, who believed in such deities required perpetual memorials of their being, and presence, and action, lest they should by a momentary forgetfulness provoke their wrath. And so Assyria had its winged bull, its man-lion, the winged circle or globe which is the constant companion of the king, the sacerdotal dress and ornaments the monarch wore as priest, the sacred tree, and the many other objects associated with the worship of deity. Phœnicia had its symbols as the coins and inscriptions witness, and the Asherah of the Old Testament points probably to one common to the Semitic race. It were needless to notice in detail the familiar symbols of Mosaism, such as the cherubim and the ark. So excessive, indeed, was the symbolism of the Semites, that it has made the interpretation of their religious ideas peculiarly difficult; misled classical writers into explaining deities, symbolically the fellows, actually the antitheses, of their own, by Greek and Latin names; misleads many modern scholars into taking some symbol, sun, moon, or planet, as expressive of the entire nature of the god. The name reveals the essential thought; the symbol is only a qualifying epithet appended by men whose conceptions were too complex to struggle into adequate speech.

One peculiarity eminently characteristic of Semitic names of God must here be noted, the ease with which they glide between an appellative and a denominative sense. They pass from general terms into proper names, or continue to be used as both in different or even the same dialects. Thus the generic *El*, which is used with the utmost latitude in Hebrew, becomes in Phœnicia the name of a distinct deity, as also in Babylon, which is simply *Bab-ilu*,* the gate or sanctuary of El or Il, the ancient God of the land and people. The Hebrew *Elohīm* becomes in the Arabic, *Ilāh*, a general term, but with the article a proper name. A rigid monotheism cannot, indeed, distinguish between the two, *Elohīm* and *Jahveh* being now to Jew and Christian alike distinct and limited in their application. Baal is certainly often a proper name,† but as certainly often a general term as well,‡ and while the God of Tyre might be raised into the Baal *par excellence*, the word needed in less eminent cases another name to define what specific god was meant, Baal-Berith,§ Baal-Peor,‖ Baal-zebub.¶ The Assyrian *Bel* bears, too, an appellative as well as a denominative sense.** *Adonim* is used both in Hebrew and Phœnician as a general term, but in the form *Adonai*

---

* Schrader, "Keilinschriften," 42.
† 1 Kings xviii. 21—26; 2 Kings x. 18—28, etc.
‡ Judges ii. 11 ; iii. 7 ; viii. 33, etc.   § Judges viii. 3?.
‖ Deut. iv. 3; Num. xxv. 1—3.   ¶ 2 Kings i. 2, 3.
** Schrader, "Keilinschriften," 80.

it becomes almost synonymous with Jahveh, while the Greeks found the name individualized in their adopted deity Adonis. Molech, too, while used by the Hebrews as the proper name of the Ammonite deity, was so indefinite a term as to have been interchangeable with Baal,* and to have needed in certain cases another word to personalize it. Jahveh, however, is distinctly personal, and never loses its denominative force.

The remarkable diffusion and fluidity of these distinctively Semitic names of God seem to warrant a double inference. (1.) There was what may be termed a common idea of God, one, too, peculiarly simple and uniform. Variety was more a matter of name than of thought. The Polytheism was real and extravagant enough, but was due to dialectical differences and tribal peculiarities crystallizing into local worships rather than to multiplicity and variety of idea. Divine names differed; divine attributes and qualities agreed. There was unity in the consciousness of God common to the family. The many specific deities invoked did not pulverize the thought, Deity is mighty, sovereign, self-existent; Man is His creature and servant. (2.) While thought and language continually moving from particular to general held within the race a more or less unconscious unity of idea, the converse movement helped it to retain, or

---

* Cf. Jer. xxxii. 35, xix. 5. But see art. "Moloch" in Herzog's "Real-Encyclop.," vol. ix. 714—721.

rather reach, as the unity became conscious, the conception of personality. The more the Semitic mind awoke to the unity of the being that had such a variety of names, the more distinctly it conceived his personality. It never in thinking of God lost the personal out of the general element, and so never, like the Indo-European mind, rarified him into an abstraction. The latter has often in many ages and on many soils created Pantheism, but the former only in some solitary thinker, who, starting from borrowed or alien premisses, has but sufficed to prove the rule.

There is no assertion here of a latent Monotheism or a monotheistic instinct in the Semitic race. All that is affirmed is this, there was in the Semitic family a mode of conceiving deity so common, yet so distinctive, as to give at once unity to their idea of God and a specific character to their religions. Mind is never so logical as when its action and inferences are unconscious. The premisses from which a people start determine the conclusions it will reach. The most extravagant *aberglaube*, to use a word Mr. M. Arnold has almost naturalized, is rooted in a prior *glaube*, and though the one may assume, according to the conditions in which it grows up, the most diverse forms, its matter is always fixed by the other. So while the Semitic religions exhibit many varieties, they are of one species, have many local peculiarities, but a common character due to their common first principle, the idea of God. The Assyrio-Babylonian empires were formed by mixed races in the Mesopotamian valley, absorbed shepherds who had on the plains watched the bright firmament and the stars which shine for ever and ever, hunters who had on the hills chased the lion and the bear, merchants who had passed by the great rivers into the interior or out to the lands that skirt the ocean, agriculturists who had tilled the fields watered by the streams, men of Turanian and Aryan as well as of Semitic blood. These empires, devoted to war, luxury, architecture, anxious to deify and propitiate the powers that ruled these, might well construct a motley Pantheon. Yet so mighty was the Semitic idea of deity that, while failing to exclude foreign elements, it stamped its peculiar character upon the national religion. The Phœnicians, seamen, merchants, agriculturists, evolved peculiarities of mythology and worship determined by their position and pursuits. The Canaanitish nations, the South Arabian tribes, the Bedouins of the desert, the Tsabians of Harran, had each religions specifically distinct, generically akin, dominated by the idea of God or gods as mighty, sovereign, the source of law and duty, whom man must speak of in symbol, and worship by sacrifice with fear and trembling.

But there is one Semitic people that claims more than a passing notice, the people in whom the Semitic genius culminated in order to realize its mission—the Hebrews. Of the controversies concerning their origin and history, literature and religion, this paper can say nothing. It were simply impertinent to attempt to do so amidst these generalities. But so much can be said—they issue out of Egypt and settle in Canaan, a branch of the Semitic race, one with it in language, cosmogonic and religious tradition. But this people's patriarchs are its own, and their significance is religious. It has its national god, Jahveh, a name which signifies existence, "He who is," and therefore the uncreated, without beginning, above time too, the present, without past or future. He stands alone, without queen, no Beltis being set over against this Bel. He is Israel's God, neither believed nor claiming to be more. Semitic fashion, He is King and Lawgiver, regulates their lives, their state, stands therefore identified with their national existence. The people know other gods, love them, serve them. Canaanitish gods, Phœnician gods, have their altars and sacrifices. But Jahvism will not mingle with these worships, is intolerant, stern after a new type, sets its face against human sacrifices, but enforces in the most absolute way righteousness, purity of thought and life. But this worship fares ill amid the lawless Hebrews, intoxicated by the wines and luxuries of Canaan, fascinated by the soft embraces of Ashtoreth. So a new class of men begin to appear, of old called Seers,* as seeing into the heart of things: now called prophets, speakers, men who ly, clearly speak what is given them, not what they

* 1 Sam. ix. 9.

think, but what comes to them, enters into and possesses them as the word or spirit of Jahveh.* These men are peculiar to the Hebrews, unknown to the other Semitic peoples; prophetism, properly so-called, not flourishing out of Israel. The prophets fight what seems a hopeless battle. The kings, seeking foreign alliances, wish to break down the stern and exclusive Jahvism that stands in their way, and to bring their religious customs and beliefs into harmony with their neighbours. The people, hating its moral severities, loving the licence their idolatrous friends enjoy, receive and worship readily the native or alien deities which the prophets denounce as false. The great powers, Egypt and Assyria, have in Israel or Judah their respective interests or parties, and these like their allies are inimical to the God identified with the independence of the land. Against these and similar forces the prophets had to struggle, with almost constant political failure, with only here and there a transient success, when a king was found who understood the issues gathered into the name and worship of Jahveh. The struggle ended only when the people, who had been carried into captivity a godless, lawless multitude, returned a united nation, with the name of

* Ewald, "Propheten des Alten Bundes," i. pp. 7 ff. Kuenen, "Godsdienst van Israël," i. 212—215. Discussion of the question as to whether Prophetism was Canaanitish in its origin is, of course, not possible here. Wherever and however it arose, the prophet became in Israel too unique a phenomenon to find an exact parallel in any other religion, and so it is no matter of much moment where the idea of prophetship originated. Israel alone realized it.

Jahveh so stamped into their hearts that the persecutions of centuries, the loss of land and laws and language, frequent and forced migrations, life for generations amid peoples of alien race and religion, have all been unable to quench their faith in Him.

But now let us look at the spiritual issues of the struggle. These prophets spoke in the name of Jahveh, declared He was one God, the only God. Other deities were false, idols, without actual or substantive being. But this monotheism was only one element of their gospel. Jahveh was King—therefore had the right to command and be obeyed. He was righteous—therefore His word was the word of righteousness, His law the standard of right and truth. He was the Creator, therefore the Father, of man, and loved the creature He had formed as a father loves his child, more than a mother loves her infant. And from these principles many great results followed. The king was bound to obey Jahveh, order his state and administer his laws according to His will. That will was man's supreme law. Obedience to it was righteousness and peace. And so morality was joined to religion, was rooted in the nature of God. Knowledge of God and the love it was certain to awaken became the mainspring of action, made obedience easy and holiness possible. And were man afflicted with the strong weakness of an unstable will, did he sin, then there was mercy with God, forgiveness that He might be feared. And how varied the expression these thoughts receive! They are uttered in curses, such curses as only Semitic lips can frame, against idolatrous kings and apostate peoples; in pictures, that seem to laugh in terrible irony, of idol gods placed alongside the only eternal Jahveh; in entreaties of weeping tenderness to the people that had been loved and had wandered to return; in proclamations of an eternal law the neglect of man can never annul, or his disobedience degrade; in descriptions, lurid as if dashed off with a brush dipt in the hues of earthquake and eclipse, sweet and beautiful as if steeped in the silent loveliness of an oriental night, or bright and luscious, full of the music of birds and the sound of many waters like an Eastern Garden of the Lord. And then, when these men turned from their mission to man to their own relation to God, how their voices seemed to change. Now we hear the muffled yet hopeful weeping of a penitential psalm, imploring the mercy of God, forgiveness of sin, a right spirit and a clean heart; again, a sweet lyrical song of trust alike in living and dying in the Lord the Shepherd. That old Hebrew literature in all its forms, in Psalms and Proverbs, in prophetic visions and lyrico-epical poems, in history and parable, tells the same tale, the sweet and winsome gospel of the God who reigns and loves, who must often punish, but who always delights to save.

Here, then, was the gift of the Semitic race in its noblest branch to the world—faith in the living, righteous

God. That faith was embodied in a sacred literature, the grandest, in its essential elements the nearest universal, mankind has ever known, and in a people exalted by enthusiasm for the divine unity into its missionaries, with their field widened into the world by their idea, in spite of all their egoism and intolerance. Their Gospel did not simply affirm there is no God but Jahveh—that had been a mere abstract and impotent proposition—affirmed also, His right is to rule, man's duty is to obey. Religion is not simply worship, is obedience, righteousness, peace. A gift so splendid might well hold in it the regeneration of the world, giving to it not only the idea of the Divine Unity, but religion changed into a mighty and commanding reality, which penetrated and inspired the whole man, dignified him with the consciousness of a divine descent, gladdened him with the hope of a happy, because a holy, immortality, quickened him with the sense of omnipotence moving everywhere to the help of man in the soft guise of infinite gentleness. He who knows what these things mean will best understand that ancient saying, "Salvation is of the Jews."

2.

The Indo-European mode of conceiving and expressing deity is in almost every respect a contrast to the Semitic. The general terms were primarily expressive of physical qualities; the proper names of physical objects or phenomena. There is no term as common to the Indo-Europeans as *El* is to the Semites. The one most extensively used is the Sanskrit *deva*, Zend *daēva*, Greek θεός (?) Latin *deus*, Old Irish *dia*, Cyme *dew*, Lith. *dēwas*.* This term, derived from the root *div*, to shine, is expressive of the physical quality brightness, characterizes God as the bright or shining one. Another very common term, the Persian *Bhaga*, old Slavonic *Bogŭ*, means the distributor, the giver of bread,† and had possibly been applied first to light or the sun as dividing time and dispensing food, and had then been extended to the being resident in or acting through these objects. The Teutonic term *cuot, guot, Gott, God*, is still of too uncertain derivation to allow any inference to be based upon it, but the most probable etymologies seem to indicate that the Germanic peoples deviated from the common Indo-European idea of God, and hit upon one that may help to explain some of the finest elements in their faith and character.‡

As were the general terms, so were the proper names, primarily denotive of physical objects or forces. The deified Heaven, usually married to the deified Earth, is the

* See pp. 25, 26, and note.
† Fick, "Indo-Ger. Wörterb.," 133. Curtius, "Griech. Etymol.," 279.
‡ Grimm, "Deutsche Mythol.," 12 ff. The most probable etymologies are either the root *ghu, gharati*, whence Sansk. *hu, havate, zend, zu, zavaiti*, to call, to invoke, or *hu*, Sansk. *huta*, to sacrifice. God is thus either He upon whom one calls, or He to whom one sacrifices. Cf. Fick, "Indo-Ger. Wörterb.," 71, 746. Pictet, "Les Origines Indo-Europ.," ii. 658—661.

foundation of the Indo-European mythologies, the sources of their multitudinous gods. Dyaus and Prithivī are in the Rig-Veda "the beneficent Father," and "Mighty Mother," the prolific parents of all creatures.* The Greeks knew the bright sky, Zeus, father of gods and men; and if philology forbids us to see in Hera, Era, Hertha, Earth, † it cannot refuse us Demeter, mother earth, "the broad-bosomed," "the mother of all things," "the spouse of the starry Ouranos." The ancient Germans knew Tuisco, the father of Mannus, sprung from the earth; Tiu, the god of the bright sky, and Hertha, or Ertha, Terra Mater; ‡ and no thought was more familiar to the Latin poets, as none was more rooted in their mythology, than that Lucretius thus utters—

> "Denique cœlesti sumus omnes semine oriundi:
> Omnibus ille idem Pater est, unde alma liquentis
> Umoris guttas mater cum terra recepit,
> Feta parit nitidas fruges, arbustaque læta
> Et genus humanum." §

All the Indo-European religions bear the stamp of this primitive naturalism, even where they deviate, as in the old Iranian faith, most widely from the family type. Almost all the deities of the Rig-Veda bear natural names, exercise functions expressive of their physical

* Rig-Veda, i. 159, 1, 2. Muir, "Sansk. Texts," v. 21—34.

† Curtius, "Griechis. Etymol.," 116. But see Welcker, "Griechis. Götterl.," i. 363.

‡ Tacitus, "Germania," c. 40. § "De Rerum Natura," ii. 991—995.

characters. Thus Indra, the great god of the Vedic Indians, "the thunderer," through fear of whom "both heaven and earth trembles," the conqueror of Vrittra, is the rain-god, who pierces the cloud by his thunderbolts, and lets the long-needed waters fall upon the thirsty earth. Varuna, the Greek Ouranos, most spiritual of Vedic deities, who knows all things, the secret as the open, who punishes transgressors, and yet is gracious to him who has committed sin, is just the open enveloping heaven. Sūrya, the all-seeing, "who beholds all creatures, the good and bad deeds of mortals," who rides in a car drawn by fleet and ruddy horses; Savitri, the golden-eyed, who illuminates the atmosphere and all the regions of the earth, are only names of deities who personify the Sun. And this naturalism appears everywhere, in Ushas, the Dawn, Agni, Fire, Vayu, the Wind, the Maruts, the Storm-gods. And if we pass to Greece, the same thoughts, only modified in their expression, again meet us. Athene is the Bright or the Blooming, without mother, daughter of Zeus, the coloured dawn coming out upon the brow of the brightening sky. In Gaia, Dione, Demeter, in Helios, Phoibos, Eos, and in the myths, familiar enough to all, that grow out of and round these and similar names, the naturalism characteristic of the race finds expression. In the Jupiter and Juno of Rome, in the Wodin and Thor of Germany, the same mode of conceiving deity is manifest, only with a difference in representation, such as was inevitable to peoples so unlike in geographical situation and political constitution as the Latin nations of sunny Italy, and the Teutonic tribes of the stormy North.

The mode in which deity was conceived and represented in the Indo-European family determined the character of its religions, the place they held, and the functions they exercised alike in the life of the individual and of the state. As naturalism furnished forms to the religious ideas, it imposed upon them its own limitations. The gods never escaped the fate of the physical objects that suggested their being and supplied their names. Their existence had a beginning, was to have an end, their power to act was limited, themselves either the subjects or victims of a dread, undeified Might, named or unnamed. Thus the Vedic Indra has a father and mother, is concealed at his birth, crushes in fight his father, and wages perpetual war against Vrittra and the Asuras. Varuna is an Aditya, a son of Aditi, who has several sons besides. Indeed, all the Vedic gods are derivative beings, are extolled as creators, yet are regarded as themselves creatures, with the same ebb and flow, struggle, failure, triumph in their lives as there are in ours. The Greek gods move within still narrower limits, are feebler, simply because more distinctly personalized, and placed in more definite and orderly relations. Zeus, though the king of the gods, can be circumvented, contradicted, resisted. The Olympian aristocracy is by no means obedient or deferential, and Hera is a queen who can often out-general and defeat her lord. But higher than all stands fate, Moira, whose decrees bind even the gods. Zeus cannot save Sarpedon, dearest to him of mortal men, because he is fated to die.* Polyphemos, in his prayer to Poseidon, recognises Destiny as higher than the god.† Poseidon wishes to lead Æneas from death, because fate has decreed his escape.‡ The very immortality, which is the distinctive attribute of the gods, is not self-given and maintained, springs from their use of nectar and ambrosia.§ And as in the Greek, so in the German mythology. The gods cannot escape their doom, must go down in a common catastrophe, the victims of Ragnarökr. There is, therefore, no self-contained existence or power in the Indo-European gods. The very names which gave them being were like the shirt of Nessus, garments that involved death.

But while the primary Indo-European conception of deity imposed such limitations on the existence and power of the gods, it helped to develop the elements of independence and freedom in the idea of man. He stood over against deity, not as a servant or slave, but as voluntary, independent, with as good a right to exist as the god, though with less power to assert or enforce it. Hence in the pure, unreformed Indo-European religions there was none of the slavish dread of deity one meets everywhere

---

* "Il.," xvi. 434.   † "Od.," ix. 528 ff.
‡ "Il.," xx. 300 ff.   § Nägelsbach, "Homerische Theol.," 42 ff.

in the Semitic. God and man not only so nearly approach each other as almost to blend in nature, but their powers are, if not well matched, yet so much akin, that the god easily becomes jealous of the prosperous man. There was even a tendency to regard the deities as somewhat dependent on human gifts. Thus Indra loves and is exhilarated by the soma juice. Without it he is like a thirsty stag, or a bull roaming in a waterless waste. All the gods hasten eagerly to partake of it, and it confers immortality on gods as well as men.* Thus, too, Poseidon goes off to the Æthiopians to a hecatomb of bulls and lambs, and is delighted with his feast.† The scent of bulls and goats, or choice lambs and kids, offered in sacrifice, pleases Apollo.‡ The same feeling is manifest, too, in those ironical pictures of the Olympian court and its contentions so common in Homer, and in the readiness to make game of the gods so characteristic of the Greeks, so unintelligible to us. The healthy Indo-European Naturalism never knew the abject prostration of spirit before the invisible powers so universal among the Semites, developed rather a somewhat super-eminent manliness that did not care to bow too low even to deity.

These peculiarities of the Indo-European religions produced another of their distinctive characteristics: they

---

* R.-V., viii. 4, 10; v. 36, 1; viii. 2, 18, 48, 3.
† "Od.," i. 20—25. ‡ "Il.," i. 40, 315.

were what may be termed *political* as opposed to theocratic. Religion did not dominate the state, but the state the religion. This, perhaps, is put a little too absolutely, but expresses substantially the truth. The Indian Aryans implored victory from the gods, and praised Indra who had hurled his thunderbolts against the Dasyus, shattered their cities, destroyed them, and given the land to the Arya.* The tragic sacrifice at Aulis, though unknown to Homer, shows what value the Greeks set upon, and what a price they thought it in certain cases right to pay for, the favour and help of the gods. But, to say nothing of the horror the legend excited in the national mind—a horror which regarded the sacrifice as a crime clamant for revenge—it is certain that, while the Greeks were always wishful to propitiate the invisible powers, their wars were never either really or formally undertaken to extend the dominion or exalt the glory of their gods. The political idea was prominent alike in the Vedic, Hellenic, and Germanic mythologies. The state made its own laws, did not receive them from deity. The king was no infallible representative and organ of heaven, had no absolute authority, had his action limited and directed by the council, while behind and above both stood the assembly. Within the state, necessary to its prosperity, but controlled, not controlling, stood the religion. It did not dare to assume the sovereignty of the nation, the direction of the individual. Impiety was a

* R.-V., i. 103, 3; iii. 34, 9; iv. 26, 2.

crime less terrible than treason. The Republic of Plato is here of peculiar significance. Greece never had a sweeter and more religious spirit, more Hellenic in its culture, more Oriental in type and character of thought. He hated the immoralities of the popular mythology, strove to develop a purer religious sense in himself and his countrymen. In his Republic his highest ideals stand embodied. It has been termed a *civitas Dei*, a church, not a state. It conceives the here as only a school for the hereafter. Man is to be so governed and educated in time as to be gratified for eternity. The general conception is religious enough, but what particular place does religion get in it? It is admitted into the state, purified, exalted; the dismal pictures of the future, the immoralities, the falsities, the mutabilities, the jealousies attributed to the gods are all removed, that the youth may be taught piety without injury to their manliness and morals; but the place it is allowed to hold is as an element in a perfect education alongside style and music and gymnastic, qualifying for the study of philosophy, which can alone construct and govern the ideal state. The condition necessary for its realization and the cessation of ill is that philosophers become kings, or kings philosophers. The Platonic church thus remains a state governed by divine ideals, working for divine ends, but a state still, where the philosopher is the priest, the idea of Good the God. The Hellenic πόλις is everywhere, the Semitic θεοκρατία nowhere, apparent.

Space does not allow us to illustrate in detail the action of these peculiarities of thought and character, determined by the primary conception of God, in the several Indo-European religions. Separated for centuries from the other branches of their stock, settling in a land where Nature is adverse to energy, favourable to contemplation, led by their conquests into the adoption of a social system which made them the one sacerdotal member of their family, the Aryan Indians evolved a religion curiously un-Aryan in its nature. They had in them in their Vedic days as fine possibilities as any section of their race. These, indeed, only accelerated the growth of the strange and terrible sacerdotalism that soon overshadowed and extinguished their original free and vigorous life. How they saw into the mercy of God, into the weakness and sin of man, let this hymn testify :—

"Let me not, O King Varuna, go to the house of earth. Be gracious, O mighty God, be gracious.
I go along, O thunderer, quivering like an inflated skin. Be gracious, O mighty God, be gracious!
O bright and mighty God, I have transgressed through want of power. Be gracious, O mighty God, be gracious.
Thirst has overwhelmed thy worshipper when standing even in the midst of the waters. Be gracious, O mighty God, be gracious.
Whatever offence this be, O Varuna, that we mortals commit against the people of the sky, in whatever way we have broken thy laws by thoughtlessness. Be gracious, O mighty God, be gracious." *

The Iranian Aryans, too, merit, though they cannot

* R.-V. vii. 9, Muir's "Sansk. Texts," v. p. 67. See also M. Müller, "Hist. Anc. Sansk. Lit.," pp. 540 f., and "Chips," i. 39 ff.

receive, more than mere mention. They had parted, possibly on religious grounds, from their Indian brethren, had transformed their primitive naturalism into a sublime moral faith, changed the old nature-gods into demons, the struggle of light and darkness into the conflict of good and evil, and had settled in the highlands of Iran as tribes that were to grow by absorption and conquest into the great Persian Empire. How their faith grew, how much of it passed into Judaism, contributing elements that helped it to expand into a missionary religion, this paper cannot now tell. But Hellenism demands more than a momentary glance. In it Indo-European religious thought passed through some of its most extraordinary phases, and became so spiritualized as to be ready, when the highest Semitic faith appeared under a new form, to blend with it into a religion universal, progressive, with the divine and human elements so united and harmonized as to change the slavish fear of the one race and the godless independence of the other into the love that made God dwell in man and man in God.

It has been common since Hegel to describe Hellenism as "the religion of the Beautiful." The Greek mind was indeed æsthestically open and susceptible to a degree men of the colder and obtuser West can ill understand, but the Hegelian formula defines Greek religion as little as "the Christianity of the Beautiful" would define the Italian religion of the *Renais-*

sance.* The Hellenic faith had as its basis or centre the common Indo-European naturalism. Its gods were nature-powers transfigured and glorified by the radiant genius of Greece; its men were free and independent worshippers touched with the peculiar Grecian grace and reverence. The mythology had many imaginative, few ethical, elements, and never so escaped from epic and dramatic uses as to become a reasonable and moral religious faith. The gods were spiritualized, but hardly became moral governors. Their authority was not exercised over or through the conscience, and sin in the Hebrew sense was unknown in Greece. Godliness did not involve righteousness. Holiness was too little of a divine attribute to make its pursuit a religious duty. The immoralities of the immortals easily apologized for those of mortals. But the old naturalism asserted its presence still more fatally in the denial of Providence or pity in the gods. They were changeful, radiant, stormful as Mother Nature. They doomed mortals to misery while they lived without care. Zeus had at his threshold two casks of gifts, one of evil, another of good; these he distributed mixed to one man, who fell now into good, again into evil; but to another man he gave the unmixed ill, which drove him miserable over the divine earth.† He knows no more wretched being than man, and does nothing to

* Welcker, "Griechis. Götterl.," ii. 168.   † "Il.," xxiv. 525—535.

lighten his wretchedness, only sneers at it. The treacherous beauty, the brilliant promise that only mocks performance, the cruel serenity which only smiles at human grief, the power to nourish, the impotence to protect man, so characteristic of Nature, characterised the Greek gods. And these qualities of deity, softened and sweetened indeed, but never essentially changed, continued to live alongside the deepening ethical consciousness of Greece, and gave to its genius the mournfulness, the tragic sense of the sad and unequal struggle between the will of man and the merciless decrees of destiny, the insight into the bitter and ironical contrast between the passion and futile endeavours of the individual and the calm order and relentless march of the cosmic whole, that created what was most sublime and pathetic in Grecian poetry and history and philosophy.

For, however few ethical elements existed in the Greek religion, the Greek nature was eminently ethical. Faith in a moral order which man could not break unpunished, has had nowhere deeper root than in ancient Greece. This faith rose into sublimest expression when the nation was in its most heroic mood,—struggled into utterance in those tragedies of Æschylos which exhibit the fateful presence and inevitable action of Nemesis, in the sweeter and more refined and less gloomy dramas of Sophokles, where the picture is softened by a milder character in God and greater reverence in man. Alongside the deepening current of moral belief flowed the stream of philosophical speculation, now metaphysical, inquiring into the cause and reality of things; again ethical, seeking to discover the origin, nature, and laws of virtue. The one unified and sublimed the idea of God; the other ennobled the nature and exalted the end of man. Greek thought could not rest satisfied with the physical conception of deity; speculated on the notion of cause and the idea of good till, transcending the received Polytheism without grasping an explicit Monotheism, it conceived an impersonal cause rather than a creator, a highest good rather than a one god. Religious thought, divorced from religion, had groped its way towards a supreme, not person, but abstraction. And so the ideas of personal reality and righteousness, moral action and rule, were associated with man rather than with God. Humanity, indeed, became the later Hellenic divinity, the vehicle of what was most divine in the universe. Art and philosophy combine to idealize man, the one to hold the mirror to what in him was beautiful, the other to what in him was good and true. Indo-European thought, which had started by finding God in the bright sky, appropriately ended in its most brilliant representative by finding deity in the heart and conscience of man.

III.

Hellenism may thus be regarded as the contrast and complement of Hebraism. The former came to reveal the dignity and divinity of man, while the latter had proclaimed the one righteous yet merciful God. Hebraism had found the supreme law in the Divine will, man's highest perfection in obedience to it. Hellenism discovered an eternal law of right written in the heart, realized in history, enforcing its authority by sanctions too dread to be despised. The prophets of the first spoke in the name of the Most High God, but the prophets of the second spoke in the name of man; were the poets who sang of his heroism, his loves, his sufferings, his struggle for life against a merciless or ironical fate, the sculptors who enshrine his beauties in forms so perfect that they needed but life to be god-like men, the philosophers who at once uttered his yearnings after the Supreme Good and pointed out the path that led to it. Neither was complete in itself. Hebraism needed Hellenism to soften and humanize it, to translate it from an austere and exclusive theocracy into a gentle and cosmopolitan religion, which could illumine the homes and inspire the hearts of men with its own sweet spirit. Hellenism needed Hebraism to pour into its blood the iron of moral purpose and precept, to keep it from falling into impotence under its own unsubstantial abstractions, and set it bare-footed, as it were, upon the living God as upon an everlasting rock. And each had thus in different, even contrary, ways, been working towards a common end. It was the old story of two streams, in source far apart, in course wholly unlike, making for a single bed. One had sprung up in the hot and blistering desert, amid thunders that seemed the voice of God, had, swollen by many a prophetic rill, forced its way round the boulders of native infidelity, between the banks, now overhanging and again meeting, of foreign oppression, and had come into a clear and open place; the other had started from the foot of Mount Olympos, had flowed onward, answering with woven and mystic music the multitudinous laughter of the Ægean, through the heroic fields of epic and the amorous glades of lyric song, had stolen through the woods sacred to tragedy, now dark and fearful as midnight, now gleaming with light that never was on sea or shore, had glided past "the olive grove of Academe," and under the porch of the Stoics, until it had broadened into a soft and limpid lake. And in the fulness of the time the long converging streams joined. In obscurity and suffering a new faith arose, had as its founder the sweetest, holiest of beings, in whom his own and after ages saw God as well as Man. His death was everywhere preached as the basis of a new but permanent religion of Humanity, and time has only served to define and strengthen its claims.

> "Is it not strange, the darkest hour
> That ever dawn'd on sinful earth,
> Should touch the heart with softer power
> For comfort, than an angel's mirth?"

But its strange might to quicken the best and subdue the worst in man had never existed had it not possessed as parents, on the one side, Hebrew Monotheism, on the other humanistic Hellenism.

Hebraism and Hellenism had thus each its own part to play in the *Preparationes Evangelicæ*. The one contributed the Monotheism, the other the Theo-anthropomorphism, which lie at the basis of Christianity. When driven out of Judaism it carried into the gentile world a few doctrines it had inherited from its fosterparent, and a few simple facts peculiarly its own. Had there been no expulsion there had been no Christianity; within the Synagogue there was room for the sect of Jesus of Nazareth, none for the religion of Christ. The Christian facts bore to the Hellenic mind another meaning than they had borne to the Hebrew, especially as they had to be interpreted in the light of the Monotheistic and Messianic beliefs of the land whence they had come. These facts were construed into doctrines which expressed and retained whatever was of ethical and permanent value in Hellenism, without losing what was universal and moral in Hebraism. The purest Monotheism, which forbade God and nature or God and man to be either confounded or compared, was married to the most perfect Humanism, and ever since Christianity has stood loyally by both the "God who so loved the world that He gave His only begotten Son" for its life, and the Son who has ever seemed "the brightness of the Father's glory," "full of grace and truth."

This essay might at this point, had space allowed, have entered on a new field of inquiry and illustration. The genius of race has contributed to the development both of Christianity in general and those specific varieties of it that are known as the Greek, the Latin, and the Protestant Churches. The Hellenic mind, educated into capacity to interpret the Christian facts through the Hebrew faith, created those theo-anthropomorphic doctrines which have ever since been regarded as the most distinctively catholic and the most essentially orthodox. The Latin mind, less speculative, more practical, political rather than theological in genius, while it touched doctrine only to exaggerate it, often in a very dismal way, was yet able to frame a Church polity on the old imperial model, to build a *civitas Dei* where the *civitas Roma* once stood, giving to its visible head such absolute authority and divine honours as the emperor had once claimed, to its subjects such rights and privileges, only spiritualized, as the Roman citizen had once enjoyed. The Teutonic mind, fresh, vigorous, childlike in its simplicity and love of reality, without either the blessing or the bane of a splendid intellectual past like Greece, or an illustrious political history like Rome, accustomed to love the beautiful as embodied in woman, to enjoy the order and freedom peculiar to lands where the national will is the highest law and obedience to it the highest duty, could not be satisfied with the inflexible dogmatism of the Greek, or the iron ecclesiasticism of the Latin Church. The Teuton loved liberty in religion as elsewhere, asserted his right to get it, to stand before God for himself, to cultivate his domestic affections free from the shadow of a sacerdotal but unsanctified celibacy. While reverent to the past as his fathers had been, he could not allow it to tyrannize over the present, or rule the destinies of the future. And so he had to force his way into a religion roomy and elastic enough to suit natures that anticipated continual progress, and the changes it brings. Christianity as an authoritative letter is Latin, as a free spirit is Teutonic. The former is the refuge of those who feel there is no safety but in adherence to an accomplished and exhausted past; the latter is the hope of those who can trust themselves to a progressive and fruitful future. The sanctities of the Latin as artificial and arbitrary are moribund; of the Teuton as natural and essential are immortal as the humanity which God inhabits and inspires.

But these are matters that cannot be touched here and now. Enough to say, Christianity does not depend for either its existence or its authority on theories of

Infallibility or Inspiration. God reveals Himself in Humanity, and His voice can cease to speak only when the organ ceases to be. As man cannot outgrow his own nature, so he cannot leave behind the faith that is rooted in it. The struggle of faith and doubt will be perpetual, renewed in every generation under fresh forms, ending in each only to enter upon another phase with another disposition of forces. The limitations within which man must think will always give to doubt its more or less plausible argument; the necessities within which man must live will always give to faith its victorious answer. And so we are certain, that while new knowledge may change, it can never abolish ancient religion—that remaining permanent as man. Science with its new conception of nature may annul the old conception of God, but the invincible faith in Him, which will ever create a new conception of Him, science cannot touch, because, on its present plane, science cannot know. As the generations behind us have transformed while transmitting the grosser ancient into the grander modern religions, so our age will purify and exalt its faith while handing it on to the future, and after ages will continue the work until, perhaps, in some distant time the old conflict between Science and Religion will cease, and the knowledge of nature and of man be found in their ultimate analysis to be—knowledge of the living yet immanent God.

PART IV.

THE RACES IN LITERATURE AND PHILOSOPHY.

I.

MAN is by pre-eminence the thinker, realizes manhood as he grows into a conscious and creative mind. Men and peoples are great in the degree in which they manifest spirit, and help the spirits of other times and lands to a higher birth and a nobler growth. The race that produces most great men is the greatest race, best serves Humanity. The orders of greatness are indeed many, and differ as star from star in glory. Yet each has its place and use. The poet like Sophokles or Goethe—creative, subtle, sensitive to the sunny and translucent as to the black and stormy cloud, reading with the intuitive eye of genius the struggle of will and destiny, life and character, and embodying what is seen in forms whose perfection secures their immortality—refines thought by refining both its instrument and atmosphere, creates ideals that, whether realized or unrealized, help men—

> " Im Ganzen Guten Schönen
> Resolut zu leben."

The thinker, like Plato or Aristotle, Spinoza or Hume, Kant or Hegel, who starts new problems, and attempts by real or possible solutions to explain the hitherto unexplained, awakens mind to many unperceived and even undreamt of realities, opens senses in it that have been shut,* and supplies it with the fine gold it can mint into common coin for common life. The highest literature is the highest revelation of mind, and mind so revealed is a barrier against barbarism of immeasurable strength, a stimulus to culture of indeterminable potency. Into it the subtlest and purest essence of the past has been distilled, that the present may drink and enlarge the mind that is by the mind that has been. When the past has become a quick and quickening spirit to the present, human progress is made not only possible, but real and sure.

If, now, thought be at once a measure and a means of progress, the peoples who have not produced most, but most stimulated others to production, have been fruitful of propulsive and progressive forces. The two ancient nations most typical of our two great families—the Hebrews and

* So Hegel describes Winckelmann as one of the men "welche im Felde der Kunst für den Geist ein neues Organ zu erschliessen wussten" ("Aesthetik," vol. i. 81).

the Hellenes—were great literary nations, not in the quantitative, but in the qualitative sense, not for what they created, but what they have made others create. To the one we owe the books that are so sacred to the Christian world, the records of its faith; to the other we owe the literature that is *par excellence* classical, living in our midst unwithered by age, clothed in the perennial freshness which belongs to perennial beauty. Round the first much of our best philosophy, history, criticism, much of our noblest poetry and eloquence has crystallized; from the second there has come, with much more, our idea of literary form, our standard of literary perfection. Heine, an apostate Hebrew, but never so Hebraic as in his apostasy, divided men into "Jews and Greeks," or "men with ascetic, iconoclastic, fanatical impulses, and men of sunny, cultivated, cultivable and realistic natures;" and a well-known English critic has naturalized the distinction, and turned it to varied and even violent uses. But Hebraism and Hellenism are contrasts, not contraries, complementary opposites, not irreconcilable opponents. The cry for a return to pure and undefiled Hellenism is vain, and false as well as vain, the expression of a one-sided and ungenerous culture. The stern and exalted Hebraic spirit was never more needed than now. Were it to be lost, our modern manhood would soon lose its greatest source of moral dignity and strength. Even our noblest and most perfect modern Greek, Goethe, was Greek only on the surface, was Hebrew at the heart, owed the balanced and beautiful forms of his thought to Italy and Greece, but its most vital matter to the illustrious Jew of Holland. The Hebrew spirit and the Hellenic culture can serve the world better married than divorced. We need the open mind that can see and enjoy the loveliness of the universe and the life it unfolds, but we also need the reverence that can make the joy divine, that can feel nature to be but the abode of Deity, whose presence, felt while veiled, makes mountain, meadow, and sea alike sacred and beautiful.

Literature is a comparatively late fruit of mind, a blossom it can bear only after ages of growth and decay. If we think of the many centuries during which Egyptian civilization stood and flourished, of its genius, industrial, political, architectural, of its wealth, refinement, knowledge, of its highly organized society, with its privileged and educated classes, of its most complex religion, at once intellectual and ceremonial, so interwoven with the social system, yet so mined and countermined with mysteries as to be at once one thing to all the people and many things to each of the initiated, it may seem strange that Egypt should have had no literature but some crude records, embedded in a multitude of names and dates, and a few stories that would be thought childish were it not for their great age. But, in truth, nothing was more natural. Before the most rudimentary literature is possible mind must have grown much on many sides, opened its eyes to many things, changed life from a struggle for existence against man and nature into a more or less conscious and happy ability to be, must have made language into a vehicle adequate to thought, invented intelligible symbols for it, and discovered a material capable of preserving them. Now, our two races do not appear in history till the older civilizations had conquered nature, discovered the more necessary arts, invented symbols for speech, and accomplished, as it were, the orientation of mind for its higher work. And so the more intellectual of the branches that first inherited the past were soon able to tell the dreams of their childhood in forms of simple grace the older peoples had not intellect enough to envy, far less imitate, and the later peoples have never ceased to venerate or admire.

II.

Language is like the raw material of literature, the stones the intellect must use whatever the structure it builds. And the material is as necessary to the structure as the constructing mind. Whatever the genius of the architect, brick can never be made to do the work of marble, or granite of freestone. And so a literature can never transcend the language it has to use. The best literary work is the work most in harmony with the material it employs. But the poet or orator does not make the language he uses, finds it, finds himself, too, everywhere conditioned and controlled by it. The men, then, that made his speech determined the limits within which and the lines along which he must work. Language is in a sense the earliest literature, parent of all the forms it may afterwards assume. In the nation as in the individual the child is father of the man; leaves in him an unconscious basis or background of thought, which, to a much greater degree than he imagines, regulates his conscious thinking. He must be an unconscious before he can be a conscious poet, speak in artlessly artistic figures before he can weave artful rhymes. And the speech of a people is the unconscious poetry of its youth, shaping the conscious poetry of its manhood. Man has now as at first to learn to speak, but he has not now as at first to make the speech he learns—only to become possessed of one instinct with the ideas and inspirations of the past, coloured by the lights and shadows under which mind first conceived nature and man. And so the childhood that made our speech made at once the medium in which our thought lives and the instrument by which it works, and thus established over manhood a sovereignty it always feels, but seldom perceives or understands.

The languages of our two races must then be looked at before the distinctive qualities of their literatures can be understood. The glance can only be of the hastiest kind, not concerning itself with the philological, but with the psychological features of the respective families of speech.

While within both families, but especially the Indo-European, there are many dialectical differences, yet there are qualities common to all the dialects that can be used for the purposes of this discussion.

The point of difference that as most superficial first strikes us is—the vocabularies. The Indo-European are rich; the Semitic, with one exception, poor. A language wealthy in words can only be the property of a people wealthy in thought. Its wealth implies that the men who speak it have observed and distinguished many objects, can give varied expression to their ideas, and discriminate the subtle differences that escape obtuser minds. A language poor in words may be spoken by a people intense and exalted, but not by one rich and varied in thought. Poverty in the means of expression implies poverty in the ideas to be expressed. And so the superficial difference involves another and deeper. The Indo-European languages are ideal and intellectual, the Semitic are symbolical and sensuous. The first tend to become abstract, to lose material in spiritual meanings and associations; the second tend to the concrete, reflect the impressions of the senses as they reflected the outer world. The object of thought is presented by the former as objective, a thing the intellect can pursue and seize; but by the latter as subjective, the symbol of a sentient state. The Indo-European are the languages of the spirit, but the Semitic of the senses, physiological where they ought to be psychological.

Thus in Hebrew to be proud is to carry the head high; to despair is to have the heart melted; to be angry is to breathe hard or quick, to be displeased is to let the countenance fall. So, too, in the region of ethical ideas. The faithful is the stable; the beautiful is the splendid; the right is the straight, the wrong the crooked. Some of our emotional and ethical terms may have been at first as sensuous, but they have long since lost, save to the skilled philologist, every reminiscence of their physical or physiological origin. Then, these verbal differences are the least; those of structure are deeper and more significant. The Indo-European languages are, as a rule, rich in inflections, and lend themselves readily to many varieties of style and expression. No work of art could be more perfect, symmetrical, transparent and flexible in form, than the Greek tongue. It has been well said that it "resembles the body of an artistically trained athlete, in which every muscle, every sinew, is developed into full play, where there is no trace of tumidity or of inert matter, and all is power and life."* The verb, with its 1200 inflections, can express every point of time, every phase or mood of mind, can be made as subtly to hint as roundly to affirm, can embody with equal ease and grace the cold, objective narrative of the historian, the impassioned appeal or invective of the orator, the swift coming fancies, changing emotions or measures of the poet, and the abstract ideas and abstruse

---

* Curtius, "Hist. of Greece," i. 24.

reasonings of the philosopher. But the Hebrew verb has few modal or temporal inflections, has, indeed, no proper tense, only forms that express an action as finished or unfinished, perfect or imperfect. Then, too, the Indo-European languages are rich in qualifying and copulative words, particles that can modify word or clause or sentence, and invest it with a meaning the practised eye alone can discover. But the Semitic tongues are, perhaps, poorer in modal, relational, and copulative particles than in anything else. And hence their capabilities are necessarily limited. Their style must be simple, can never become complex. They are lyrical rather than epic or dramatic, descriptive rather than metaphysical or oratorical.* They are so sensuous as to be eminently picturesque, but as eminently unscientific. As M. Renan † has said, "To imagine an Aristotle or a Kant with such an instrument is as impossible as to conceive an Iliad or a poem like that of Job written in our metaphysical and complicated languages." And as is the speech, so is the mind it expresses. The qualities of the tongue are the qualities of the spirits that speak it.

And as the languages are, so have the literatures been. The Indo-European, whether his home has been India or

---

* Ewald, "Ausführliches Lehrbuch der Heb. Spr.," p. 30, 6th ed.

† "Hist. des Langues Sémit.," 18. The views of M. Renan are admirably epitomized and illustrated by Mr. Farrar, "Families of Speech," pp. 118-128. I have also to confess my obligations here to Professor Steinthal's "Charakteristik der Hauptsächlichen Typen des Sprachbaues," pp. 241 ff.

Greece, Italy or Persia, England or Germany, has been able to shape his elastic and mobile speech into every variety of poetry. He has been lyrical, now in songs glowing with the warmth or moving to the rhythm of man's strong love, and again in hymns, here gushing from the soul like the spring bursting from the dark earth into the glad sunlight, there gliding like the hidden brook under leafy shades. He has been epical, too, now in an Iliad, where gods that are but magnified men and men that are hardly diminished gods gloriously mingle in battle and victory and defeat; now in a Ramayana or a Maha-Bharata, where are reflected the struggles through many centuries of priests and princes, peoples and faiths; now in a Nibelungenlied, with its old yet ever fresh story of valour and love, jealousy and revenge. He has been dramatic, too, has made the tragedy the mirror of a moral order that could not allow its majesty to be insulted, and the comedy express his hatred of the new evil that was corroding the ancient good. But the Semite, intense and narrow, unequal to the sustained and lofty march of the epic,[*] to the subtle analysis and complex action of the drama, has been great in the lyric, the song the impassioned son of the desert sings to the maiden he waits to

---

[*] The Assyrian discoveries have, indeed, revealed the existence of Babylonian legends of an epic character, but they can hardly be regarded as Semitic *pur et simple*. See Schrader, "Die Höllenfahrt der Istar," p. 58. On the other hand, Steinthal, "Der Semitismus," "Zeitschr. d. Völkerpsychol.," vol. viii. pp. 339 ff.

bear away on his swift steed, in the psalm in which the penitent weeps his sorrow for sin, or the worshipper praises Him who is from everlasting to everlasting, or the victorious warrior extols the Lord who hath triumphed gloriously. The Indo-European has been philosophical and scientific, questioning nature, inquiring at man; but the Semite has been incurious, intuitive, so satisfied with his theistic conception as seldom to feel the need of travelling beyond it. The languages of the first are rich, but the second poor in oratory. The man who guides the Indo-European state is the orator, wise and persuasive in speech, able to save or serve the state as he can, by brave words give courage to her warriors, by prudent counsels guide her fathers, or by reason and passion weld into unity of action and purpose the incoherent demos. But the man who claims to guide the Semitic state is the seer, the prophet, the speaker for God, who in vision or ecstasy has received the word which he must speak to king and people and which they ought to obey. These are real, not imaginary, differences, patent in the respective languages and literatures, latent in the minds that made them. The races approach man and his problems from different standpoints, conceive and solve them differently, and the differences which have thus arisen explain the work they have respectively done in the world of thought.

III.

The purpose of this paper is to exhibit these differences

in their reciprocal and complementary action; in other words, to show how the mind of the one race has at once stimulated and supplemented the mind of the other. But before attempting to deal historically and critically with the differences, we must attempt to indicate their source.

The Indo-European and Semitic minds seem to differ in the general notion of nature and man, which is, as it were, the unconscious or implicit basis of all their conscious or explicit thought. The Indo-European appears to have had as its common first principle or starting-point a monistic, or natural, or cosmic conception; but the Semitic a conception dualistic, supernatural, theistic. To the one nature was living, self-existent, creative; but to the other dead, caused, created. The Indo-European deities were natural, stood within, not above, nature, elements of the abiding yet transitory universe; but the Semitic were supernatural, stood above, not within, nature, its causes, not its creatures. Hence, as we have seen, the gods of the one family differed in names and nature, attributes and powers, from those of the other. To the one the idea of a divine creator was native, to the other alien. The Indo-European religions were all transfigured naturalisms. The one that became most ethical and spiritual—Zoroastrism—bore in its most distinctive features the evidences of its descent. Light and darkness, transformed into ethical entities, became

Ahriman and Ormuzd, the good and the evil spirit; and personalized Time, the infinite, creating, governing, yet devouring all things and beings. But the Semitic religions were in general supernaturalisms. Their gods were creators and lords, sources of life, causes of death, unwithered by time, untouched by decay.

Now, this difference in what may be termed the implicit premiss of every mental process, may be traced to a double cause, an ideal and a real, or a material and formal. The ideal or material cause was psychical, mental; the real or formal was physical, natural. There was a creative faculty which gave the matter, and a stimulating nature which supplied the form of the primal idea. The Indo-European, familiar with a varied and fruitful nature, conceived it as living; the Semite, with one monotonous and desert, conceived it as dead. To the one the physical, to the other the personal, was the great creative force. The Indo-European, pre-eminently imaginative, conceived the whole as alive and the source of life; the Semite, pre-eminently ethical, conceived the individual as the source of being and authority. The one was objective, the other subjective; and so their standpoints were respectively natural and impersonal, and supernatural and personal.

These differences of standpoint and idea distinctly emerge in the respective mythologies. The Indo-European were cosmological, but the Semitic theological and genealogical. The first were objective and natural, the second subjective and historical. The Indo-European mythologies are simply the interpretation of nature by the imagination, acting spontaneously. They became unintelligible to a later age, because the later lost the mind of the earlier, the eyes with which it looked on nature and read into it a meaning too simple to be seen by self-conscious and inquiring men. The notion that they must have been concealed science, or disguised philosophy, or distorted traditions, or misunderstood history, was the result of a reflective trying to interpret through itself a spontaneous age and faith. But the interpretations, though often both violent and ingenious, could find no sense or reason in the old mythologies, could not, because seeking what did not exist. They had arisen without purpose or design, even, it might be said, without thought. They were creations of the imagination clothed in forms supplied by the senses and the memory. To it heaven and earth were alive; the words that denoted natural denoted living objects. There was no death. The dread thing so named was by its very name realized and vivified. Nature and man so interpenetrated that it lived in his life, supplied his fancy with forms it personalized, real then, though grotesque now, and radiant with a light the cultured imagination of to-day can never restore. The universe pulsed with multitudinous life; what was in man was in it: in it, therefore in him. The forest was musical with living voices, the midnight heaven alive with listening stars, the pale-faced moon full of weird influences, and the glorious sun as it broke from the bosom of the dawn a glad presence scattering the darkness that terrified. And when these fancies were thrown into speech the speech formed a mythology, a veracious reflection of mind in a period of beautiful yet creative simplicity, a dark enigma to mind perplexed with a thousand problems, seeking in the ancient beliefs a wisdom higher than its own.

But the Semitic mythologies had an essentially different character. It is necessary, indeed, to be here cautious. Certain myths hitherto believed to be distinctively Semitic are being traced to Turanian sources. But this only allows us to be more definite and precise, to perceive what are really the essential features of the Semitic mythologies. They were theological and historical. They are not imaginative interpretations of nature. Their nature is dead, owes its being, life, and energy to the gods. They are eminently cosmogonic, concerned with the beginnings of things as the oldest Indo-European myths never are. And as they are, on the one side, theological, they are, on the other, historical. As the Semitic conceived the person to be the great force in nature, he also conceived him to be the great force in history. The living present ever seemed to him made by the men of the immemorial past. He was greater, indeed, in memory than imagination, and so became the genealogist of the world, marking time and making nations by patriarchs. His mythologies were thus intensely subjective and personal, cosmogonies on the one side, genealogies on the other, persons being to him supreme alike in nature and history.

Mythology is nascent literature, spontaneous poetry. And poetry is the form the first conscious literature everywhere assumes. Here, then, the poetries of our two families ought to have been exhibited as mirrors of the racial mind. But the subject is too vast to be here handled. Enough to say, the poetry of the one family has been imaginative, objective, representing the infinite variety of elements in nature and man, but that of the other has been emotional, subjective, expressing devotion or passion, love or hate, as God or man, friend or foe, was addressed. Indo-European poetry has grown with the race, has claimed whatever was man's as matter it could make its own, has widened with mind, deepened with thought, become varied and complex as experience has multiplied the material it could idealize and represent. It has been sensitive to every shadow that has fallen upon the spirit, to every change in the relations of mind to nature and man. In ages of action, when men loved the heroic and the chivalrous, it has been full of adventure and enterprise, oblivious of the thinker's questions, alive to the glory of strength and courage and warlike achievement.

In times of ease and luxury, it has known how to indulge the heart, how to idealize the lust of the eye and the pride of life. In seasons when patriotism has sublimed, or faith transfigured, or doubt perplexed, or discovery widened and enlarged the spirit, its poetry has responded to its mood. Æschylos may weave into his tragedies the ancient legends of his people, but he informs them with a new spirit and meaning, makes them speak of a moral order, an inflexible law, which inspires with a strength and touches with a terror the men of the Homeric age never knew. Sophokles may find the material of his dramas in the stories current among his countrymen, but he makes them the vehicles of his own thoughts, expressive of a new and more perfect idea of man, the consciousness of the ethical worth and significance of life which marked the age when philosophy turned from speculating about nature to inquire at man. Shakespere may find in history or old romance the material of his plays, but he makes his matter the home of a universal spirit, inspires it with a meaning that enables men ever after to feel more deeply the immensity and the mystery of life. And ever has Indo-European poetry been as progressive as Indo-European mind, most objective when it seemed most subjective. The subject has been but a conscious object, mind aware of self as a mirror of the universe, the one as an eye that reflected the all. The *Divina Commedia* represents the faith not of a man, but of an age; "the thought it lived by stands here, in everlasting music." *Faust* is not Goethe, but the universal student, athirst for knowledge, in search of truth, mocked by the empty forms that hide while they profess to reveal it. Wordsworth's was a universal subjectivity, the modern spirit aiming at the higher and more conscious imaginative interpretation of nature. As thought has increased in mass, variety, and complexity, imagination has developed the energy that could poetically represent and present it. "Le silence éternel de ces espaces infinis m'effraie," says Pascal, contemplating a starlight night; but out of the terror caused by the deepening sense of the infinite space and time lying round our little conscious moment, there has ever come the material the creative phantasy could shape to its own high ends, making its creations as varied and manifold as the universe they reflect.

But Semitic poetry has not been rich and progressive, but intense and exalted, subjective and passionate. It has been sensuous rather than imaginative, the symbol of strong emotions rather than the vehicle of creative thought. It has represented with unequalled power the intensities of love and hate, the feeling of a man in the ecstasy of admiration or aversion. It has prayed to and praised God, has blessed and cursed man as no other poetry has done. It is seldom ideal, almost always real and personal. The very strength of the Hebrew Psalms is the intensity of the personal element. The subjective state is objectified and realized the object of faith is known, trusted, loved like an object of sight. The Semite believes as he perceives, his faith is, in a sense, sensuous. And hence its peculiar force, its power to inspire him, to utter itself in words that can inspire us. The Hebrew Psalms stand alone in poetry, mightiest and most moving utterances of faith in an invisible but realized God. What made the Semitic spirit so potent here made it impotent elsewhere. It has, indeed, in one of its most beautiful and perfect creations striven to become dramatic, to use the drama, too, as a theodicy. The Hebrew seldom felt that his sublime Monotheism needed defence. The ways of God justified, or would justify God. If they were dark and perplexing to the present, they would be bright and serene enough to the future. But there was one thing that puzzled even the Hebrew— the prosperity of the wicked, the misfortunes of the righteous. Once he had thought that a happy and prosperous life was the reward of God, certain to the obedient, impossible to the disobedient. But facts were too strong for his simple faith. The bad were often seen great in power, the good desolate and oppressed. Why these inequalities of lot? Why should a man serve God? For wealth or health, or something better, though less perceptible, than either? Out of these questions came the Book of Job, the nearest approach to a dramatic composition the Semitic spirit ever made. It has, indeed, a significance far higher than the poetical; yet as a poem it has helped us to see in the Semite capabilities other than lyrical, real, though unrealized.

IV.

The reciprocal and complementary action of the Indo-European and Semitic minds in the field of philosophy is a great subject, worthy of patient and penetrative study. Here we can present it only in the baldest outline.

1.

The older Semitic peoples were non-philosophical. The later Greeks, indeed, seemed to regard the East as the wonderland whence all knowledge had come. The men of the Neo-Pythagorean and Neo-Platonic schools loved to send the fathers of Greek philosophy wandering through the Orient, gathering by intercourse and initiation and curious inquiry the secret lore of the ancients, and then to make them return to teach at home what they had learned abroad. But these pictures are for the most part fanciful and fictitious.* The older

---

* I regret that it is impossible to discuss here the many interesting and important questions connected with the relation of Greek philosophy to older and foreign thought. I hold Greek philosophy to have been, down to Aristotle and in a less degree after him, in everything essential native to Greece. The contrary was long the dominant opinion, but it

Greeks knew nothing of an imported philosophy. There was no philosophy for them to import. The East stimulated the West to philosophic thought, but not by giving it philosophies. It sent knowledge of men and nations, of the means of intercourse, of arts and industries, of individual doctrines or sciences, but not of any constructive or interpretative science of nature and spirit. The Semites were without the intellectual needs that create philosophy. They were related to nature

was mostly based on authorities too recent to be trustworthy. The men of the Alexandrian schools were the great believers in the oriental origin of the Greek systems. Obligations acknowledged by the older Greeks relate chiefly to single doctrines in science. Herodotos (ii. 81, 123) believed that the Pythagoreans borrowed certain of their rites and their doctrine of transmigration from Egypt; but he does not go the length of deriving Pythagorean philosophy from a foreign source. Demokritos, as we know from himself (Clemens Alex., "Stromata," i. c. xv.), was the most travelled man of his time; had seen and learned more of distinguished barbarians than any contemporary Greek. But he expressly says that the Egyptian mathematicians did not excel him. The later story of his journey to India is evidently mythical. There is a passage in Plato on which both Ritter ("Hist. of Philos." vol. i. 151) and Zeller ("Geschichte der Philos." i. 23) lay great stress ("Repub." iv. 435), where love of money, the passion of the merchantman, is ascribed to the Phœnicians and the Egyptians, but love of knowledge, the passion of the philosopher, to the Greeks. If the latter had been obligated to the former to the extent that Philo and Iamblichus and Clemens represented, it is impossible Plato could have so denoted their distinctive characteristics. It is certain that the Greek mind was greatly stimulated by contact with what are called, with vague and inaccurate generality, the oriental nations, but the stimulus was not due to philosophies which existed there. Travel was a greater means of culture then than now, and the culture it gave helped to develop the philosophical capacities of the Greeks—a much better thing than giving them philosophies.

by sense rather than by intellect, interpreted it by faith rather than by reason, Their religion explained its being; and the explanation was sufficient. To desire more had been not only superfluous, but impious.

Philosophy was the peculiar and distinctive creation of the Indo-European spirit. Its faith idealized a living and present nature, had no dim intuition or distant theory of how it had begun to be. The Indo-Europeans did not think of asking in their spontaneous and imaginative period, how has nature come to exist. They were satisfied with the existing, the cosmos, which lived and created life. It was enough to know that Earth, the all-fruitful Mother, was folded in the embrace of Heaven, the all-fertilizing Father. The gods were by their very names held fast in nature, parts of the universal system, its first and highest born, but still its children, unable to transcend the limits imposed by their birth. Indra was to the Hindu the all-conquering, the beautiful, ruddy and lustrous as the sun, hurling thunderbolts which could pierce the clouds, the cities of the Asuras, but his functions were natural, not supernatural, those of a creature, not of a creator. Zeus was to the Greek the cloud-compeller, the wielder of the thunderbolt, the bright and beneficent deity to whom the Athenians prayed—

ὖσον ὖσον, ὦ φίλε Ζεῦ,

but he was active in the system as made, had no relation to it as a maker. The Indo-European could not, like the

Semite, "through faith understand that the worlds were made by the word of God," for his god was in the world, one of its phenomena, needing to have his own being and becoming explained.

But a world unexplained by faith was a perpetual challenge to reason. The man could not remain for ever an imaginative interpreter of Nature, satisfied with the present, incurious as to the past. Its interpretation by the intellect was as necessary to the man as its interpretation by the imagination had been necessary to the child. The more the reason grew, the more it was confronted by the question—How has this universe of gods and men come to be? Once it was asked it could not but be repeated, each attempted answer but provoking another, the mind being at once fascinated and stimulated by the immense and gloomy depths into which it was compelled to look. Yet the search for the answer would be along lines determined by the implicit premiss. As there was no idea of a cause that transcended nature, the cause would have to be sought within it. But the search, though starting from one premiss, might be along two divergent lines, a subjective and objective. The subjective would seize the life immanent in nature and man, and resolve all phenomena into an emanation from it; the objective would seek the primal cause in what seemed the most active element in the world of visible appearances. The one would be metaphysical, the other physical, but each in the blind and imperfect way inevitable in a science trying to begin to be.

Now, this exactly represents the process by which philosophy was born. The two great philosophical peoples of antiquity, the Hindus and the Greeks, were both Indo-European. To both philosophy was in the truest sense native, a plant indigenous to the soil. Both were roused to speculation by the same cause, a world without a maker, a universe unexplained, ceaselessly asking the intellect to explain it. But while starting from a common premiss, they followed different lines, the one the subjective or metaphysical, the other the objective or physical. The Hindu, living amid influences repressive of action, provocative of meditation, feeling everywhere the community of life in the one and the many, in the person and in the person-creating All, groped after an immanent cause, a creative entity, an immense abstraction, and found it at first in a Nameless Something, which no word could qualify. The Greek spirit, unfolded under the happiest natural and ethnic influences, free, active, heroic, its imagination vivified, perfected, and immortalized by the ideal of man and the state which to it had succeeded the early ideal of nature, was not only late in becoming speculative, but became it by asking the most pervasive and potent elements in its bright world whether they could tell whence and how this universe had come to be. The introspective Hindu mind tried to evolve nature from an inexpressible entity; the observant Greek mind, apparently simpler, really subtler, attempted to build the world out of the forces it saw most actively and creatively at work.

The differences here of the Hindu and Hellenic minds and methods are most significant, and might be amply illustrated. But one illustration must suffice. In the tenth Mandala of the Rig-Veda there is a celebrated hymn which asks, though it can hardly be said to answer, the question which the Indo-European naturalism forced upon the Indo-European mind. It begins with the idea of a state, if state it can be called, prior to existence, when "nothing that is, was; and even what is not did not then exist;" "death was not, nor immortality, nor distinction of day or night." Then "that One breathed breathless by itself;" and "there was nothing different from it or above it." "Darkness there was, and all at first was veiled in gloom profound, as ocean without light." The nameless "One," which "lay void and wrapped in darkness, was developed by the power of fervour." Then "desire arose in It, the primal germ of mind," "the bond that connects entity with nonentity." But bold as is the thinker and far as he has gone in the path of affirmation, he has to confess his problem insoluble both to himself and the gods, and even to the most high seer in heaven. Here is the hymn in full.*

* The translation is Dr. Muir's "Sansk. Texts," vol. v. p. 356, where another and more literal version will also be found. The hymn

"Then there was neither aught nor naught, no air nor sky beyond.
What covered all ? Where rested all ? In watery gulf profound ?
Nor death was then, nor deathlessness, nor change of night and day,
That One breathed calmly, self-sustained ; nought else beyond it lay.
Gloom hid in gloom existed first—one sea, eluding view.
That one, a void in chaos wrapt, by inward fervour grew.
Within it first arose desire, the primal germ of mind,
Which nothing with existence links, as sages searching find.
The kindling ray that shot across the dark and drear abyss—
Was it beneath ? or high aloft ? What bard can answer this ?
There fecundating powers were found, and mighty forces strove,—
A self-supporting mass beneath, and energy above.
Who knows, who ever told, from whence this vast creation rose ?
No gods had then been born,—who then can e'er the truth disclose,
Whence sprang this world, and whether framed by hand divine or no,—
Its lord in heaven alone can tell, if even he can show."

Now here is a most characteristic specimen of early Hindu speculation. It is neither theistic nor physical, but metaphysical, a speculative search after the common cause of gods and men. Its source is a One, a something which can be properly denoted by no term borrowed from the regions of reality, reason, or faith. Yet the thinker, while compelled by the laws of thought to seek a cause for the universe, hesitates to affirm that he has found the alone real and absolute. His intellect on its sublime speculative summit is paralyzed by doubt. The cause may or may not be a person, a mind. What or who it was neither he, nor the gods, nor even, perchance, the highest in heaven can tell.

may also be read translated in Max Müller's "Sansk. Lit.," 564, but cf. pp. 557, 563 ; Prof. M. William's "Indian Wisdom," p. 22.

But the early Greek method was in almost every respect a contrast to this. It did not proceed by introspection and a regressive movement of thought, but by the observation and interpretation of physical phenomena. Thales perceived that all things were nourished by moisture, that the seed of all things was humid, that water was the principle of the humid, and so he formulated his doctrine, "the principle of all things is water." Anaximenes saw that the air was infinite, surrounded and sustained the world, and so he argued "the primeval substance of all things must be air, for all is produced from it and resolved into it again." Herakleitos, observing the creative force of heat, said, "The one world was made neither by God nor man; but it was and is and ever shall be an everliving fire, in due measure self-enkindled, and in due measure self-extinguished." These were crude but courageous efforts to interpret nature objectively, through elements the senses perceived in active and resultful operation. To conceive them as either conscious or unconscious breaks with Greek religion is to misconceive utterly the basis and matter of Greek thought. Philosophy was never more perfectly in harmony with religion than it was then. The religion was natural; the dualism which distinguished matter and spirit, God and nature, was then unknown. Nature could be interpreted only in terms intelligible to the Greek spirit, and in methods it could pursue. Where religion and thought were so permeated with naturalism, the philosophy could hardly be other than physical.

Philosophy thus alike in India and Greece rose out of the naturalism common to both, rose to supplement its deficiencies, yet was clothed in forms it suggested or supplied. Their thought pursued very dissimilar courses, but yet came here and there to remarkably similar results. Their divergences were mostly due to their different methods; their coincidences to the similarity at once of their problem and their premiss. There is no evidence that Greek speculative thought was in its creative period influenced by India. The one had but few opportunities to know the other. The nations that divided them were but poor interpreters. Persia was of ancient Indo-European states the most intolerant of foreign faiths and systems, and Persia was the great channel through which the earlier knowledge of India reached Greece. The expedition of Alexander first made the countries directly and really known to each other. But the knowledge came too late to do much for Greek philosophy. Its greatest period was then just coming to an end, its work too well and too nearly done to be much affected by material it could so little assimilate or even understand. For to know a country is not necessarily to know its higher and abstruser thought. That implies somewhere or other such a knowledge of the minds that made the philosophy and the language they

used as is not won in a day. The Greeks cared too little
for foreign tongues to care much for foreign thought,
studied the first too little to get readily initiated into the
mysteries of the second. Aristotle might be indebted
to Alexander for the means of enlarging his knowledge
of nature, but hardly for his metaphysics. The objects
the naturalist studies might be sent from Asia to Greece;
but philosophy is not quite as transmissible as plants and
animals, especially when it speaks in an unknown tongue.
In short, it is not only unproved, but eminently im-
probable, that Greek thought down to Aristotle was in
any way influenced by Indian.

Yet their very independence of each other makes their
differences and similarities peculiarly significant to the
student of the history of thought. They had, it has just
been said, the same problem and premiss, and different as
were their methods of solution, they could hardly fail
now and then to agree in their results. Greece had its
Demokritos, India its Kanada; and of the two atomic
theories the Indian is the more clearly conceived, the
more patiently and consistently developed. The shadows
of the Platonic cave have a distant resemblance to the
illusory world of the Vedanta, though the realities that
are behind the appearances of the Greek show on how
much nobler an idea of being his thought was founded.
The Prakriti, or nature, of Sankhya, and the matter, the
πρώτη ὕλη, of Aristotle, are in many respects similar,

unproduced, yet productive, the potential which is the necessary condition of real existence. The Purusha, the ungenerated and ingenerative spirit of the Indian, has a certain resemblance to the νοῦς of the Greek, the creator who moves all things while himself unmoved.* But these are developmental coincidences, points were minds busied with the same problem touch each other, where the analytic and synthetic methods meet, though only to part. Yet beneath these superficial resemblances the real differences lie. The ideas of nature and person, being and man, radically differ. To the subjective Indian life was one, though its forms were many; to the objective Greek the one was as real as the all. Indian philosophies are to a much greater degree than Greek theories of knowing; Greek are to a much greater degree than Indian theories of life and action. Both are rooted in nature, but while the

---

* In a recent German work, Prof. Schluter's "Aristotele's Metaphysik eine Tochter der Sankhya-Lehre des Kapila," an attempt is made to affiliate Aristotle's metaphysics to the Sankhya system. But the attempt is most unsuccessful; is unsupported by any critical or historical evidence. It is not enough to prove that there are resemblances between the two systems; it is necessary to prove that the resemblances are due to derivation or appropriation. And this the author never tries to do. The resemblances are, as they are named in the text, "developmental coincidences;" and mark profound and radical differences. The idea that coincidences or similarities of doctrine involve derivation, was made by Röth and Gladisch the ground of their endeavours to affiliate the successive Greek philosophies to oriental parents. But their efforts were not of the kind to encourage imitation—though evidently they have not checked it.

Indian dissolves the idea of the person in the idea of the universal life, one in its essence, infinitely varied in its manifestations, the Greek sees in the person the highest and most imperishable product of the creative power. Personal being is the calamity of the Hindu, but the glory and joy of the Greek. To lose it was the great desire of the one, to realize it the great end of the other. The practical aim of every Indian philosophy is to teach the soul how its personal existence may be made to cease; but the aim of the greater Greek philosophies is to teach the man how his personal being may be perfected. The first have little, but the second preeminent, political significance. The great Indian thinkers were too anxious to escape from the present and the personal to be concerned with the state; but the great Greek thinkers were so anxious to exalt the present and the personal that their chief practical problem was, how to make each citizen contribute to the perfection of the state and the state to the perfection of all its citizens. Indian philosophy may thus be said to be man interpreted through nature, but Greek, nature interpreted through man. The subjective starting-point results in the sacrifice of the individual to the universe; but the objective in the glorification of the universe through the individual.

Enough has been said to show the necessity of philosophy to the Indo-European mind, and to indicate the reasons why and the points in which the philosophical Indo-European peoples of antiquity at once differed and agreed. Here we ought to discuss the influence of their philosophies on the history of mind. But that is so great a subject that we hardly dare even glance at it here. Enough to say, while India exercised a vast influence in ancient Asia, especially through Buddhism, which had a philosophic basis if not a philosophic birth, a much less and late and chiefly indirect influence in Europe, Greece through her philosophy became at once, and has ever since continued to be, in the proportion in which she has been known, an enormous intellectual power. The worth of the Greek philosophies is to be measured not by the amount of truth they discovered, but by the strength of the stimulus they have given and continue to give to mind. It is easy to be the critic alike of their matter and method, but not so easy to be the impartial judge of their historical and intellectual worth. They might be said to exhaust the premisses that lay in the Indo-European idea of nature and man. The pre-sokratic schools were physical and mathematical; nature was studied without man while by him. They all assumed that truth could be known, a cause discovered, and looked in the surrounding world for what they believed to be. But the Sophists arose, denied that truth was discoverable, or that man could by speculation find it, and declared that what man ought to seek was the knowledge of things practical and practicable. Then came Sokrates, leading philosophy to its object through its subject, making it ethical and psychological, the study of nature with and through man. In Plato speculation centres in and circles round man, begins to inquire into the nature and origin of knowledge, the kinds and the qualities of the objects known and their relation to the knowing mind, the essential character of ethical acts, the true, the beautiful, the good, the relation of the sensuous to the intellectual, the transient appearance to the permanent reality, the man physical and mortal to the man spiritual and immortal, the constructed universe to the constructive mind. In Aristotle philosophy becomes encyclopædic, methodical, scientific, aims at being real and comprehensive, describing and interpreting what is. In the post-Aristotelian schools Greek thought swings round from speculative and scientific to practical aims, passes through Stoicism and Epicureanism to Scepticism. The Stoic was eminently ethical, but in the true Greek manner, not by submission to authority, but by obedience to nature, the realization of the idea given in his own being. Epicurus cultivated philosophy as a means of happiness, not as a search after truth; the science which did not promote pleasure was worthless and superfluous. And the Sceptic, anxious, too, to be practical, became it in his own way, denied either the reality or the possibility of knowledge, and turned from the impossible or the delusive to do and to be satisfied with the probably best.

Now, it can only be the shallowest of all possible criticisms that seeks to estimate Greek philosophy by its inglorious end, though its end is not so inglorious as it seems. The problem was too complex and immense to be solved by the minds that first essayed it; but their essay has been at once the basis of every other and the stimulus to it. Their very failure was in one respect a splendid success—made their work the more creative of mental action and the energy and growth it brings. It was not possible that thinkers starting from the simple premiss which was the implicit principle of all Greek thought should have solved the problem of existence. It had not been good had it been possible. Man had more to gain by the search after truth than by its premature discovery; and Greece has been at once a leader and a light in the search.

> "Die Wahrheit ist in Gott,
> Uns bleibt das Forschen,"

and we thankfully confess our obligations to the great thinkers who have so directed and strengthened us in our quest.

2.

The point our discussion next reaches is one where the Semitic family and the Greek people seem alike broken and powerless. Rome has conquered and rules. Freedom and philosophy have together forsaken Greece; and can hardly be said to live in Rome. Cicero has written elegant, if not very profound or original, disquisitions on various things philosophical. Lucretius has sung the praises of Epicurus, and done his best to show how atoms could become a world. Stoicism, a creed congenial to the sterner Roman spirit, is making, and is for long to continue to make, noble men in swiftly degenerating times. But philosophy, as a creative search after truth, has not found a home in the imperial city, and is looking for one elsewhere. The Semitic family seems doomed; its great nations are either dead or dying. Assyria has ceased to be. Phœnicia, aged, withered, feeble, is hardly alive. Carthage is eclipsed; against her the *delenda est* had gone forth. Israel, proud, subject, weeping under an alien king, sits cold in the lengthening shadow of national extinction, and scarcely dares to dream of her ancient hopes. Hebrew has died; Aramæan lives. Syrians are everywhere, swarm in the capital,

"In Tiberim defluxit Orontes,"

and are everywhere useful, used, trusted, despised. The Jew is becoming a citizen of the world, has penetrated to India, to China even, has quarters and colonies in every city of the empire, can count his thousands in Rome and Alexandria. In Nazareth one who shall make the name of Jew at once illustrious and infamous for all time, is beginning to move to love or hate the minds of men. In Tarsus a youth is awakening to the world about him, asking many things, what it is to be, to be a Jew, a Greek. Everywhere within the old the seeds of a new order are falling, and shall yet fructify, causing death while creating life.

In Alexandria the thoughts and faiths of men from many lands met and mingled. The Greeks were the sons of the men who had followed Alexander, more cosmopolitan than the old Hellenes had been. Yet they loved, as men ever do when planted on a foreign soil, to glorify their fatherland, and to enrich themselves with the treasures of its genius. The literature of Greece was collected in Alexandria, and the place felt the inspiration of its presence. There were, too, in the city children of the soil, sons of the ancient empire, contributing their quota to the collective mind and its wealth. There, too, were Jews, many thousands of them, breathing the spirit of the place. They were far from Judea, and by and by its polity, institutions, temple, worship, even its speech, grew strange to them. Without these, Judaism tended to become less a formal authority, more a quickening spirit. The rabbinical tradition was broken; the inflexible sacerdotalism of home was softened. The Scriptures were translated into Greek; and the new speech created a new order of ideas. The old tongue had been sacred, had preserved many distinctive and exclusive associations; but the new tongue was at once common and classical, the tongue of the market and the schools. The place Hellenized the men, and the language their Scriptures. In the museums, libraries, and academies they studied the literature of Greece; and in the synagogue they heard the Book their fathers had revered as the Word of God speak to them in Greek. Plato was read with eyes accustomed to Moses, and Moses with eyes accustomed to Plato, and a spirit whose existence was before unguessed was unsphered in both. Hebrew faith and Greek science were alike loved. Heathen wisdom was made an effluence of the divine. The antitheses or incompatibilities of the letter were overcome by a method of interpretation which left the interpreter fancy free, able to make the words and records of the past reflect the mind of the present. The philosophy of Greece was evolved from Moses, and the God of Moses was proved to have lived, ruled, and been believed in Greece.

The Judeo-Greek philosophy, whatever may be thought of its intrinsic worth, must be judged of the highest historical importance. In it Semitic religion and Greek knowledge consciously met and consciously tried to unite. Philo's system may be in the highest degree artificial and arbitrary. His allegorical interpretations may be forced, fanciful, often ridiculous. He may have put too much of Plato into Moses, too much of Moses into Plato. His notion of Deity may have been crude and inconsistent. He may have too absolutely translated the Hebrew idea of the inexpressible Name into the Greek idea of the inconceivable Being. His method of establishing relations between the Absolute and the relative, God and the world, may have been violent and without any basis in reason. But once criticism has said its last word against his system, it still remains true that he and his school mark the beginning of a new era in the history of philosophy and philosophic thought. They have about equal significance for Neo-Greek philosophy and Christian theology, prepared the way for both, and made the work of both more possible, supplying in the one case new principles and premisses, in the other appropriate and appropriable modes of thought and speech.

Neo-Platonism may be said to be, in a sense, an attempt to construe from the Greek side and in the Greek method Semitic faith, as Philo's had been an attempt from the Judaic side to translate Greek philosophy into Hebrew religion. It was certainly rooted in the older Greek thought, owed much to the Eleatics, Plato, Aristotle, the Stoics. Its problems, too, were, in great part, the same, yet significantly construed from the subjective rather than the objective side. It tried to conceive Being, absolute and relative, as some of the older schools had done, so combining their once independent and opposed ideas as to form its own Trinity, the abstract or pure Being of the Eleatics, the reason, the νοῦς of Aristotle, and the creator, the δημιουργός of Plato. But the distinctive peculiarities of Neo-Platonism were on the subjective side. It was religious as no earlier Greek system, not even the Pythagorean, had been. It was indeed essentially a philosophy doing its best to become a religion. It tried to reach its object by faith, not by reason, by intuition, not by speculation or inference. It believed in ecstasy rather than science, visions, lustrations, mystic rites and symbols rather than open-eyed inquiry and patient study of nature and man. It had indeed a most un-Hellenic but strongly Oriental contempt for the body, and respect for self-denials, penances, and ablutions. Plotinus thought it would be folly to leave to posterity an image of himself, and so would not allow his portrait to be painted, or even tell the day of his birth, the names of his parents or his native land. It is true the Neo-Platonists were ostentatiously Greek, but they were it as Philo was ostentatiously Hebrew. Their system was evolved from the ancient mythologies and philosophies, as his had been from Moses, by a method of interpretation which left the interpreted at the mercy of the interpreter. Neo-Platonism was a splendid and even tragic endeavour of Greek philosophy to appropriate, disguise in its own forms, and turn to its own uses Semitic religion. Julian was at once the symbol of its history and the prophecy of its fate. It died while still young, amid forces it had tried at once to assimilate and resist, conquered by the Galilean, the religion of the future, which no philosophy of the past could either express or vanquish.

It does not fall within the scope of this paper to discuss the conception of God evolved and formulated in the Christian schools of Alexandria. But this much may be said—it was, perhaps, the most notable result of the meeting of Semitic belief and Indo-European thought. The one supplied the facts and the faith that had to be interpreted, but the other the interpretation. The influence of Neo-Platonic philosophy on Christian theology has been well, though it can hardly be said sufficiently, discussed, especially on what may be termed its negative side. There is no harder problem either in religion or philosophy than, How ought we to conceive God? How can He be made an object at once of thought and of love and worship? The reason ever tends to deprive Deity of the qualities that win the heart and touch the imagination. As He is refined by the one He becomes lost to the others. Thought, too, can ill conceive the relation of the Infinite to the finite. Are not these indeed contradictory and mutually exclusive notions? Does not infinite by its very nature exclude finite Being? God must be absolutely perfect; but how can an absolutely perfect Being be a Creator? Does not creation imply that He was either less than perfect before or more than perfect after it? Then, if to escape the difficulties of Atheistic Dualism, thought falls back on a theistic Monism, what is the result? It may evolve an Akosmism or Theopantism, which is but the apotheosis of nature; or an Emanationism, which makes the universe of phenomenal and finite Being an efflux of the real and infinite. But Deity so universalized and transformed is Deity annihilated. Pantheism and Pankosmism are but the ideal and real sides of the same thought. The pantheist is a metaphysician, the pankosmist a physicist, and are distinguished by what is but a verbal difference. In neither case can what occupies the place of Deity be an ethical and personal Being.

Now, ancient thought had conspicuously failed to find a God the reason could acknowledge and the heart love. The Hebrews had believed in a personal God and Creator, but they had been intuitive theists, not rational philosophers. The Judeo-Greek school had discovered the difficulty of conceiving the relation of God to the world, and had tried to vanquish it by the fiction of a semi-personal, semi-impersonal Logos, graduated orders of being, losing in divinity as they retreated from the divine. Neo-Platonism had felt the difficulty in a much more eminent degree. Their Absolute was too absolute to be in any way limited or qualified; their Perfect too perfect to sustain any relation to an imperfect creation or creature. As he was made inconceivable, he was made inaccessible; as he was denuded of qualities, he ceased to be a Being that could be reached by the reason, represented by the thought, or loved by the heart. So their idea of God helped the evolution of the Christian conception by showing what God ought not to be, how He might live in name while He was in reality dead. And with this other and more positive influences combined, eminently the influences of the great Christian facts, which were interpreted as revelations of the sublimest ethical qualities and relations in the Godhead. God was conceived as a unity, but not as a simplicity; as an absolute, but as an absolute to whom relations were immanent and essential. He was a Being capable of loving, capable of being loved; for by a necessity of His nature He had been eternally at once object and subject of love. He could know and be known; for to be as He was and what He was, was to be both the known and the knower. He could act, for action was necessary to His essence. The impossibility, that had so perplexed ancient thought, of conceiving an unchangeable related to the changing, the impassible related to the passible, was overcome by the idea that made the active and transient relations to the universe but the transcript of the relations living and immanent in God. The Christian theologians, with genuine, though unconscious, genius, concerned themselves with the objective problem, How God ought to be conceived, not with the subjective, Whether and how man could know Him. Their question was theological, not psychological; and they tried so to deal with it as to lift the idea of God from a rigid and barren abstraction into a living and fruitful thought. And so, significantly enough, a new theology was struggling into being, while the philosophy which had gathered into it the noblest elements of the older systems was passing its meridian and beginning to slope slowly to the west and eternal night.

3.

There is, perhaps, no more extraordinary phenomenon in history than the sudden emergence from obscurity to empire of the Arabs. "While Europe had been marching for centuries in the way of progress and development, immobility had been the distinctive characteristic of the innumerable tribes who wander with their tents and herds over the vast and arid deserts of Arabia."* They had been untouched by the waves of conquest, by the revolutions of thought and religion that had been sweeping round and carrying away the ancient civilized nations. As their fathers had been they were, without a literature, without a polity, a multitude of kingless tribes, who each said, " We know no master but the Master of the universe." Yet, at the very time when the progress of Europe was stayed and decay was superseding development, this nation of isolated and independent tribes, stationary and illiterate for so many centuries, suddenly issued from its deserts, spread like a resistless stream northward, eastward and westward, till it could boast an empire from the Atlantic to the plains

* Dozy., "Hist. des Musulmans d'Espagne," vol. i. p. 1.

of India and the highlands of Thibet. In the West Rome had fallen before barbarians who had no aim but plunder, or a home pleasanter than the one they had left. In the East an exhausted civilization was dying a most pitiful death, hurried forward by miserable court intrigues and ecclesiastical follies. But the desert tribes of Arabia, fused into unity and raised into heroism by a great faith, came to do a needed work, help the exhausted past to die, the future with all its potentialities and promise to live.

Into the causes of this extraordinary apparition we cannot here inquire. New thoughts and beliefs, native, Jewish, Christian, may have been fomenting in Arabia. The children of the dispersion may have helped to form the new Moses; the voice of the old prophets may have awakened the prophetic spirit in the son of the desert, who so believed in his own mission that he was able to make the men who knew him best the strongest believers in himself and his destiny. However it was, the faith that inspired Mahomet inspired and unified his Arabs, gave them at once their mission and the purpose and power to fulfil it. Without a past, they made themselves a splendid present; without a history, they vaulted at a bound into the highest historical eminence. The people was like its speech, the most perfect of the Semitic tongues. "This language, before unknown, shows itself to us suddenly in all its perfection, with its flexibility, its infinite richness, so complete, in a word, that from then till now it has suffered no important modification. There has been for it neither infancy nor age; once we have described its appearance and conquests, all has been said that need be said. I do not know if we can find any other example of an idiom entering into the world like this, without an archaic state, without intermediate degrees or preparatory stages." *

The significant point for us here is the influence of the Arabs on philosophy. They began as iconoclasts in literature as in art; but they soon became its admirers and missionaries. Mahomet hated and cursed the poets of Arabia; Omar detested and destroyed the philosophers of Greece. But another and sweeter spirit possessed their sons. In Persia the Semitic met the Aryan, found the thought and fancy of the old world in forms he could assimilate. And when, with much Aryan blood in his veins, he pressed westward, crossed into Europe, and settled in Spain, he began to build cities, to love the arts and cultivate the sciences he had once hated. The Moorish was rooted in two ancient cultures, the Hebrew and the Greek; and it strove to wed the faith it owed to the one with the philosophy it had derived from the other. But it was only a fragment of the latter that the Moor understood and appropriated. He was a poet; but not in the spirit and after the model of the Greeks. Tragedy he could only despise; Homer was to him impious; a book of supreme immortality, with too many gods to please the man

* Renan, "Hist. des Lang. Sémit.," 342.

whose mission was to proclaim the being and authority of One. Even Plato he disliked, having too little imagination to understand him. But Aristotle was his delight. In him he found a theory of the universe he could understand and use as a scientific form for his Monotheism. And so Aristotle became to the Moor the wisest of the Greeks, the father of science, the creator of logic, physics and metaphysics, a man who deserved to be called divine, so great that he had had his eminence recognised by the Koran, and was a conspicuous instance of the superiority God gave to whom He willed.

The Arab philosophy was in the schools alike of Bagdad and Cordova essentially of one type, unless, indeed, we make an exception as regards Gazali, the greatest thinker it had. It had two fundamental doctrines, which it derived from Aristotle, the eternity of matter and the theory of the intellect. The first, matter, was incapable of definition, being simply possibility, potential existence, the ability to be. The power which caused the potential to become the actual, the possible the real, was the reason, the intellect, the unmoved, but all-moving God. There was no creation, only generation. The individual was a transitory form of the eternal, the impersonal reason personalized, but only to be again depersonalized and absorbed in the universal intelligence.

But there must be here no attempt at an exposition of the Arab philosophy. What needs here to be noted is, it forms the transition from ancient philosophy to modern; with it indeed the latter may be said to begin to struggle into being. And it is at its beginning essentially distinguished from ancient. Modern philosophy starts with God, while ancient started with nature. What was given in the Arab faith was meant to be explained by the Arab philosophy. Theology and philosophy became in the hands of the Moors fused and blended; the Greek scientific theory as to the origin of things interwound with the Hebrew faith in a creator. And so speculation became in a new and higher sense theistic; and the interpretation of the universe the explication of God's relation to it and its relation to God.

The point now indicated essentially distinguishes modern from ancient speculation. Our great questions, as to cause, as to personality, as to creation and providence, did not perplex the Greeks. They had not personalized the First Cause, had not identified God and Creator, had not to reconcile the idea of Person and Infinite. These are the offspring of faith and speculation, Christian theology and Greek philosophy; and though the offspring be now and then more troublous than mind can well or peacefully bear, he must be shallow alike in head and heart who would not gladly suffer the trouble for the discipline and the strength, the glory and the joy it brings.

The relations of Moorish to Jewish and scholastic, and through them to modern, philosophy cannot be here traced historically. Had it been possible to do so, it might have helped us to see the source and meaning of many of our modern tendencies. Our problems were set for us by our fathers. Our present are the children of past controversies, and the parent often explains what is inexplicable when the child is studied alone. Man can never again approach Nature as the Greek or Hindu did. He can never annihilate in his own consciousness what it owes to the past, can never see the questions that perplex him as the men did who lived before the Semite told the Indo-European, "In the beginning God created the heavens and the earth." Our philosophies cannot escape the spell which faith has woven round our spirits. A science or a system that would explain the becoming of the universe without a Divine cause, is atheistic in a sense proper to the modern world alone, and can never lose the consciousness that it has to start with a negation that will not allow it to reach a positive and assured conclusion. God is to us the cause of Nature, and Mind, whether scientific or philosophical, critical, sceptical, or constructive, can never approach its ultimate problems as it did when Nature was conceived as either the home or the cause of the gods.

Here our inquiry must pause, not venturing to cross, even by a single step, the threshold of modern philosophy. While it has been, in the main, a creation of the Indo-European mind, the Semitic has largely supplied the inspiring ideas and influences. The universe is varied, and needs varied minds to penetrate its mysteries and tell its meaning. If the Naturalism of the one race has done much for modern science, the Supernaturalism of the other has done no less for modern philosophy. It is significant, indeed, that the spirit which, though not of this century, has most stimulated its highest speculative thought was a Semitic spirit. Spinoza might be the logical consequence of Descartes, but while he owed his formal principle to the great Frenchman, the material was his own. His philosophy was modern and influential, not through its notion of nature, but through its notion of God. Pantheism is a modern word,* and, in its proper sense, a modern theory. In a sense predicable of no ancient system, Spinoza's was pantheistic. The κόσμος was evolved from the θεός, not the θεός from the κόσμος. The world was construed through God, not God through the world. And so the system, unlike the so-called ancient and oriental Pantheisms, was most ethical in character, penetrated and sub-

---

* Toland, the English Deist, was the first to use the words "Pantheist" and "Pantheism." Aristotle used the word πάνθειον, but in the sense familiarized to us by Pantheon, a temple devoted to all the gods. (Schol. Aristoph. Plut., v. 586). So little was the word known, even after Spinoza had created the thing, that Bayle could only name him an Atheist, and his system Atheism. "Pantheist" stands in the sub-title of Toland's work, "Socinianism truly Stated," 1705; and Pantheism receives a quite distinct definition in his "Pantheisticum," 1720. See Böhmer's interesting treatise, "De Pantheismi Nominis origine et usu et notione," Hal. Sax., 1851.

limed by the most exalted religious ideas. Its comprehensive synthesis seemed to combine and unify the antitheses of infinite and finite Being, matter and spirit, God and man. And when thought had grown weary of a Dualism whose terms it could not surrender and whose contradictions it could not reconcile, it turned to Spinoza for rest and quickening. And so he found voice after he had been dead and silent for more than a hundred years. He freshened and fertilized the later mind of Lessing, and suggested some of the wisest and weightiest things the great critic ever said. He opened the eyes of Goethe to the divine life that beat and breathed in the universe, and his ear to its silent harmonies. He made Schleiermacher alive to a nobler than the traditional saintliness, and through him created in theology a deeper consciousness of God, the sense of a Divine Presence everywhere and in everything, a joy in God that made the feeling of dependence on Him a source of daily inspiration and daily delight. He helped to awaken in Schelling the idea of an all-comprehensive Absolute, appearing in the co-ordinate forms of nature and spirit; in Hegel the notion of an Absolute which united the infinite and finite, the real and ideal, the temporal and eternal, nature and spirit, and was no inflexible and unproductive abstraction, but a living process, an eternal Becoming. In England, too, he lived, dropped fruitful germs into the mind of Coleridge; and we may perhaps hear a distant echo of his voice in the sublime verses which tell how the poet feels—

> "A Presence that disturbs me with the joy
> Of elevated thoughts; a sense sublime
> Of Something far more deeply interfused,
> Whose dwelling is the light of setting suns,
> And the round ocean and the living air,
> And the blue sky, and in the mind of man;
> A motion and a Spirit, that impels
> All thinking things, all objects of all thought,
> And rolls through all things."

Spinoza's system was anything but a final or exhaustive philosophy. It was splendid as an endeavour, not as an achievement; and the degree in which it has stimulated thought but proves that the modern spirit possesses a need of God unknown to the ancient, and craves some mode of conceiving and expressing Him and His relation to the world true at once to the greatness of His own nature and the necessities of the human reason and the human heart.

www.ingramcontent.com/pod-product-compliance
Lightning Source LLC
Chambersburg PA
CBHW050846300426
44111CB00010B/1148